Terrarium and Cage Construction and Care

by R. D. Bartlett and Patricia Bartlett

Consulting Editor: Fredric L. Frye

More than 100 full-color photographs

Illustrated by Michelle Earle-Bridges

The Authors

R. D. Bartlett, a herpetologist, is author of three books and coauthor of 11. He has also written more than 500 articles. He lectures extensively and has participated in field studies across North and Latin America. In 1970, he founded the Reptilian Breeding and Research Institute, a private facility at which more than 200 species of reptiles and amphibians, including endangered species, have been bred, some under captive conditions for the first time in the United States.

Bartlett is a member of numerous herpetological and conservation organizations, a co-host on an on-line reptile and amphibian forum, and a contributing editor of *Reptiles* magazine.

Patricia Bartlett, a biologist and historian, is author of five books and coauthor of 12. A museum administrator for 17 years, she has worked in history and science museums. She received the American Public Works Association Heritage Award in 1985 and serves in several local and state organizations.

Copyright 1999 by Barron's Educational Series, Inc.

All inquiries should be addressed to:
Barron's Educational Series, Inc.
250 Wireless Boulevard
Hauppauge, New York 11788
http://www.barronseduc.com

Library of Congress Catalog Card No. 98-38742
International Standard Book No. 0-7641-0673-2

Library of Congress Cataloging-in-Publication Data
Barlett, Richard D., 1938–
　　Terrarium and cage, construction and care /
R.D. Bartlett and Patricia P. Bartlett; consulting editor
Fredric L. Frye.
　　　　p.　cm.
　　Includes bibliographical references (p. 211) and index.
　　ISBN 0-7641-0673-2
　　1. Captive reptiles. 2. Captive amphibians. 3. Reptiles as pets. 4. Amphibians as pets. 5. Captive reptiles—Housing. 6. Captive amphibians—Housing. 7. Vivariums. 8. Reptile cages. I. Bartlett, Patricia Pope, 1949–　. II. Frye, Fredric L. III. Title.
SF515.B38　　1999
636.3'9—dc21　　　　　　　　　　　　　　98-38742
　　　　　　　　　　　　　　　　　　　　　　　　　CIP

Printed in Hong Kong
9 8 7 6 5 4 3 2

Photo Credits

All photos by R. D. Bartlett except for pages 17, 22, and 58 by Billy Griswold and Karin Burns. *Hemitheconyx caudicinctus,* albino specimen, on page 45, courtesy Don Hamper and Bill Brant.

Important Note

Much enjoyment can be experienced in keeping terraria; however, the reptile and amphibian owner must exercise common sense at all times.

The authors and publisher urge readers to be prudent in handling terrarium plants and animals. Some plants cause allergic reactions in sensitive individuals. If you experience swelling, redness, or itching after working with terrarium plants, consult your physician immediately.

Also, caution should be exercised when handling snakes; the bite of even nonpoisonous snakes can cause serious injury. Large lizards, especially the green iguana, can also inflict a harmful bite. See a doctor immediately after any snake or lizard bite.

Handling giant snakes requires experience, alertness, and caution. Carelessness can be fatal! Snake keepers who are inexperienced or who have children or mammalian pets are strongly advised not to keep large boas or other giant serpents.

Some toads, as mentioned in the text, excrete a toxic substance that, if ingested, can be fatal to pets and extremely irritating to the skin of humans. Wash your hands thoroughly immediately after handling these animals.

Electrical appliances used in terraria must carry the UL Approved marking. Everyone who will use the equipment must be aware of the dangers associated with it. It is strongly recommended that you purchase a device that will turn off the electricity in the event of an equipment failure. A licensed electrician can install a circuit protector that performs a similar function. Make sure a pool is securely fenced, so no children can enter.

Some states and localities have laws that specify height and type of fencing to be used around outdoor pools. But even if it's perfectly legal for you to have an unfenced pool, don't risk a tragic accident. Make sure the area around your pool or pond is securely fenced, so no children can enter.

Table of Contents

tiles, among them great green and spiny-tailed iguanas, large monitors, and giant snakes, might do best in a room or half a room. You will need to install waterproof flooring and ascertain that the room is escape-proof. Window screens will need be strengthened and firmly secured to prevent accidental or intentional escape, and doors will require dead-bolts or locks to prevent accidental opening by either unauthorized persons or the inhabitants.

If you don't already know it, you'll quickly realize that big reptiles can be messy. If they're not fully tame, they can also be dangerous, and even if fully tame, if the species you're keeping happens to be a giant snake 10 feet (3 m) or more in length, you should *never* enter the cage when you're alone. A big snake with a bad attitude can equal big problems, big time! *Always* use the buddy system when caring for your giant "pets"— have a friend with you at all times.

Whatever cage furniture—shelves, logs, rocks—is provided must be sturdy enough to withstand prolonged use by the animals.

Providing a suitable water receptacle is especially important. It must be sufficiently large to accommodate the animal's needs, including the overflow caused by total body immersion, yet must be always clean and fresh. In the case of a large python or anaconda, it might be necessary to provide a receptacle the size of a bathtub. Many herps defecate in their water container, so unless you provide direct

A shower stall can provide a habitat for large reptiles.

plumbing, keeping the water clean will be a chore of which you will quickly tire. Never use any phenol based disinfectant, including pine oil cleansers, when cleaning your facility.

Every snake enjoys a room of its own.

9

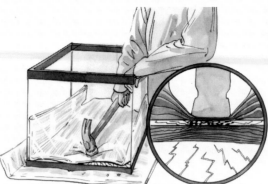

Be careful when you knock the bottom out of a tank.

Stacked Terrarium

A stacked terrarium may consist of two or three aquaria stacked one on top of the other. The glass bottoms of all but the lowest aquarium (the base tank) must be carefully removed. To do this, take the tank to a quiet area and set it, bottom down, on a flat surface thickly covered with newspaper. Cover the inside surface of the bottom with several layers of newspaper, then tap the bottom soundly with a hammer. Using extreme care, remove all pieces of loose and broken glass. Dispose of this properly, and be very careful of stray shards when you are working and removing the broken glass. Remember also that once the bottom is removed from a tank, the tank loses much of its structural integrity. Handle such tanks *very* gently and *very* cautiously! Adding a horizontal corner brace in one or more corners of each tank will do much

Corner braces stabilize your tank.

to stabilize the tanks. The brace, a simple triangle of glass or Plexiglas of the desired size, can be securely held in place by aquarium sealant, and if the brace is fronted with a strip of glass or Plexiglas, that also can be held in place by sealant. These mini-shelving units can be planted with humidity-tolerant vining plants such as philodendron or Epipremnun (pothos). The presence of the vines will not only serve as areas of security for the inhabitants, but also increase the humidity in a terrarium.

Once aligned on top of each other, the tanks in the stack can be held in place by taping two frames together with 2-inch (5.1 cm) wide transparent plastic shipping tape. A more permanent method is to run a bead of latex aquarium sealant along the top of one frame before setting the next tank up on top of it.

You must remember that servicing a tall tank is more difficult than servicing a low one. You may need a stepstool. You

can make the servicing of stacked terraria easier by placing the stacked tanks a foot or so from a wall. Tape only the back edges of the top and second tanks. By tipping the top section backward against the wall when you need access, you can reach easily into the tanks.

Plastic Containers

Plastic shoe, sweater, and blanket boxes are often used to house rather small, sedentary amphibians and reptiles. They

Tip the top section back for easy cleaning.

Be sure lids fit securely.

and usually ventilate all four sides. If an aridland rat snake is being kept, we ventilate the top as well.

Cabinets that hold a dozen or more plastic boxes are now available, many with heat tapes built in. These are advertised in most reptile magazines and are available at many reptile dealers.

Gallon Jars

These small terraria are ideal for housing tiny amphibians and reptiles, especially while you're acclimating them to captivity.

Apartment building for small reptiles and amphibians.

work well as temporary housing. These receptacles are all available in most hardware and department stores. They are very functional, but are too small to permit any accessorizing. Be sure the lids fit securely or can be secured with tape or Velcro strips.

If plastic boxes are used, sufficient air (ventilation) holes must be drilled or melted to provide air transfer and to prevent a buildup of humidity. We prefer ventilation on at least two sides

Ventilate sides and top.

Small geckos, treefrogs, and the smallest woodland salamanders can be housed in a gallon jar set up as a small woodland terrarium, with a carpet of moss, a small twig, and a sprig of pothos or philodendron growing in it. As an aquarium, it can house one or two small tadpoles or invertebrates. Cleanliness, of course, is of great importance in such a small, fully enclosed receptacle, and you will have to remove inhabitants and furniture periodically to sterilize the jar.

General Caging Notes

Wild-caught amphibians and reptiles of many species are nervous and quick to become frightened. Unused to transparent restraints such as glass, particularly skittish examples may continually batter their noses in their efforts to escape. Visual barriers such as horizontal and diagonal limbs and vining vegetation—either real or artificial—may help these specimens feel more secure. You can also minimize stress if you move slowly when you are near the vivarium.

In extreme cases it may be necessary to tape sheets of paper or plasticized backings over most of the glass surfaces of the cage. These opaque barriers not only give the animals a feeling of additional security, but also enable them to know when they are near the edges of their vivarium. Over time, it is usually possible to remove most, or all, of the paper shields.

Accessories

Plants and Furniture

- For all terraria except the desert terrarium, vining plants such as philodendrons and pothos are excellent choices. All thrive in reduced light and high humidity typical of most terrarium setups.
- Nonvining (also called self-heading) forms of philodendrons and anthuriums are also available and usually do well.
- Small species of bromeliads (airplants) can be either positioned in the soil or wired onto limbs. If misted occasionally and given sufficient light, they will thrive and will multiply by throwing off "pups."
- Small epiphytic orchids can accompany the bromeliads on elevated boughs. If conditions are suitable, some of the hardiest forms will multiply and bloom.
- Pieces of tree limbs, many festooned with arboreal ferns and lichens, can be picked up in many wooded areas; we use some of the most attractive ones in our terraria.

Desert, woodland, and rainforest tanks can be decorated with rocks, manzanita branches, cholla (cactus) skeletons, and other nonliving decorations purchased from pet stores or found in the wild. Be sure to secure rocks or heavy limbs so that they cannot shift position.

Elevated horizontal or diagonal perches, preferred by many terrarium creatures, can be held in place with U-shaped beads of aquarium sealant (open side up) on the glass ends of the tank. Arboreal amphibians and reptiles kept in groups that use limbs or rocks for basking above ground level need several perches. If only one perch is available, only the dominant animal will enjoy it.

You can provide hide boxes and plastic caves, some incorporating water dishes in their designs, which are stocked by many pet stores, and are easy to clean and sterilize.

Items such as hot rocks and heatlimbs are available, but we do not encourage the use of these (see comments on page 14).

Substrates

Various kinds of substrates are available, some more natural-looking than others. Certain species seem to prefer certain substrates. Tortoises, for example, in simple indoor terraria or cages, will do fine on a substrate of alfalfa pellets such as compressed rabbit food or another substrate that gives them a firm toehold. Dry river rock—too large to be swallowed—and mulch, or pieces of indoor-outdoor carpeting cut to the size of the enclosure, are also fine. Newspaper, while suitable for snakes, doesn't give enough foothold purchase for lizards and tortoises, and it's too dry for amphibians.

Each substrate has its advantages and disadvantages:

- River rock is easy to wash when dirty, and provides traction.
- Textured paper towels have the advantages of newspaper and offer some traction, at least until wet, when they should be changed anyway.
- Aspen, cypress, or pine mulch provide good footing and are absorbent and virtually inert.
- Cedar shavings and cedar cage furniture, on the other hand, con-

tain phenols, which are harmful, or, in strong concentration, even fatal, to herps.
- An inch (2.5 cm) or so of dead leaves such as those of the live oak, *Quercus virginiana,* form an ideal substrate for most reptiles and amphibians.

Whichever type you use, monitor its condition, and wash or change it as needed.

To sterilize substrate, cage furniture, or the terrarium itself, use a diluted solution of either Ro-Cal or chlorine bleach. Follow the instructions on the bottle of Ro-Cal or use a 1:10 ratio of bleach to water. After cleaning and sterilizing the items, be sure all are thoroughly rinsed with clean, fresh water. This applies to your hands as well.

Note: Do not use pine oils or other phenol-based disinfectants for cleaning amphibian and reptile cages. Herps do not tolerate phenols well, and even the lingering odors could be harmful.

Thermoregulation

Every amphibian and reptile has a body temperature at which all daily functions are optimized. These preferred temperatures are attained by using external heating or cooling sources; the behavior is called *thermoregulation*. Thermoregulation may be accomplished in many ways. Certain species, especially nocturnal and/or high-altitude forms, may lie

This spotted turtle, Clemmys guttata, *was sunning early in the morning in a garden pond.*

on top of or under sun-warmed rocks or logs. To cool themselves, they merely move away from the warmed object. These species are called *thigmothermic*. Other species are *heliothermic*; that is, they warm themselves by basking in the sunlight. These latter species are physiologically and physically adapted to light and to being warmed primarily from above.

We suggest that warmth-producing flood- and spotlights directed onto or into basking areas are much more satisfactory for thermoregulation than are the heated artificial tree limbs and rocks now available.

Hot Spots

Use a terrarium/aquarium thermometer and try different wattages of bulbs to achieve the desired temperature of your tank and the tank's hot spot. The hot spot will be the brightest, hottest part of your tank that will be used for sunning and thermoregulation. Generally speaking, it needs to be from 95° to 110°F (35° to 43°C). Vary the wattage of the bulb according to the terrarium size, by the distance from the bulb to the area being heated, and by the ambient temperature that surrounds the terrarium. You may need to use a spotlight bulb for heating the hot spot. Attaining the suitable temperatures in a stacked or 100-gallon (378.5 L) terrarium may require a 100- or 200-watt bulb. Heating a terrarium will require smaller bulbs in warm climates than in cooler ones.

Keep an eye on your tank when you're setting up the lights. The directed rays of even a rather small bulb can easily melt the plastic edging now used on aquarium frames. The heat from large bulbs, if too close, can break aquarium glass. Too large a bulb can overheat your terrarium and the temperatures can be lethal to the inhabitants. Rays from misdirected or oversized bulbs can burn and kill plant leaves.

Undertank Heaters

Undertank heaters, used in conjunction with directed overhead lighting, may also be useful. Such heaters, made specifically for this purpose, are available in most pet stores. Human heating pads may also be adapted as undertank heaters, but no matter which type you use, only heat half the tank this way, to allow the animal to choose the warmth it needs. The use of an undertank heater under the water receptacle may make the water too warm for the animals to drink and will assuredly increase cage humidity. Warmth and a great deal of additional humidity may be gained by placing an aquarium heater in a tall, slim jar of water and taping the jar in place in a not easily seen corner of the tank. If you do use this method, make sure that your animals cannot purposely or acciden-

tally enter the jar and drown. Add only warm-to-hot water to daily replace the evaporated water, or the temperature change might break the heater.

Flood Lamps and Full-Spectrum Lighting

Indoor caging facilities should be provided with both a heat-producing flood lamp (we use "plant-grow" bulbs for this function, but color-corrected incandescents are also available) and full-spectrum fluorescent lighting to provide your specimens with at least a little UV-A and UV-B. Note that UV availability does not seem to be a prerequisite for successfully keeping snakes. Although the necessity of having ultraviolet rays in *all* reptile husbandry remains undetermined, the full-spectrum bulbs do seem to induce a rather normal activity pattern and may assist reptiles in synthesizing vitamin D_3 or in metabolizing calcium. Certainly, you should do everything possible to provide your captive animals with the conditions that best promote the most normal life and lifestyle.

Suggestions for preferred habitat and temperature range are provided in the species accounts for each kind of terrarium habitat. If you are unsure of what temperature your species prefers, use other information sources and services such as pet care sheets found on-line, your local library—libraries have books, magazines, recordings, videotapes, and access to on-line information on reptiles, and it's all free—your local reptile society, your pet store, nature center, or the nearest university, college or junior college.

Watering Techniques

Not all herps will use water dishes. This is especially true of persistently arboreal species, which in nature lap dew and raindrops from leaves and limbs. Gently misting your terraria until pendulous droplets form on leaves and perches is the most suitable way of providing water for many arboreal species. Do this daily.

Some arboreal herps will lap water from dishes in elevated positions so that they may drink without going onto the ground. This is especially so if the surface of the water is roiled by a bubbling aquarium airstone. A bubbling watering dish with a connection for an air pump is now on the market; it could be placed arboreally or on the tank floor.

Most but not all terrestrial species will lap water from dishes. Many desert herps metabolize much, if not most, of their moisture necessities from their food items; however, providing moving water via an airstone or a commercial bubbler bowl will often induce even reluctant specimens to drink. If you use a bubbler bowl in a desert terrarium, turn the bubbler on for only a few minutes each day to avoid increasing the humidity beyond the inhabitants' tolerance level.

Chapter Three
Woodland/Rainforest Terraria

Woodland and rainforest are two terms that are often used interchangeably for heavily planted terraria without an aquatic area. If a difference is noted, *woodland* should probably be reserved for terraria housing seasonally active temperate plants and herps, and *rainforest* for terraria housing (nearly) always active tropical plants and herps. Of the two concepts, the temperate woodlands are the more difficult to duplicate or emulate.

The woodland tank can be an ideal home for temperate small salamanders and frogs, and occasionally for some of the hardier and more northerly distributed skinks and wall lizards. You may be able to collect some of these in the field. Among other species, red-backed and other woodland salamanders, gray and European treefrogs, five-lined skinks, sand and viviparous lizards, brown and red-bellied snakes, and smooth green snakes are candidates for a temperate woodland terrarium.

The tropical rainforest terrarium, active and vibrant throughout the year, is a suitable home for many small reptiles and amphibians commonly offered in the pet trade. A daily misting with a hand-held sprayer will add humidity to the cage. There are commercially available cage foggers that will keep your rainforest tank humid, but can also be used to rehydrate distressed frogs and lizards.

Because of the host of easily grown potted house plants and scientifically formulated soils available, rainforest terraria are among the most easily constructed and maintained of the various terrarium types. To successfully maintain the plants in

Temperate species such as Amur rat snakes, Elaphe s. schrencki, *thrive in properly appointed naturalistic cages.*

either setting, it will be necessary to assure that their roots remain damp, but not soggy, and to provide them with adequate lighting. The river rock below the air conditioning filter or the screening acts as a reservoir that will prevent excess water from destroying the roots of your plants if you should happen to overwater. Of course, if you regularly overwater, or overwater too excessively, the reservoir will become filled and provide little benefit to the setup.

Even shade-tolerant philodendrons, pothos, and syngoniums will require several hours of fairly strong light daily if they are to survive.

Woodland and Rainforest Creatures

Green and Brown Anoles (Temperate/Subtropical Woodland Terraria)

Lizards that can change color have always been of interest to humans. Several of the New World anoles (family Iguanidae) are well known for this ability. There are currently more than 290 described anole species, mostly in the West Indies and the neotropics. Some have distendable throat fans, which they use during territoriality displays. The colors and patterns displayed on the throat fans are distinctive for each species.

The brown and the green anoles are the species most commonly

seen in the American pet trade. Longevity of wild-caught adults can range from four to eight years. Now that some species are being captive bred, longevity records of more than a decade can be expected.

The green anole, *Anolis carolinensis,* is native to the southeastern United States. It is a small lizard, with an adult size of about 6 to 7 inches (15 to 18 cm).

Green anoles are highly arboreal but occasionally may be seen on the ground. They are commonly seen in cypress heads, among stands of oaks, in understories of rosemary and wax myrtle, in pine/palmetto scrublands, and even in certain tall native grasses. Populations of this lizard diminish as the land is developed. They are uncommon to absent in many urban and suburban settings.

Stress, temperature, humidity and light intensity—not the color of the lizard's background—trigger the green to brown color changes. When cool, basking anoles are brown, a color that quickly absorbs heat. When warm, if in the open, the lizards are often a pale green; in the shade they may remain brown. When active, green anoles are often just that, a bright green. When they are involved in aggression, they are green with a black patch behind each eye. A lighter vertebral line is often present. Males are slightly larger than the females, and their tail base is heavier. The throat fan in the female is vestigial to nonexistent. Over most of the range, the male's throat fan is usually a pale pink.

Some males in south Florida have white or pale cream throat fans.

Males defend their perceived territory against interloping males by expanding their body to appear larger, doing push-ups and head bobs, and distending the throat fan. They also may elevate a low, vertebral ridge. If this does not dissuade the interloper, the defending lizard will then sidle broadside toward his rival, then dart forward and actually skirmish with the offender. The fights can be fierce, and will last until the intruder rushes off or the defender is deposed.

Although the green anole is primarily an insectivorous species, individuals will also lap at nectar, pollen, and tree sap, and actually consume an occasional brightly colored flower petal or two.

Breeding: As with all other anoles, the green anole is oviparous. From late spring throughout the summer, the female lays a single egg at fortnightly intervals. Each incidence of ovarian development is stimulated by a courtship sequence. Since sperm can be stored in viable condition for periods exceeding eight months, actual copulation before each egg deposition is not essential. If a nest is prepared, it is a rather haphazard affair. A shallow scrape only slightly deeper than the diameter of the egg may be made in moist ground. As often as not, the egg is merely placed in leaf litter, amid trash heaps, or in similar moisture-retaining sites. Incubation averages two months. It may be some-what less in hot weather, somewhat greater if climatic conditions are cool. Hatchlings are relatively large, often exceeding 2 inches (5.1 cm) in total length.

Originally restricted to the West Indies, the brown anole, *A. sagrei* ssp., is now one of the most abundant lizard species in Florida. Other populations have been reported in Texas and in the New Orleans, Louisiana, area. It is more aggressive than the green anole, unable to assume a green color, and better adapted to life in high population densities and in disturbed or modified landscapes. It is also the more terrestrial.

Typical of most anoles, male *sagrei* are much the larger of the two sexes both in length and proportionate heaviness of body. Males approach 8.5 inches (21 cm) in length. They are also the darker of the two sexes and usually lack all but traces of the dark-edged, scalloped, or straight middorsal stripe typical of the juveniles and females. The throat fan of the males varies from yellow-orange to orange and has a whitish border. When not distended, the border of the throat fan forms a light streak on the throat of the male lizard. Some males have well-developed tail crests. Erectile nuchal crests are well developed and a vertebral crest slightly less so.

Except for the noted differences, all comments made about the green anole apply equally to the brown anole.

Woodland and Rainforest

You Will Need:

Woodland Terrarium
- Terrarium and stand
- Appropriate substrates
- Air-conditioning material or screen
- Seasonal plants, which will probably have to be collected from a woodland
- Cage furniture
- Lights and top

Rainforest Terrarium
- Terrarium and stand
- Appropriate substrates
- Air-conditioning material or screen
- Plants (available at a nursery)
- Cage furniture
- Lights and top

Build Your Terrarium

1 Place the chosen terrarium on its stand. If the setup is to be a seasonal woodland tank, it would be best to use a stand or table that can be wheeled into a cold, dark area

2 Place river rock in the tank to the selected depth.

3 Place filter material or a double thickness of plastic screening on top of the river rock.

4 Arrange all heavy cage furniture (rocks, logs, and so on), setting them firmly in place

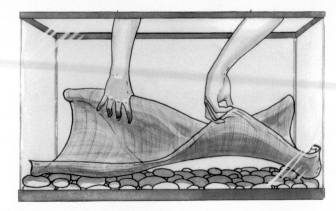

Place filter material atop river rock.

over the pebble substrate or affixing them in place with aquarium sealant if it appears that the herp inhabitants will be able to move these and trap themselves.

5 Add the topsoil, contouring it as desired. From an inch (2.5 cm) to several inches of topsoil may be used.

6 Add plants.

7 Add a suitable top and lighting. The lighting will vary greatly according to its purpose. If the terrarium is housing only amphibians, fluorescent full-spectrum lighting may be all that is necessary. Reptiles of most kinds will require one or more hot spots for basking. To provide optimum conditions, it may be necessary to provide one basking spot on land and another directed at a limb or rock protruding from the water.

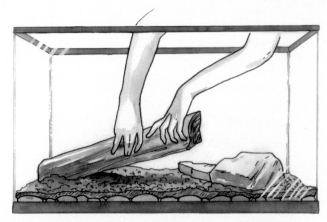

Arrange rocks, logs, and other furniture before adding plants.

This latter arrangement is especially important for basking turtles.

The kind of top you select depends on where you live. It should be noted that the more tightly closed a terrarium is, the more heat and humidity it will retain. Thus, in arid areas of the country, keepers of a woodland/rainforest terrarium may choose to have solid tops, while an open screen top may better suit a terrarium being maintained in humid areas (such as the Southeast or in fogbelts).

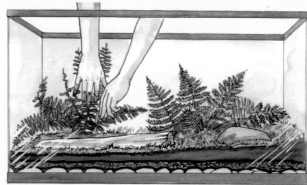

Ferns and mosses can be transplanted from your garden or purchased from a nursery.

Woodland Terrarium

Spotted wintergreen, pipsissewa, native ferns and mosses, and jack-in-the-pulpits can be taken carefully from nearby woodlands and planted in the terrarium. Most of these plants undergo a considerable period of dormancy during the winter months, and will do best if allowed to do so in the terrarium. To accomplish this, the entire terrarium can be moved into a darkened area that drops into the low or mid-40s°F (4°–7°C) for the months of December, January, and February. Reduce watering during this period, but do not allow the tank to become entirely dry.

Do not use native orchids such as showy orchis and lady's slippers in a woodland tank. They are often protected; moreover, they have complex growing requirements involving symbiotic fungi. Most will not live in a terrarium.

Rainforest Terrarium

Philodendrons, pothos, spathyphyllum, tropical ferns, prayer plants, or any number of other types can be purchased in nurseries. Plantings can be sparse or profuse.

If kept humid, the stems of pothos and philodendrons will quickly root from the leaf and stem nodes and will soon, if lighting is adequate, form a jungle. Other rooted plants may be set directly into the terrarium soil, or sunk in their pots up to the pot rim in the gravel and soil. Mossy logs and stones can be easily and artistically incorporated into the design.

Five-lined Skink
(Temperate/Subtropical
Woodland Terraria)

Besides being occasionally available in the pet trade, the five-lined skink, *Eumeces fasciatus,* is often collected from the wild by reptile enthusiasts. It ranges widely throughout much of the woodlands in the eastern half of the United States, and is often found under water's edge trash and debris.

Beautiful and adaptable tropical house plants are available in most neighborhood nurseries and garden centers.

When young, the five-lined skink has scales of shining black, five yellowish longitudinal lines running from head to tail, and an electric blue tail. Females tend to retain the juvenile pattern, but body colors lighten to tan or light brown, and the tail also fades to brown. Males usually lose their striping, are clad in warm olive brown body and tail scales, and develop reddish heads that are brightest in the spring of the year. The five-lined skink usually has only four large upper labial scales with the central row of scales beneath the tail (the subcaudals) noticeably widened. These two facts are important in differentiating the five-lined skink from the similarly sized southeastern five-lined skink, *E. inexpectatus,* and the larger broad-headed skink, *E. laticeps.* The five-lined skink attains an adult length of about 8 inches (20 cm).

Five-lined skinks thrive on vitamin-enhanced insect diets, and will occasionally accept canned cat food, a pinch of fresh, soft fruit, or flower blossoms. They are oviparous, with the female guarding her eggs throughout the incubation period.

Ground Skink
(Temperate/Subtropical
Woodland Terraria)

The ground skink, *Scincella lateralis,* is one of eastern North America's most common lizard species. It may be encountered in urban, suburban, and woodland habitats where it darts from the cover of one leaf to another. These lizards often hide under logs, boards, and other man-made and natural ground litter. The ground skink is common both in suburban and wild habitats. Its diet consists of tiny insects, but captives may accept canned cat food as well.

This active little lizard, once called the brown-backed skink, is of an overall dark coloration. The broad, dark brown dorsolateral stripes, which extend from the snout to well onto the tail, separate the light brown dorsum from the even lighter sides. There is no light brown striping. The top of the head may be copper colored, especially on juveniles. The tail also may be a copper or the same color as the body. Juveniles are especially pretty, and gleam in the sunshine like burnished copper. The legs are tiny but fully functional and bear five toes each. Although it is not easily seen, there is a transparent area, often referred to as a window, in the lower eyelid.

Although fully functional and used when the ground skink is moving slowly, the legs are folded against its body and the lizard relies on serpentine squirming when frightened or pursued.

The ground skink may occasionally reach 5.5 inches (14 cm) in total length, but 3.5 to 4.5 inches (9 to 11 cm) is more typical.

Breeding: Unlike many skinks that provide their eggs with maternal care, the ground skink does not do so. Although up to seven eggs are reported, most clutches contain from two to five. When properly cycled, a healthy female may lay

The color-changing green anole, Anolis carolinensis, *is a perennial favorite and adapts well to woodland terraria.*

several clutches of eggs at four- to five-week intervals during late spring and summer. Incubation duration is in the 50 to 60 day range.

Brown and Red-bellied Snakes (Temperate Woodland Terrarium)

These two tiny natricine snakes are common in many regions, but are seldom seen. They may be found under human-generated trash as well as under natural ground cover such as rocks and fallen trees. Both occur over much of eastern North America.

The Florida brown snake, Storeria dekayi victa, *is a tiny, live-bearing snake that feeds well on earthworms.*

The brown snake, *Storeria dekayi* ssp. is the more widely distributed and is represented by eight variable subspecies. The dorsum is variably brown, usually with a row of tiny darker spots on each side of the back. The spots may be connected across the vertebral area. The belly is white to whitish pink.

The red-bellied snake, *Storeria occipitomaculata* ssp., is represented by three confusingly similar subspecies. These are normally a rich brown to russet dorsally, but grayish or even black individuals occur. A light vertebral stripe and/or four thin dark stripes may be present. The belly is usually yellow-red, salmon, or bright red-orange. This, too, may occasionally be dark.

Both species are adult at from 8 inches to 1 foot (20 to 30 cm) in length, but occasional individuals may exceed 15 inches (38 cm). When found, these little snakes may huff, puff, and make feinting strikes. They also coil, inflate their body with air, flatten their head, and writhe strenuously. All are harmless. If grasped, they usually immediately discontinue the show of bravado, instead smearing cloacal contents on the hand of their captor. Even a 3-inch-long (7.6 cm) neonate will indulge in these displays. Clutches usually number between 3 and 12, but large females may have 20 or more. A period of winter dormancy may be necessary to cycle captive snakes reproductively.

Brown snakes feed primarily upon worms; red-bellied snakes feed upon slugs but may accept worms.

Green and Black Arrow-Poison Frog (Tropical Rainforest Terrarium)

The green and black arrow-poison frog, *Dendrobates auratus,* is the most frequently seen and easily bred of the arrow-poison frogs. It is also one of the most beautiful. Although it is usually a velvety green-spotted or banded with black, specimens with ground colors of cobalt blue, turquoise, gold-green or nearly entirely black are occasionally seen.

This frog attains about 1.5 inches (3.8 cm). It occurs from Costa Rica to extreme western Colombia and has been introduced in Hawaii.

Males are the smaller and less robust sex. An aggressive species, both males and females grapple with members of the same gender. Only males that hold territory can successfully breed, and to attain and retain that right they will mercilessly bully or even kill their rivals. Subordinate specimens are likely to be so severely stressed that normal feeding is impossible.

Diet: Arrow-poison frogs have prodigious appetites. In the wild, they consume gargantuan portions of ants. In captivity, probably because of a lack of ants in their diet, even the most toxic of arrow-poison frogs seem eventually to lose most or all of their toxic properties.

Captive frogs should be fed daily, and amply. Termites, springtails, suitably sized field plankton (small insects netted from insecticide-free fields or meadows), and vestigial-winged fruit flies are eagerly accepted. Pinhead-size crickets and aphids may also be given.

A malformation of the forelimbs may occur during development. Called *spindly leg syndrome,* this is thought to be a diet-related problem. Feed all frogs—especially breeding ones—highly nutritious diets augmented with vitamin D_3 and calcium. Feed the tadpoles well and often.

Breeding: The poison-arrow frog is a nonspecialized breeder that deposits small clutches of four to ten eggs on leaves. They do not indulge in amplexus. The males may sit on the backs of females or grasp them by the head usually before, not during, the expulsion of the eggs. The frogs utilize much tactile stimulation, such as stroking each other's back, sides, and cloacal areas with the foretoes. Egg deposition and subsequent fertilization usually occurs while the frogs sit in a vent-to-vent position. There may be several minutes between egg laying and fertilization, with the male sometimes first leaving the site, then returning to fertilize the eggs. The male frequently returns to keep the eggs moist while they incubate, and takes the new hatchlings to water. Some captive specimens enter water solely to accomplish the release of tadpoles, although these frogs live near forest streams in their natural habitat.

Terrarium essentials: Because arrow-poison frogs are extremely territorial, it is essential that their terraria be provided with many visual barriers, such as plants and hiding places. Philodendrons, epipremnums, pipers, fittonia, maranta, and other such moisture- and heat-tolerant tropical plants are ideal. Place plastic huts, halved coconut shells punched full of holes, and shallow water receptacles, such as petri dishes, around the terrarium.

Arrow-poison frogs have well-developed finger and toe discs that allow them to climb nearly as adeptly as tree frogs. Keep the terrarium tightly closed to prevent their escaping.

Don't crowd, overcool, or otherwise stress your specimens. High relative humidity and a temperature

Mantella aurantiaca, *the tiny golden mantella from Madagascar, also occurs in a red phase.*

range of 73° to 87°F (23° to 30.5°C) are ideal.

Golden Mantella Frogs (Tropical Rainforest Terraria)

Mantella aurantiaca has three separate color morphs, of which the golden phase is the best known. It is found in the isolated patches of rainforest habitat that remain in southeastern Madagascar. The golden mantella is just that—an intense, rich, golden hue sometimes overlain with just a blush of red. The golden mantella is reported to be a lowland form; therefore, it is capable of withstanding more warmth than highland species.

Two other morphs of this species appear less frequently on dealer lists. The first of these, often called the ruby mantella, varies from an intense tomato red to vermilion. The third morph is similar to the ruby morph but has a black spot on the tympanum (external eardrum). Those specimens of the two red phases we have seen seem to be slightly smaller than the golden phase. Although the colors of the mantellas may serve a warning or aposematic function, little is known about the actual toxicity of the skin secretions.

The mantellas are sufficiently distinct to form their own subfamily, the *Mantellinae*, in the family *Ranidae*.

While a 5-gallon (19 L) terrarium may be of sufficient size for a couple of mantellas, larger quarters are better. Mantellas are territorial and feisty frogs. In asserting dominance and establishing territory, male mantellas will engage in lengthy wrestling bouts in which the weaker contestant is actually flipped upside down onto the substrate. It is, of course, the winner that breeds the female.

Mantellas are weak swimmers that shun deep water.

Diet: Fruit flies, termites, and field plankton seem to be more eagerly accepted than baby crickets. If wild insects are provided as food, vitamin/mineral augmentation will probably not be necessary. If crickets and fruit flies are the main diet, they should be dusted occasionally with a good, finely powdered vitamin/mineral supplement. We prefer to provide our frogs with numerous smaller, as opposed to a few larger, food insects.

Breeding: The males' vocalizations draw the females to secluded terrestrial areas near pond edges.

The females lay their clutches of 12 to 30 large eggs on land, adjacent to water. The eggs are immediately fertilized by the dominant male. The eggs undergo terrestrial development, and the tadpoles either wriggle their way to the nearby water or are washed into the water by rivulets during storms. The tadpoles grow and metamorphose rapidly and some six to eight weeks later the mantella froglets emerge from the water to begin their terrestrial existence.

Sexual dimorphism is slight in the mantellas; the males are less robust and slightly smaller than the females. Males often sit in a more upright position with straight forelimbs. Only the males vocalize, but the calls are soft and may be difficult to hear, even in a terrarium.

Although mantellas have occasionally been bred when kept as pairs, success is more assured with a group of four or five males to a single female.

Woodland Salamanders (Temperate Woodland Terraria)

The various woodland salamanders (genus *Plethodon*) are rare to abundant inhabitants of cool, moist, temperate woodlands in both the eastern and western United States. Some species have a remarkably restricted range; others range widely over vast areas. Although some species are habitat generalists, others have more specific habitat needs. Several, for instance, prefer talus slopes, and are absent from even nearby woodlands; none are found in the Great Plains and desert areas.

Unlike most other salamanders, which have an aquatic egg and larval stage, the woodland salamanders deposit their eggs in moist, protected, terrestrial situations, and the larvae develop while in the egg capsule (direct development), emerging as tiny replicas of the adults. Although none of the members of this genus have been bred in captivity, the intricate breeding sequences of many are known.

Males and females locate one another by following pheromone trails. Females choose the male with which they wish to breed. Courtship includes complex front-leg motions, nuzzlings, the raking of the female's nape by the male, and a curious straddling walk with the male under the female. Near the end of the courtship sequence, the male deposits a spermatophore. The female picks up the sperm cap with her cloacal lips, and fertilization of the eggs occurs. The eggs are enclosed in individual gelatinous packets and either laid against a moisture-retaining substrate or dangled from the roof of protected cavities. The female remains in attendance of the eggs for the entire developmental period.

It is possible that moving the entire terrarium into a cool—42° to 52°F (5.6°–11°C)—dark room for the months of winter would cycle woodland salamanders for breeding.

Woodland salamanders, such as this Appalachian red cheeked morph of Plethodon jordani, *are ideal choices for a temperate woodland setup.*

Comparatively little is known about the life history of many species.

Red-Backed Salamanders

A common and widespread example of the woodland salamander is the red-backed salamander, *P. cinereus.* This species occurs not only in the typical red- (occasionally straw-) backed phase, but also in an all-gray (lead-backed) and an all-red (erythristic) phase. The red-backed salamander, once one of the most common species in northeastern North America, seems to be diminishing in numbers in many parts of its range. It is adult at 5 inches (13 cm) or less in total length. From five to about a dozen eggs are laid.

The larger—to 7 inches (18 cm)—Appalachian woodland salamander, *P. jordani,* is immensely variable geographically. In general, it is an entirely dark, nearly black to mostly black salamander, which in certain areas of its range has red cheeks, red legs, or golden flecks on its dorsum. Eggs number from about 6 to more than 15. The Appalachian woodland salamander remains common over much of its range.

Diet: These salamanders feed on small invertebrate prey, being particularly fond of termites, sow bugs, and earthworms. Most captives readily accept all manner of small insects and worms. Offering these salamanders small sections of earthworms on a broomstraw is a quick and efficient way of feeding them.

Most of the various wart or star plants of the genus *Haworthia* thrive amid the rocks in a savanna terrarium. Some have comparatively tender leaves, while the leaves of others are tough and almost indestructible. These plants have rosettes of leaves and may be either a squat, rather broadly opened rosette, or rather tall with the leaves clasping the stem.

Purslane or *Portulaca* is sold by nurseries for both hanging garden baskets and as bedding plants. They are fragile, drought-tolerant succulents that require very bright lighting. Because they are inexpensive and bear beautiful blossoms, these plants are occasionally used as expendable terrarium plants. Tortoises and herbivorous lizards readily eat both the foliage and blossoms.

Creatures for Savanna Terraria

Following are descriptions of several species of amphibians and reptiles that are adapted to the savanna habitat. As you read further in this book, you'll find that many species of amphibians and reptiles discussed in the desert terrarium section are equally suitable for the savanna terrarium. This is because these animals choose the microhabitat closest to their preferred microhabitat, whether it's a dry savanna or a slightly damper desert.

European Green Toad and Colorado River Toad

The European green toad, *Bufo viridis*, may exhibit bright green patches against a ground color of gray, but it is more often of such a muddy hue that the green is all but imperceptible. While in the wild, this species may occupy a variety of habitats—except deep forest—and it is often associated with dry, sandy habitats such as old fields and savannas.

Like all amphibians, this species will require a terrarium with the substrate kept just on the moist side of dry, and a low dish of clean water, to which you've added a commercial aquarium water dechlorinator. It acclimates easily to captivity. It is adult at about 3 inches (7.6 cm) in length; females are the larger sex. The parotoid (shoulder) glands are well developed. The skin is weakly tuberculate. Males have a long, pleasing trill, but this is seldom voiced by captives.

The green toad, Bufo viridis arabicus, *is a hardy savanna amphibian, but it is unable to withstand absolute dryness.*

At an adult snout to vent size of more than 7 inches (18 cm), the Colorado River toad, *B. alvarius*, is the largest toad native to the western United States. It also has the most toxic secretions. Wash your hands carefully after handling this toad, or any other for that matter. The dorsal skin is quite smooth, but both the parotoid and tibial glands are prominent. The voice is a rather weak chirp. Despite being thought of as a desert toad, the Colorado River toad is often associated with moisture-retaining areas. It may be encountered near garden pools and along the banks of ponds, lakes, and canals, but it may also be found far into the drier desert and savanna habitats as well.

Diet: A fair number of these toads refuse to eat in captivity; however, those that acclimate will live long lives as captives. Besides insects, larger examples of this interesting toad will accept an occasional pinky mouse. These toads will sit in a shallow dish of fresh dechlorinated water to replenish their body moisture.

Because of their large size, Colorado River toads can soon lay waste to all but the most substantial savanna plantings in a terrarium. This should be considered when you formulate the plans for your terrarium and its inhabitants.

Tortoises

Factors such as space constraints and the ambient humidity of the region where you live are important considerations before you purchase a tortoise. Large tortoise species should not be confined in small spaces, those that stay fairly small may still outgrow your tank, and those adapted to arid regions may languish if kept in humid areas.

If you can devote only the space of a small indoor terrarium to the creature, you should certainly purchase only a young—and small—species of tortoise that stays small when adult, from 6 to 10 inches (15 to 25 cm). Plan as well to increase the size of your terrarium as your tortoise grows, and/or set up an outdoor enclosure for the warmer months. This is a pet that will live, with proper care, for 20 to 40 years.

Several species of tortoises are well adapted to the savanna terrarium. Among them are European and Central Asian tortoises, the star tortoise of the Indian subcontinent, and the bowsprit tortoise of southern Africa. Young Bell's hinge-backed tortoise, although seldom bred in captivity and usually badly in need of deparasitizing, may also be a good inexpensive choice.

Diet: Tortoises are largely, but not exclusively, herbivorous. In the wild, many will consume carrion, insects, or even nestling rodents or birds if they happen across them. Captives of most species will eagerly eat dark leafy vegetables such as romaine, kale, collard greens, and escarole; pulpy vegetables such as squashes and the like; fruits such as apples, pears, kiwis, papayas, and mangoes; and a small prepared tortoise diet or dog kibble. A diet too heavy in protein may cause shell malformations and metabolic problems, so when in doubt, offer vegetables and fruits. There are several tortoise diets now on the market that claim to be a complete diet, but we would still recommend variety. A D_3 calcium supplement should be periodically given. Vitamin/mineral supplements are given more frequently to rapidly growing young tortoises than to adults.

Breeding: Many tortoises will breed throughout the year; others, especially species from temperate areas or tropical areas that have well-defined rainy and dry seasons, have one or two well-defined breeding seasons annually. In most cases, the initial breeding and egg deposition will occur in the spring when the hours of daylight are increasing.

The starred tortoise, Geochelone elegans, *of India and Sri Lanka, one of the world's most beautiful species, is now being captive bred in some numbers.*

Digging the nest can be a lengthy process. Depending on soil composition, it may take two to four hours to complete the nesting sequence.

Egg incubation should be accomplished in a barely moistened substrate at a temperature of 81° to 84°F (27° to 29°C) with a relatively high humidity in the incubator.

All species discussed in this section enjoy a well-illuminated, heated basking area with a surface soil temperature varying between the mid-90°s F and 100°F (35° to 38°C), but nighttime temperatures can drop into the 70°s F (24°C). Fresh water should always be present, and food items should be fresh and well hydrated.

The European Hermann's tortoise, Testudo hermanni, *is a European favorite that is now becoming popular in the United States. Protected in the wild, captive bred babies are readily available.*

Hermann's Tortoise
Supracaudal (usually) divided
No enlarged tubercles on thigh
Tail tipped with horny spur
5 to 10 rows of small scales
    on anterior of forelimb

Mediterranean Spur-thighed Tortoise
Supracaudal (usually) undivided
Enlarged tubercles (usually)
    present on thigh
Tail (usually) not tipped with
    horny spur
3 to 6 rows of large scales on
    anterior of forelimb

Hermann's and Mediterranean Spur-thighed Tortoises

These two look-alike species can be difficult to differentiate. Of the two, the Hermann's tortoise, *Testudo hermanni* ssp., seems the hardier and most personable. It is a small—to 7 inches (18 cm) when adult—attractive tortoise that occurs on both the southern European mainland and on many of the adjacent islands. It favors savannas, open woodlands, and similar xeric habitats. Hermann's tortoise has a highly domed carapace that is variably patterned in black and horn. The rear margin of the carapace may flare outward moderately. The posterior lobe of the plastron is weakly hinged. Hermann's tortoise has long been a favored pet species. Besides the standard tortoise fare, they like broccoli florets and particularly favor clovers, dandelions, and buttercups.

Breeding: This species has been bred for many decades. Hibernation is probably necessary for the long-term physiological well-being and breeding of this species. Males breed the females aggressively, butting and biting to immobilize their mates. Nests are flasked and about 4 inches (10 cm) deep. Several clutches of from two to ten—occasionally more—eggs are laid annually by adult females. At from 83° to 86°F (28° to 30°C), incubation takes from 80 to 100 days. The hatchlings are hardy in the savanna terrarium and grow quickly. It is suggested that minimal animal matter be fed to the hatchlings of this tortoise species.

The Mediterranean spur-thighed tortoise, *T. graeca* ssp., is similar in appearance to the Hermann's tortoise. Its regimen of care in captivity is also similar.

Although not as commonly seen in the pet trade today as in past years, the Mediterranean spur-thighed tortoise is still one of the most commonly offered species. Specimens in some populations may attain 1 foot (30 cm) in length, and their adult size makes it hard to maintain them in cages.

T. graeca can be difficult to acclimate to captive conditions, especially in perpetually humid areas. When maintenance is attempted in such areas, respiratory ailments are common. These often worsen or recur despite treatment, and can be fatal. It is somewhat easier to succeed with this tortoise species in dry-to-arid regions.

To do best with this species, it is necessary to know where your specimen originated. In some areas of its range, this tortoise hibernates (brumates) in winter and estivates in excessively hot summer weather. In other areas it may do one or the other, and specimens in yet other populations remain active all year.

Central Asian Tortoises

Testudo horsfieldi is a rather plainly colored tortoise that occurs over a wide range in Central Asia. This species attains an adult length of 6 to 8 inches (15 to 20 cm) and tends to lack much of the dark pigmentation on its horn-colored cara-

Most Central Asian tortoises, Testudo horsfieldi, *seen in the pet trade are still collected from the wild and can be difficult to acclimate.*

pace. The carapace is also somewhat wider in proportion to its length and less highly domed than those of the Hermann's and Mediterranean spur-thighed tortoises. Additionally, the Central Asian tortoise has only four, rather than five, claws on its forefeet.

The Central Asian tortoise seems to metabolize much of its water needs from the vegetation diet it prefers, harsh though this diet may be during much of the year. It avidly eats grasses, leaves, succulents, and fruit.

In America, this tortoise species is considered more difficult to keep than many. This is often because the tortoises arrive here so debilitated by collection and shipping stresses that they don't have a fair chance. If acquired when in good condition, treated for parasites when necessary, given a nutritious diet and adequate temperatures, the Central Asian tortoise can be hardy and long lived.

Star Tortoise

The 6- to 11-inch-long (15 to 28 cm) star tortoise, *Geochelone elegans*, of the Indian subcontinent is now being captive bred in fair numbers. The largest examples occur in Sri Lanka. Hatchlings are about 1.25 inch (3.6 cm) long.

The star tortoise is unquestionably one of the world's most beautiful tortoises. Its black carapace is elongate, highly domed, and vividly marked on each scute with a series of bright yellow radiations. Its plastron, light with dark radiations, reverses the color scheme. It is associated with relatively humid savanna and open forested areas and is most often encountered during the rainy (monsoon) season. Star tortoises forage early in the day during dry periods.

Breeding: Males of this beautiful tortoise are very aggressive toward both other males and females during breeding attempts. They indulge in considerable ramming, butting, and biting. Wheezing chuckles are voiced by breeding males.

Female star tortoises are noticeably larger than the males. The females dig deep, flasked nests in which from 2 to 10—usually 4 to 6—eggs are placed. In a humid incubator, at 84° to 86°F (29° to 30°C), incubation lasts from 85 to 95 days. Natural incubation may be nearly two months longer. The babies are vividly, but not as intricately, marked as the adults.

Star tortoises are primarily herbivorous, but will eat some fruits and a small amount—not to exceed 5 percent—of animal protein. Some specimens develop immensely pyramided carapacial scutes, a condition thought to be the result of too much animal protein in the diet.

Bell's Hinge-backed Tortoise

Bell's hinge-backed tortoise, *Kinixys belliana*, is an inexpensive East African tortoise that is still readily available in the American pet trade. This is unfortunate, for it is a fairly delicate tortoise that can be quite difficult to acclimate to captive conditions. This is especially true of specimens severely stressed and dehydrated by improper collection and shipping techniques. Even

The rear carapacial lobe of the East African Bell's hinge-backed tortoise, Kinixys belliana, *is movable.*

prompt veterinary intervention may not save these tortoises.

Unlike any other tortoises, all species in this genus have a hinge in the carapace that allows the back portion of the shell to draw down tightly against the bottom shell to afford protection to the legs and tail. Bell's hinge-backed tortoise is an elongate, highly domed species that attains an adult length of about 7.5 inches (19 cm). Young specimens in the pet marketplace usually are about 3 inches (7.6 cm) long.

This tortoise is a dweller of brushy savanna and grassland habitats and is often encountered near water holes. Well-defined wet/dry seasons predominate within the range of this species and the tortoises often estivate when water sources are dried. Bell's hinge-backed tortoises bask extensively.

Clutches are small (from one to four eggs) and incubation may last four or more months. Juveniles are more colorful than adults, having well-defined radiating carapacial markings. This pattern may be carried over to adulthood, but usually fades dramatically. Some adults are a uniform horn color.

The several species of *Kinixys* are more omnivorous than many other tortoise species. Besides grasses and other greens, pulpy vegetables and fruits, these tortoises eat slugs, snails, worms, and other invertebrates and carrion. They will even chase down and consume young mice.

Although not as colorful as some species, the nocturnal South African Bibron's gecko, Pachydactylus bibroni, *is a hardy and robust species.*

Lizards

Bibron's Gecko

This large, robust South African gecko is known scientifically as *Pachydactylus bibroni*. It attains a heavy-bodied 7-plus inches (app. 18 cm) in overall length. It is an inhabitant of savannas and rocky dry sclerophyll woodlands but is associated with human habitations in many regions. It is active virtually throughout the year and is persistently nocturnal.

Bibron's gecko has a ground color of tannish buff or gray and has five well- to vaguely defined darker chevrons on its tuberculate dorsum. A few lighter spots are often also present. The subdigital pads are broad and well developed. Displaying males vocalize in chirps and clicks. Skirmishes are common and a carelessly restrained example will readily bite the hand that holds it.

Bibron's geckos are not especially active and a pair, or even a trio, can be easily maintained in a 15-gallon (57 L) or larger savanna terrarium. They are voracious feeders that will eagerly accept all manner of insects and, occasionally, pinky mice. These geckos lick droplets of water from freshly misted rocks, plants, and terrarium glass.

Breeding: This species has frequently been bred in captivity. Other than being somewhat more precisely patterned, the hatchlings are 3-inch-long (7.6 cm) replicas of the adults. A slight winter cooling and a natural photoperiod seem all that is necessary to cycle these lizards reproductively. The two eggs may be laid in rock crevices or on the substrate against a rock or a grass clump. The shells are very fragile and the eggs must be handled carefully. They will hatch in 54 to 60 days at 82°F (28°C).

Moorish Wall Gecko

The Moorish gecko, *Tarentola mauritanica*, is of fair length—to 6.5 inches (16.5 cm), and robust build. Prominent pointed tubercles are arranged in well-separated rows along this gecko's back, sides, and tail. Prominent rounded tubercles are present on the sides of the neck. The coloration of this interesting lizard is of variable earthen tones that usually blend well with its background. It has a clicking call and is quite vocal if restrained. It is principally nocturnal during warm weather, but may be active by day during cool periods.

This, too, is a dweller of savanna scree slopes and other rocky habitats, and is becoming thought of as a "house gecko." The toe pads are prominent and extend to the very tips of the toes. The lamellae are single (undivided) across their entire width. The inconspicuous claws are present only on the third and fourth toes of each foot.

Moorish geckos are insectivorous and prefer to lap water from the sides of their terrarium and from plant leaves. The species can withstand a four- to six-week period of winter dormancy, but can be bred successfully if merely cooled to the low 70°s F (21° to 23°C) during the day, and with nighttime temperatures in the 60°s F (16° to 20°C) during the winter months. They will need less food and smaller insects at this time.

The two eggs—several clutches can be laid each year—are weakly adhesive, and if laid in a rock crevice may be difficult to remove to an incubator. If this is the case, a film canister or other small plastic protector may be placed over the eggs to help retain satisfactory humidity and temperature. Incubation takes from 55 to 60 days at 81° to 83°F (27° to 28°C).

Although not at all colorful, this species has caught hobbyist interest and Moorish geckos are now being extensively bred in captivity. They are indigenous to the warmer

Paroedura picta, *the terrestrial Madagascan ocelot gecko, is a prolific breeder that is becoming a popular terrarium animal.*

Mediterranean coastal areas but may be seen in some inland locations. They are also found on the Canary and Ionian Islands, in Crete, and in North Africa.

Ocelot Gecko

The ocelot gecko, *Paroedura pictus*, is a small—to 5 inches (13 cm)—basically terrestrial species. Males are slightly the larger of the two sexes. Juveniles are somewhat more prone to climb than are the adults.

The ocelot gecko is a nocturnal endemic of Madagascar's rocky, dry savannas. It occurs in both prominently banded and striped morphs. Both patterns diffuse somewhat with advancing age. The ground color is deep brown.

Juveniles are somewhat more brilliantly colored and precisely patterned than the adults. Both dorsal and lateral surfaces bear prominent tubercles. These slender geckos have a large head. Each toe bears two leaflike pads under the toe tip.

Male ocelot geckos are capable of producing clicks and squeaks. They are especially vocal during the breeding season. Because of the tropical latitudes in which the ocelot gecko is found, breeding activity may actually occur over much of the year. The developing eggs can be seen as diffuse light areas through the body walls of the female.

Breeding: Breeding activities seem to be stimulated by a slight

More subtly colored than some of the day geckos, Standing's day gecko, Phelsuma standingi, *is a beautiful large species.*

peratures of 82° to 88°F (28° to 31°C). A drop of several degrees at night is perfectly acceptable.

Standing's Day Gecko

Phelsuma standingi is a magnificent diurnal gecko of the open woodlands and savanna edges of southern Madagascar. It is highly arboreal and at maturity may measure nearly 1 foot (30 cm) in overall length.

Standing's day geckos are alert, active, fast, and, because their skin tears easily, difficult to handle. They are best moved when necessary by shepherding them into a glass or jar, then slipping a piece of cardboard over the mouth of the receptacle.

The hatchlings of Standing's day gecko are much more colorful than the adults. These 2-inch (5.1 cm) rainbows have a ground color of terra-cotta or russet that is patterned on the head with pale green, on the trunk with pale blue, and on the tail with brilliant turquoise. The limbs are blue and terra-cotta. These colors fade quickly in intensity with growth. Adults are most brightly colored anteriorly. Anteriorly, the adults are dark mottled green, but fade to a slate gray, which is marbled with pale green posteriorly. This species can make the usual repertoire of gecko clicks and squeaks but is usually silent.

Although they may be slow to begin breeding, once acclimated they will produce several sets of two eggs each during the summer months. The eggs may be laid on the substrate within a hollow log or

lengthening in the photoperiod and by increasing humidity. Females will often nest in a small, covered, plastic refrigerator dish containing about an inch of a slightly moistened, peat/sand mixture. At a temperature of between 83° and 86°F (28° to 30°C), the incubation time will be a day or two on either side of two months.

Although ocelot geckos are now captive bred in fair numbers, most offered in the pet marketplace are still wild-collected specimens.

Diet: Ocelot geckos feed readily on half-grown crickets, waxworms, and other similarly sized insect fare. They will drink water from a flat dish. Food insects should be dusted with a vitamin D_3 calcium supplement at least once weekly. These tropical geckos prefer daytime tem-

other such hiding area or may be laid completely in the open. At 86°F (30°C), they hatch in 55 to 66 days.

Besides the more traditional insect diet, day geckos are fed a vitamin-calcium fortified fruit and honey concoction. This is provided in shallow dishes on elevated platforms.

Standing's day geckos are quite temperature-tolerant. Summer hot spot temperatures of 90° to 95°F (32° to 35°C) are utilized extensively by the big lizards. Nighttime temperatures are in the 70°s F (21° to 26°C). Both day and night temperatures may be allowed to drop by a few degrees during the winter months.

Male Standing's day geckos are very territorial, and no more than one of this species should be housed per cage. They are also antagonistic toward males of other large day geckos.

Banded Geckos

Coleonyx elegans (southern Mexico, northern Guatemala, and Belize) and *C. mitratus* (El Salvador and Honduras to Panama) are two of the largest and prettiest members of this genus. Both have tuberculate dorsal skin. In most external appearances these two species greatly resemble each other. The most significant external difference between *C. mitratus* and *C. elegans* is in the head patterns and the formation of the claw sheaths.

Unlike other *Coleonyx*, their congeners, all denizens of open or rocky desert and semidesert and associated cliffs and escarpments,

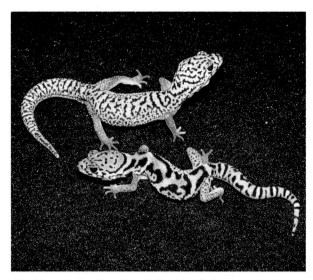

The Central American banded gecko, Coleonyx mitratus, *is among the largest species in this genus*

C. elegans and *C. mitratus* inhabit dry open forest, thorn scrub and seasonally wet secondary forest. Both species are variable in coloration and pattern. In fact, in certain areas of the Yucatan Peninsula, *C. elegans* occurs in both a banded and a striped morph.

Leopard Geckos

Although subspecies are known, because of generations of captivity-induced intergradation, it would be almost impossible to assign a subspecies to the leopard geckos now being produced in American breeding programs (see pages 69–74). *E. macularius montanus* originates from the vicinity of Quetta, West Pakistan. *E. m. fasciolatus* of Pakistan's coastal lowlands and adjacent India is also imported.

Like others of the genus, Coleonyx elegans, *the Mexican banded gecko, is a hardy terrestrial species that wags its tail when foraging.*

Leopard geckos are a hardy, long-lived species; captive records of 15 to 22 years are not uncommon.

The distinctive black and yellow bands of the juveniles tend to break into a pattern of spots and reticulations as the lizards mature. Breeders strive to produce aberrant colors, working particularly for a reduction of black pigment. Leucistic examples, inordinately dark specimens, and other color aberrancies are known.

Because of their inactivity, terraria for leopard (and other eublepharine) geckos can be relatively small. A terrarium made from a 10-gallon (38 L) tank will house one male and three females without overcrowding. Use an inch (2.5 cm) or two of sand, finely ground oyster shell, finely granulated calcium carbonate, small

pebbles, or dry cypress mulch for substrate. Preformed caves, cork-bark tubes, or curved pieces of pine bark all make good hiding areas for these nocturnal lizards. A low receptacle of clean water should always be present.

Fat-tailed Gecko

The African fat-tailed gecko, *Hemitheconyx caudicinctus*, is also a commonly seen pet trade species.

Fully adult male fat-tailed geckos attain an overall length of more than 8 inches (20 cm). Females are noticeably smaller.

This beautiful tropical West African gecko is an inhabitant of dry, rocky woodlands and savannas and their environs. It is a terrestrial gecko that is adept at secluding itself under natural and man-made debris. It also seeks out deserted burrows of small mammals in which to hide.

Male fat-tails squeak and click when they are upset or involved in territorial disputes.

Fat-tailed geckos occur in several color phases, but remain less variable than leopard geckos. Typically, the lizard is broadly banded in contrasting shades of tan and dark chocolate, either with or without a white vertebral stripe. Occasionally, on both banded and striped phases, the light areas are suffused with peach and the dark cross-bands suffused with orange. As might be imagined, the effect is startlingly beautiful and efforts are being made by private breeders to perpetuate and even enhance the color. Juveniles, clad in bands of dark chocolate and yellow, are much more brilliantly colored than the adults. Albinistic and leucistic fat-tailed geckos have recently become available. Males have larger preanal pores than females, and also have hemipenial bulges at the base of the tail.

Once only sporadically captive bred, today African fat-tailed geckos are being produced in large, ever-increasing, numbers. Although they are considered by most hobbyists to be slightly more difficult to keep and breed than leopard geckos, once their slightly different caging necessities have been met, they have been found to be both easily kept and bred. Fat-tails prefer their terrarium conditions slightly

Fat-tailed gecko, normal.

more humid than do leopard geckos. This may be accomplished with a substrate of bark nuggets, a medium that, in perpetually humid areas such as Florida, holds slightly more moisture than sand. In dry

Fat-tailed geckos, Hemitheconyx caudicinctus, *are now bred in both normal (top) and albino (bottom) morphs.*

The short-lined skink, **Eumeces tetragrammus brevilineatus,** *is secretive and subtly colored, but a hardy captive.*

areas of the world, fat-tails can be provided with a suitably sized receptacle of barely moistened, unmilled sphagnum moss into which they can crawl. Plastic refrigerator dishes meant for sandwiches are ideal. Some keepers keep these tightly covered, cutting an access hole in the top. Fat-tail geckos drink readily from low water dishes and avidly accept most types of insects and new-born mice as prey.

The eggs of this lizard are typically eublepharine; they have soft shells. Like those of the leopard gecko, the moisture content of the incubation medium containing fat-tailed gecko eggs must be neither too damp nor too dry.

Prairie Skink and Short-lined Skink

These are two pretty skinks of the central United States that are more readily collected from the wild by an enthusiast than found on dealers' lists. Both are adult at about 6 inches (15 cm) in length.

Adults of the prairie skink, *Eumeces septentrionalis* ssp., have buff to grayish tan backs—occasionally with two darker paravertebral stripes bordering a lighter vertebral stripe—and two well-defined yellowish lateral stripes contained in a dark field on each side. Adult breeding males have orange on the face and sides of the head; juveniles have a blue tail.

Adults of the short-lined skink, *E. tetragrammus brevilineatus,* are mostly a warm brown, but have short stripes on each side. Breeding males have a wash of orange on the face and sides of the head; juveniles have a blue tail.

These skinks are both adapted to savanna/aridland environments and live well as captives. Both are essentially insectivorous but may lap at saps and nectar and will readily drink the vitamin-calcium fortified fruit-honey mixture described on page 204. Both are oviparous, but there are no captive-breeding programs in place for either species. Like other members of the genus, the females remain with and try to protect the eggs during incubation.

Eastern Fence Lizards

The fence lizards, *Sceloporus undulatus* ssp., are small—to about 6.5 inches (16.5 cm)—active, heliothermic (basking) iguanid lizards

Southern fence lizards, Sceloporus undulatus, *are active lizards in which the sexes are colored differently (female left).*

that can be commonly seen in the open pine and mixed woodlands of the eastern United States. Besides sunbathing in trees, they frequent sun-warmed woodpiles, fallen trees, debris along pasture edges, and sometimes even fences. They are ideal first lizards for beginning hobbyists.

The Eastern fence lizards are clad dorsally in scales that mimic the grays of the bark of the trees on which they live. On the back of female fence lizards is a series of well-defined posteriorly directed chevrons. The chevrons are less discernable on the males. Ventrally, the two sexes are very different. Males have prominent, elongate, patches of bright blue to bluish green along the sides of the belly. These are bor-

dered along their inner edge by black. Males also have a black-bordered blue patch on the throat. Females have a greatly reduced amount of blue on the belly and scattered black flecking. Females from the Deep South tend to have more black ventral speckling than females from the North.

Hobbyists collect these lizards from the wild or purchase them from dealers. Several clutches of from 4 to 10 eggs are produced annually by adult females. At 80° to 84°F (27° to 29°C), the young hatch in about 60 days.

The fence lizards in general are hardy insectivores that require a well-illuminated and warmed basking spot in which to thermoregulate. If this, in combination with a natural

The emerald swift, Sceloporus malachiticus, *is a colorful but delicate and difficult-to-keep species.*

photoperiod and a period of winter hibernation, is provided, these lizards will breed easily in captivity.

Emerald Swift

Although the emerald (or malachite) swift, *Sceloporus malachiticus*, has become a mainstay in the pet industry, it is also a difficult species to maintain for long periods. This is a high-elevation, live-bearing species from Latin America. They are seen most often on rocks and fallen trees in montane forests from Mexico to Central America. Males are adult at about 6.5 inches (16.5 cm) in length. On their back and sides male emerald swifts are brilliant green, either with or without dark markings. Ventrally they have bright blue patches that have black inner edges, and orange and blue throats. The females are smaller and much duller and the neonates are even duller.

Diet: Besides insects, emerald swifts will eat blossoms and some sweet fruits.

Emerald swifts enjoy cooler daytime temperatures of 72° to 80°F (22° to 27°C) with a well-illuminated, warmed basking spot of about 94°F (34°C). Nighttime temperatures can be allowed to drop to the high 60°s F (19° to 20.5°C). Even with exemplary care, emerald swifts seldom survive captivity for more than a few months. Those kept in cool climates and in large terraria or cages with many branches and rocks on which to climb seem to do the best.

Snakes

Numerous snake species are well adapted, at least as babies, to life in a savanna terrarium. If the terrarium is large, and planted with sturdy vegetation, many of these snakes will do well throughout their lives. If snakes are kept in a savanna terrarium, unless they are insectivorous species, it will probably preclude keeping anything *but* snakes. Lizards, frogs, even baby turtles, will simply eventually provide a meal for all but the smallest and least predaceous of snake species.

Racers and Whipsnakes

Because of their persistent feistiness, racers and whipsnakes are often avoided by hobbyists. They are smooth-scaled and often have a satiny rather than a shiny luster to the scales. Although the designations of racer and whipsnake are arbitrary, the common names for these snakes are pretty well standardized: The members of the genus *Coluber* are usually called racers, while those of *Masticophis* are called whipsnakes or, in the East, coachwhip snakes. All North American members of these genera are large. The Mexican racer, *C. constrictor oaxaca*, which has restricted distribution in the United States, is typically the smallest, but even this snake attains a slender 3-plus feet (91 cm) in length. Like all members of both genera, the Mexican racer is an opportunistic feeder, consuming frogs, lizards, insects, and probably quantities of fiddler crabs.

The most common racers are the various black racers or black snakes of the eastern United States. They are larger than the Mexican racer, often attaining or exceeding 5 feet (152 cm) in length. Most of these are solid satiny black both above and below, but have a white to brown chin. Other racers are bluish with a yellowish belly, and some, such as the buttermilk and tan racers, have scattered blotches of blue or brown on a black, blue, or tan dorsum. Hatchling racers of most races are tannish or gray with many darker saddles or bars.

In the East, the whipsnakes are often, but not always, dark anteriorly and pale tan posteriorly (some are solid black); in the West, they are reddish and almost unicolored or prettily striped. Hatchlings of eastern and western nonstriped coachwhips are patterned similarly to the racers; however, hatchlings of the various striped whipsnakes are patterned similarly to the adults.

Racers and whipsnakes have a rapid metabolism, tend to be nervous as captives, and may strike and bite animatedly if handled carelessly or sometimes if just approached. They are also usually heavily parasitized. Unless treated by your veterinarian, parasites will quickly stress

All kingsnakes, such as this desert king, Lampropeltis getula splendida, *are hardy, but are voracious predators on other reptiles, amphibians, and small mammals. Cagemates for these and other snakes must be chosen very carefully.*

and debilitate these nervous snakes.

All racers and whipsnakes are oviparous and a healthy female may produce more than a single clutch annually. The eggs have a pebbly surface and will hatch in about 60 days if incubated at 84°F (29°C).

The racers and whipsnakes can be an interesting challenge for hobbyists wanting snakes that are just a little bit different.

Desert Kingsnake

Although the popularity of this pretty aridland snake is eclipsed by that of several other races, *Lampropeltis getula splendida* is well adapted to life in the savanna terrarium. Hatchlings and juveniles are especially well suited to even small terraria, but the 4 to 5 feet long (122 to 152 cm) adults will require a ter-

rarium 30 or more gallons (114 L) in size. Because desert kings are moderately active, the cage furniture and plantings should be substantial and well secured.

It is also important to remember that king- and milksnakes will eagerly constrict and eat most cagemates, including others of their own kind. Desert kingsnakes are no exception; therefore, they should be housed separately.

The desert kingsnake is variably colored, but typically most heavily speckled on the sides. The dark dorsum is divided into numerous—often 35 to 45—saddles by narrow light crossbars. The belly is mostly dark.

Like all kingsnakes, the desert race lays one or more clutches of from 5 to 14 eggs that will hatch in about 60 days if incubated at 84°F (29°C). The eggs are often adherent, and no effort should be made to separate them for incubation.

Red Milksnake

Because of their bright colors and hardiness, the various tricolored kingsnakes and milksnakes are always of interest to hobbyists. Many subspecies have a body completely encircled with bands of red, yellow or white, and black, but others, such as the beautiful red milksnake, *Lampropeltis triangulum syspila*, have black-edged, red saddles on a dorsal ground of grayish white, and black and white checkerboard bellies.

These snakes are powerful constrictors that will usually readily accept laboratory mice. Although they are usually 30 inches (76 cm) or smaller, red milksnakes occasionally exceed 3 feet (91 cm) in total length. This is a milksnake of our central states.

Like all its relatives, the red milksnake is a secretive creature that persistently hides under rocks and debris. It can and will burrow in loose soils.

These beautiful snakes do very well in a savanna terrarium. Even if provided with darkened caves, they are very likely to burrow deeply into the substrate but will often emerge in the evening, especially following the watering of the plants.

One or more clutches of from 3 to 15 eggs are produced in the spring or early summer. At 83° to 85°F (28° to 29°C), incubation lasts from 50 to 60 days.

Baird's Rat Snake

Elaphe bairdi, is a moderately sized—to 5 feet (1.5 m)—pretty, quiet, and hardy rat snake. Dorsally, adult Baird's rat snakes may vary from a dusty pearl gray through a powdery orange-brown to a rather warm burnt orange. Adult males are usually suffused with more and brighter orange than females. Adults have four dark to orangish stripes of variable intensity and contrast. The pair of dorsolateral stripes are usually the better defined. Specimens of Mexican origin are usually more brightly colored than those from more northerly areas. Hatchlings and

The red milk snake, Lampropeltis triangulum syspila, *is a hardy and beautiful, but secretive, snake of moderate size.*

juveniles are grayish with a busy pattern of many narrow dorsal saddles. Lateral blotches are also numerous and rather well defined. A curved dark bar crosses the snout immediately anterior to the

Baird's rat snakes, Elaphe bairdi, *are now becoming a popular pet species. The hatchlings are very different in appearance from the adults.*

51

Trans-Pecos rat snakes, Bogertophis subocularis, *occur in a blonde, normal, and silver phase in the wild. All are popular with hobbyists.*

eyes and a dark postocular stripe runs from eye to mouth. With growth, both markings pale, eventually to disappear completely. The head of an adult Baird's rat snake is entirely without markings.

Texas Rat Snake

In contrast to the Baird's rat snake, the Texas or Lindheimer's rat snake, *E. o. lindheimeri*, is a belligerent species that is often slow to tame.

The Texas rat snake retains a pattern of blotches throughout its life. The ground color can vary from straw yellow to orange, but is most often tan or light brown. The dorsal blotches are rather elongate, fairly narrow and medium to deep brown, either with or without light centers. The contrast between the dark dor-

sal blotches and the lighter ground color is not very great. The lateral interstitial skin can vary from yellow to orange. The interstitial color may spill over onto the leading edges of some lateral scales, but since the trailing edge of the preceding scales overlaps, the little brilliance may not be seen unless the snake is distended with food or tightly coiled.

Albino (amelanistic) and leucistic Texas rat snakes are more popular with hobbyists than are normal, wild-caught specimens. Of the two, the albino is the less pretty, being white (almost translucent when hatched) with pink saddles. The colors intensify somewhat with increasing age. The dorsal saddles of older adults are usually pale strawberry. The eyes of the amelanistic are pink.

The leucistic morph is a beautiful creature. It is a solid, unpatterned white and has gray-blue eyes.

Both the Baird's and the Texas rat snakes seem to reproduce best if hibernated; however, hibernation is not invariably necessary, especially with captive-bred and -born snakes that have reached sexual maturity. For these, little more than a slight winter cooling and a reduction of photoperiod may be necessary. Clutches number from 4 to 10 eggs. Incubation nears 90 days at 82° to 86°F (28° to 29°C). The hatchlings almost always feed readily on newborn mice. Large, healthy, females often produce two clutches annually. Hatchlings are about 1 foot (30 cm) in length.

Trans-Pecos Rat Snake

The overall distribution of *Bogertophis s. subocularis* is from central New Mexico and western Texas southward to the Mexican states of Durango and Nuevo Leon. Three color phases are rather commonly offered in the pet trade.

The "normal" phase of *B. s. subocularis* has a straw to olive-yellow ground color. The neck is marked with a pair of usually distinct black dorsolateral stripes that fade and become H-shaped blotches on the body. The arms of each H are formed by a darkening of the dorsolateral stripes. The crossbar of each H may be as dark as the arms, be considerably paler, or be lacking entirely. This latter seems especially apt to occur on captive-bred and -hatched specimens. Poorly defined lateral blotches are often evident.

The "blonde" morph is much yellower than the normal and the dorsolateral striping—even that on the neck—is either muted or absent. Body markings are in the form of light-centered, irregular saddles. Lateral blotches may or may not be present.

The third form remains the rarest. It has a ground color of pale to steel gray and is often referred to as the silver phase.

Although these snakes reach a fairly large size and bulk, captives prefer small prey items. Adults do best on a diet of baby mice or newborn rats. Although these snakes can constrict, they often do not do so. Hatchlings prefer small lizards, espe-

Once acclimated, glossy snakes, Arizona elegans, *are long-lived captives.*

cially the side-blotched lizard, *Uta stansburiana*, or anoles, *Anolis* sp.

In size, the Trans-Pecos rat snake may reach 5.5 feet (165 cm).

Trans-Pecos rat snakes often do not begin breeding until June and the three to seven eggs are laid in August or September. The eggs should be incubated at from 82° to 86°F (28° to 30°C).

Long-nosed Snake

Throughout most of its range in our southwestern states and Mexico, the long-nosed snake, *Rhinocheilus lecontei* ssp., is prettily patterned with saddles of black and red that are narrowly separated by yellow. The red fields are speckled with black, and the black fields with yellow. In some parts of their range, there is a tendency for long-nosed snakes to lack both the red and

Praying mantids are interesting predaceous insects, that occasionally appear in the pet trade and can also be found in the wild.

is light in color and unmarked. This kingsnake relative is able to constrict its prey, but often does not. Many specimens prefer lizards to mice and some are problematic captives. Long-nosed snakes are preferentially crepuscular and nocturnal. Frightened long-nosed snakes often void and smear cloacal contents on a handler.

Breeding: These are oviparous snakes that lay one or more clutches of eggs annually. Each clutch may contain from two to nine eggs. Hatchlings emerge after about two months of incubation at a temperature of 83° to 85°F (28° to 29°C). Nearly all long-nosed snakes that are offered in the pet trade are collected from the wild.

This snake is aided in its burrowing proclivities by its pointed nose. Even when provided with hiding caves and other darkened areas of seclusion, captives may burrow deeply. This activity can uproot and topple nonpotted plants. All cage furniture should be securely anchored.

most of the contrasting speckling. These snakes have, instead, broad bands of yellow or cream and black. There may be a lateral patch of yellow speckled with black contained in each black band. The belly

Glossy Snake

The glossy snake, *Arizona elegans* ssp., is a smooth-scaled bull snake relative. Although wild-collected, glossy snakes are often offered for sale at inexpensive prices. Many are reluctant to feed in captivity; of those that do, most prefer lizards over mice. In its many subspecies, the glossy snake ranges widely over the American West and Mexico.

Bark mantids are among the most effectively camouflaged of all predatory insects. This adult rests on a pine tree in Florida.

The cream dorsal ground color may, with advancing age, become heavily suffused with brown. This, in combination with the brown saddles and lateral markings present at all ages, may combine to produce a snake that is almost entirely brown. The belly is light. Glossy snakes can constrict, but many do not do so. Glossy snakes are essentially crepuscular and nocturnal. They are persistent burrowers that will uproot nonpotted plants. They seem to be hardier captives in areas of low humidity than in our humid eastern states or in fogbelts. An oviparous species, females may produce from 3 to 18 eggs, with the larger females producing the most. At 83° to 85°F (28° to 29°C), hatchlings emerge after about two months of incubation.

Insects

Mantids

Mantids (family Mantidae) are ideal inhabitants for the savannah terrarium, and range in size from 3 to 6 inches. If the showy exotics are not available to you due to legalities (several states forbid the importation of these creatures due to possible impact on agriculture) or cost, those you find in your own area will do just fine. The native species may be your best choice in any case, because of the availability of food and natural adaptation to the regional climate. No matter what the area of origin, the care requirements for native and

The palmetto stick insect is of stockier build than many species. It is an abundant species in Florida. The male is smaller than the female.

exotic mantids are much the same.

Mantids have a mobile triangular head with large compound eyes at the upper two corners and the mouth at the third. Their first pair of legs are adapted for grasping, with grasping barbs and a serrate comb along the back edges of the first and second leg segments. These legs are held up in mock supplication in front of the body, which gives rise to the common name, praying mantis. They are carnivorous, feeding on other insects, and occasionally small frogs, lizards and hummingbirds. The female of some species (there are some 1,800 worldwide) may devour the male while mating.

Of the 11 species in the United States, perhaps the most familiar and most widespread is the green Carolina Mantis, *Stagmomantis car-*

olina. It is found from Virginia to Florida, and westward to Mexico and California. Nymphs may be purchased from companies that provide biological gardening controls.

Mantids need savanna caging with a source of moisture. They are arboreal, spending their days perched in branches above the ground, swaying back and forth with tiny air currents, awaiting prey. Their insect diet includes crickets, moths, small wasps and bees, true bugs and caterpillars. Nymphs will feed on fruit flies; they prefer the wingless varieties to the winged ones because they are easier to track. Although mantids don't need a hot spot light as reptiles do, they do need enough bright lighting in their cage to initiate natural behavior in their prey. Daytime temperatures of 75°F (24°C) are adequate; nighttime temperatures can go as low as the low 60's F (16° to 18°C) for mantids from temperate areas. Mist a portion of the cage daily so they can drink, and make sure the caging is well ventilated.

Stick Insects

Walking sticks (family Phasmidae) have a greatly elongated body, a tiny head, and long slender legs. In the United States, they are found from Florida northward along the Atlantic coast, and westward to New Mexico and Alberta. Tropical species such as the Indian walking stick *(Carasius morosus)* or the giant spiny stick insect *(Eurycantha*

catcarata) have been popular imports, but new regulations may make these pets hard to obtain. Many stick insects—particularly the Indian walking stick—are parthenogenic, and will drop several eggs a day during deposition season. Since these feed on the foliage of deciduous trees and shrubs, such as grapes and oaks, the potential damage is enormous.

Walking sticks have two defensive mechanisms. When threatened, they fall off their twig to the ground and remain motionless until they feel the danger has passed. Faced with imminent danger, they can shed several legs as a diversion. The legs are quickly regenerated. Three of the walking sticks found in the United States are the northern walking stick, *Diapheromona femorata* (males are 3 inches [7.6 cm], females are 3.75 inches [9.5 cm]), the giant walking stick, *Megaphasma dentricus* (3 to 6 inches [15 cm]), and the palmetto walking stick, *Anisomorpha buprestoides.*

Walking sticks are arboreal, and need sticks at least the diameter of their bodies to perch upon. Place potted food plants in the cages, or add new branches each day for food leaves, inserted into a small jar filled with water. Walking sticks won't eat dried-out foliage. Mist a portion of the foliage each morning so the walking sticks can drink; they may get enough from the foliage but it's hard to determine if their needs for moisture are being met.

Chapter Five
Desert/Aridland Terrarium

Deserts are dry areas, with less than 10 inches (25 cm) of moisture a year. The plants have reduced leaves—the cactus spines are a good example—or bear leaves only during the rainy season, like the ocotillo cactus. Reptiles and amphibians that dwell in the desert exhibit wonderful modifications for a terrestrial and saxicolous—rock-dwelling—existence. They may have palmate feet, to avoid sinking into the sand, or dark skin, to heat up faster in the morning before the heat becomes too intense, or reduced limbs, to make "swimming" through sand easier. Some, like the leopard and banded geckos, collared lizards, bearded dragons, and the sandfish skink, feed readily and adjust easily to captivity and to captive breeding. Others, like the horned lizards (horny toads), are specialized feeders that do not live long in captivity and that should not be collected.

Desert terraria are among the favorites of hobbyists; they are not difficult to build, and can be constructed at several levels of complexity. Properly arranged desert terraria provide attractive habitats that stimulate both the interest of the hobbyist and the normal and natural behaviors of the inhabitants.

Substrate

Over the years, we have noted concerns about the use of sand as a substrate. The principal concern seems to be the possibility of intestinal impaction if the sand is ingested by the inhabitants. It is suggested that comparatively slow-moving, heavy-bodied, desert omnivores and herbivores, such as bearded dragons, chuckwallas, and spiny-tailed agamids, are more prone to intestinal impaction than insectivorous species. However, over a period of more than 40 years that we have kept and bred her-petofauna, we have never lost a lizard, nor even had a serious problem, from impaction. After all, what is a desert if not sand?

Multiple factors may also intervene to prevent impaction in the

of sand. As with nearly any other naturally occurring substrate, sand comes in a variety of grain sizes and mineral composition. We urge, if the chance of sand-related problems does worry you, that you choose a smooth-grained desert sand. Several brands are now available. The use of smooth, variably sized river gravel can also be considered. Do not use sharp-sided silica aquarium gravel as a substrate.

The depth of the substrate can vary. If only a fine covering, your tank will, of course, be lighter, but will not be suitable for animals that burrow. If 3 to 6 inches (7.6–15 cm) of substrate is used, you will be able to better maintain the barely dampened bottom layer and the dry top layer preferred by many burrowing lizards, snakes, and toads.

Desert setups may be as small as a gallon jar, or as large as this room-sized enclosure at the Jardin des Plantes in Paris. The lizards are Moroccan spiny-tailed agamids, Uromastyx acanthinurus.

wild. A wild amphibian or reptile has a far more active lifestyle than that of even the best-kept captive. It seems probable that normal hydration, a normal diet, and a metabolism elevated by a normal activity pattern may assist in moving accidentally ingested sand through the digestive system of a wild specimen.

That said, we are the first to admit that there are different kinds

Cage Furniture

Rock ledges and caves, individual basking rocks, potted aridland plants, corkbark hiding areas, and cholla cactus skeletons can be provided both for decoration and the psychological well-being of your specimens. Since most desert-dwelling reptiles are adapted to low humidity, the terrarium should be in a well-ventilated area. A screen top will prevent a buildup of cage humidity that could be detrimental to the health of your desert pets.

Long-nosed snakes, Rhinochellus lecontei *ssp. (top left), and shovel-nosed snakes,* Chionactis occipitalus *ssp. (top right), are both burrowing aridland species. Both the Queensland bearded dragon,* Pogona brevis *(left), and the lesser bearded dragon,* P. minima *(bottom left), thrive in aridland terraria.*

Desert Terrarium

Choose a tank of suitable and adequate size. Since most desert herps are relatively active, the larger your terrarium, the better, especially if you intend to keep several specimens of one kind or to have a desert reptile and amphibian community. Our most successful and easily maintained desert terraria have been 50 to 150 gallons (189 to 568 L). It seems that the larger the tank, the more forgiving it is of errors and oversights. Of course, if you are intending to keep only a single pair of desert or leopard geckos, a burrowing skink or two, or a couple of arid-adapted toads, a 15-gallon (57 L) tank will be adequate, but a 20-gallon (76 L) will be better. Be *certain* that the stand on which the terrarium will be placed can safely hold the weight.

Materials Needed

- Terrarium and stand.
- Substrates; fine upper layer (sand) and coarse lower layer (pea-sized river rock).
- Drought-tolerant plants (cacti and succulents).
- Rocks and/or other terrarium furniture (rocks, contorted branches of grape and manzanita, cholla skeletons, corkbark—both flat and tubular sections—water receptacle), and camouflaged hide boxes.
- A piece of air-conditioning filter material the length and width of the terrarium, or enough plastic screening to fold into two layers between the two substrates.
- Nontoxic sealant to hold rocks or heavy cage furniture safely in place.
- Undertank heaters
- Terrarium top; metal-framed screen or wire top is best. Full glass tops are not acceptable.
- Lighting fixtures and bulbs (full-spectrum fluorescent and heat-producing, directed-beam, color-corrected, incandescent bulbs).
- Small ventilation fan (optional).

Setup Procedure

1 Place the tank on its stand with the undertank heaters in place. Follow directions carefully when placing and connecting the heaters.

2 Place and seal any heavy cage furniture (rocks, limbs, and so on) in place. This is a particularly important step, for if these items are just placed on top of the surface sand, herps can burrow under and allow the rocks to settle on themselves. This can cause injury or the death of the animals. Allow a minimum of 24 hours for sealant curing.

3 Place the large, smooth, variably-sized river rock on the bottom of the tank to the depth desired—we suggest 2 to 3 inches (5–7.6 cm). Do not use aquarium gravel.

4 Lay the air-conditioning filter material on top of the gravel—a double thickness of plastic window screening will also suffice.

5 Pour the fine sand over the filter material or screen to a depth of several inches. If you prefer a textured surface, you can mix a few pieces of variably sized river rock with the sand.

6 Place the plants where you wish them. We prefer to leave the plants in their pots and sink the pots to the rim in the sand. This contains the moisture and plant food better when the plants are watered and prevents extensive areas of sand from becoming overly moist or saturated with fertilizer. If the plants begin suffering from insufficient light or other growth problems, it is a simple matter to replace them.

As an alternative, the plants can be removed from their pots and planted directly in the sand. Extreme care will then need to be used in watering and fertilizing, and replacing the plant is more difficult.

7 Arrange any remaining *lightweight* cage furniture on the sand surface, or partially buried, as desired. Depending on the number and compatibility of the specimens to be kept in the tank, from one to several secure hide boxes or a hiding area should be included.

8 If the lighting is inside the terrarium, position and affix

the fixtures. If the lighting fixtures are to be positioned above the tank, install the top, make sure it is escape-proof, and correct the angle and closeness of the lighting.

Lighting and Heating

We feel that a minimum of two (preferably four) fluorescent bulbs be used in a large desert tank. These should include one BL type black light and from one to three full-spectrum tubes. These will supply at least some of the beneficial UV-A and UV-B rays provided in the wild by natural, unfiltered sunlight. Additionally, directed-beam incandescent bulbs should be used to provide basking hot spots for the day-active (diurnal), heliothermic reptiles; the necessary thermal gradients can be provided either, or both, vertically and horizontally. To provide vertical gradients, direct the bulb at the summit of a high rock. Adjust the bulb size or distance

until the top of the rock is warmed to a temperature determined to be suitable for the species being maintained. The desired temperature may be as high as 110° to 115°F (43° to 46°C) for lizards such as chuckwallas, spiny-tailed agamids, and bearded dragons. Temperatures of sand-surface basking areas can be adjusted in the same manner. Sufficient lighting is as important for the live plants as for the animals.

Cage Furniture

Rocks and, occasionally, corkbark can be affixed to the back and/or side glass of the terrarium. There are lightweight plastic rock backgrounds that offer dozens of small lookout and concealment areas. These treatments can offer additional beauty, complexity, and balance to your desert terrarium, and provide a feeling of naturalness and security to escarpment-inhabiting amphibians

and reptiles. It is important that any rocks and other components used in a terrarium ledge be affixed both to each other and to the aquarium glass against which they are stacked. Clear silicone aquarium sealant is often used for this purpose. Do not depend on the integrity of the sealant alone. Rather, build your ledge carefully, depending on the materials to support each other. Consider the sealant only a part of the system that prevents the terrarium inhabitants from moving or dislodging rocks. Apply the sealant liberally, but assure also that it is not visible when the terrarium is viewed from the front. Be absolutely certain that any hides or planters built into the ledge have sufficient integrity to withstand the rigors of time and the efforts of the inhabitants to dislodge them. Periodically check the integrity of the ledges and reaffix them as necessary.

Plants for Desert Terraria

You must pay as much attention to the choice of plants as you do to the selection of your animals. Remember that the nearer the tip of a leaf is to an incandescent lightbulb, the more light and warmth present. Thus, although the top of a sansevieria leaf may be receiving sufficient light for proper growth, the leaf may be severely burned by the heat from the bulb. Choose and position plants and bulbs sympathetically. Be ready to change plant species if necessary from those requiring high light situations to less demanding species if growth becomes spindly or discolored.

Cacti

Many species and cultivars of common and easily grown cacti are available at stores and nurseries. Most grow well under intense artificial lighting, and some flower freely under such conditions. Despite their obvious armament, we have used cacti in our terraria over the decades and have never had any problems. Among others that grow well are the genus *Mammillaria*; several of the less lethally armed fishhook cacti, *Ferocactus*; star cacti, *Astrophytum*; and the comparatively spineless beaver-tail cacti, which are cultivars of the genus *Opuntia*.

Euphorbias

Euphorbias are the Old World counterpart of cacti. Members of the genus *Euphorbia* vary from tree-sized succulents that drip quantities of a quite toxic, latex-like sap when injured, to tiny spherical tennis ball-sized species that are

Exotic cacti and succulents are now available in nurseries across the world.

Euphorbia globosa, the "baseball plant" is a delightful species that thrives in desert setups.

ideally suited for a desert terrarium. Other examples include the varied crowns-of-thorns that, despite their spiny aspect, make fine terrarium plants when small. Like cacti, many euphorbias are readily available in nurseries and garden shops. Most of the smaller euphorbias will grow well under dry terrarium conditions, but few have significant flowers.

Some individuals develop a severe sensitivity to euphorbias. If you notice redness or itching, contact your doctor immediately.

Haworthias and Gasterias

These are commonly grown nursery plants that cluster readily into impressive, dwarfed thickets. Most of these lily relatives have leaves tipped with a rather weak spine and weakly serrate, spiny leaf edges. Of the two genera, the haworthias seem the easier to cultivate and require little in the way of winter cooling. The gasterias, on the other hand, do enjoy cooler and drier conditions during the short days of winter. Most of the commonly offered species in both

genera will grow well in somewhat less light than most cacti and euphorbias.

Sansevierias

These are ideal moderate- to high-light terrarium plants available in myriad species and cultivars. Some are so tall that they will be suitable only for the tallest terraria; others are dwarfed and form attractive, clustered rosettes of green. For enthusiasts who like a little variety in terrarium plants, many of the sansevierias are available in both normal and variegated forms.

Pachypodiums

Choose the species of *Pachypodium* carefully. Some of the commonly offered varieties will quickly grow to heights of more than 15 feet (4.6 m)! However, a few of the small species are interesting, contorted plants that grow well in brilliantly lit terraria. These are specialty plants that you may have to search out at mail order dealers or at plant sales at botanical gardens.

Desert Invertebrates

Tarantulas

Tarantulas are members of the spider family Therapsidae. They are found in temperate and tropical areas the world over, and are characterized by their large size, largely terrestrial habits, and fangs that move up and down instead of

Tarantulas of many species are popular as captives. Here we have the Costa Rican zebra, Aphonopelma seemanni *(top), and the Mexican fireleg,* Brachypelma boehmei *(bottom).*

sideways like all other spiders. Like many other spiders, tarantulas are cannibalistic.

Housing and maintenance: Tarantulas have modest housing and maintenance needs. They must be kept singly, of course, fed regularly, and provided with enough moisture that their lungs don't dry out. They dine quite happily two or three times a week on crickets, a few mealworms or other insects, and an occasional pinky mouse. The amount of moisture needed is partially determined by their area of origin or the species. Those from the American West are desert dwellers, and need less ambient moisture than species from the rainforest. All types must have a water dish in their tank at all times; use a hand-held sprayer to mist the cage at least weekly. Add a few potted plants to increase the moisture levels for tropical species. The lungs, which are layers of folded cuticle, are called book lungs because they look like the pages of a book. Air exchange takes place across these cuticle layers.

Humidity is important not only for breathing, but for movement. Tarantulas extend their legs—or walk—by reducing and then increasing the blood pressure in their legs. If their surroundings are too dry, they lose body moisture across the lung surface. Reduced body moisture results in decreased blood pressure, which means the legs don't work.

Physical description: Having functional legs is important not only for the ability to move around, but also in sensing the world around the spider. Tarantulas have very poor eyesight from their tiny eight paired eyes. They rely instead on sensory organs in their feet, which respond to the sensations of both scent and touch.

Tarantulas rely on their sense of touch to keep them out of trouble, and most of the New World species have added an unusual fillip to their defense mechanism—the short barbed hairs that copiously cover their body and legs are irritating, much like tiny porcupine quills. When the tarantula is upset, it rubs its legs against its body and sends a shower of irritating hairs toward its aggressor.

Behavior: Tarantulas can spin silk, which they use several ways. The first is to line their burrow. Some species wrap their prey in silk while the venom/digestive juices begin to work. A third use for the silk is to literally lay a trail for the wandering tarantulas' return. They follow their silk back to their burrow or lair. These are largely sedentary hunters, waiting patiently at the mouth of their burrow or on a cliff face or tree trunk for any food that happens by. The only time the tarantula wanders is during the breeding season, when the urge to find a mate is the strongest.

Breeding: Both male and female tarantulas have their genital opening on the underside of the abdomen. The male uses a modified structure on his pedipalp called the embolus to transfer the sperm packet to the female. When the male and female mate, the female rears back, exposing her genital opening, and the male places the sperm packet into the opening. She will retain the sperm until she lays her eggs, generally two weeks to several months after mating. The eggs are deposited into a silk-lined bowl the female has dug into the cage substrate. Once the eggs are laid the female will roll the eggs and their silken wrapping into a sphere. She will generally hold the sphere in her mouth or keep it underneath her until the eggs hatch. After the spiderlings hatch, they molt several times before they begin feeding. When you see them beginning to eat each other, offer them wingless fruit flies, pinhead crickets, and other tiny insects. Egg sacs generally contain as many as 200 eggs, so you'll probably have lots of babies.

Sexual maturity is the beginning of the end for male tarantulas. Once the males become sexually mature, they have only a few months to live. Both sexes may take up to 10 years to reach sexual maturity; the female, once mature, has another 10 to 20 years to live. If you're looking at tarantulas with the thought of acquiring one, be sure you get a female.

Selecting a tarantula: In buying your tarantulas, ask for guidance from the vendor. The basic guidelines are simple: Buy the biggest, fattest female you can find and be cautious about buying one with a bare abdomen—it could be a male on his way out.

When you get your tarantula home, place it in a desert/woodland tank with enough substrate to permit it to burrow. The ground dwellers, which include the large Goliath bird-eater *(Theraphosa blondi)*, and the Colombian lesser black tarantula (*Xeristhis immanis*), may dig their own burrow, but generally prefer to use one already made. The arboreal or off-ground species, which include the Trinidad chevron (*Psalmopoeus cambridgii*), the pinktoe (*Avicularia avicularia*), and the Trinidad mahogany tarantula (*Tapinauchenius plumipes*), prefer to be off the substrate, in a road bank, on trees or cliff faces, or in agricultural crops. Offer them a site raised off the substrate, either a small shelf or some bark slabs secured in one corner. If you use a vertical cage format, with the former top of the cage now the side, your tarantula will have room to build its retreat in one of the upper corners. Use a hand-held mister filled with dechlorinated water to lightly mist the tank; your tarantula may lap up the water droplets or just enjoy the increased dampness. Do not spray her—or him!—directly; point the spray bottle upward so the mist falls like gentle rain.

Leave your tarantula in its new cage for a few hours or overnight, and offer it live food. If it doesn't eat immediately, you can leave the insects in overnight; your tarantula may not be hungry, or it may need additional time to settle in.

Shedding: These spiders shed frequently when young and less fre-quently as they mature. Shedding is presaged by the spider lying on its back with its legs extended. The spider will not respond to a gentle touch and may seem dead. This sleep mode occurs when the new skin and the old skin are separat-ing, so the spider can literally lift itself, abdomen first, out of its old skin. The moisture level in the cage is important during this disengage-ment. The spider is very vulnerable before and during shedding, and must not be moved or disturbed in any way. An interrupted molt is almost always fatal to the spider.

Use large forceps to handle your tarantula, or shepherd it into a con-tainer that you have placed in its cage. Tarantulas can be handled, but you want to avoid stressing your pet to the extent that it rasps off its body hairs in defense, and you don't want to take the chance of it becoming frightened and jumping off your hand. Although tarantula venom evolved as a food-procuring device, you also don't want to find out if you're sensitive to any of the components. As time goes on and you feel more comfortable with your spider, you can use one hand to gently urge it to walk onto your other hand, but remember that this kind of handling places your spider at risk for falling and may induce it to release its barbed hair.

Scorpions

Scorpions are found both in the Old and New World, and most adapt readily to aridland or desert terrariums. Although they may vary in size and toxicity of venom, all look pretty much alike. They bear a pair of pinchers on the front end, a recurved tail with a venom-containing stinger on the back end, and four pairs of legs on the abdomen. They are related to the spiders, but are in a separate order, *Scorpionida*. There are 1,500 to 2,000 species of scorpions worldwide, approximately 70 of which are found in the United States.

Scorpion fanciers commonly keep the hairy scorpions (genus *Hadrurus*, family Luridae). These are long lived (to more than two decades), highly predacious—even cannibalistic—species of moderate size and varying toxicity. Adapted to arid surroundings, some can evidently obtain all their moisture needs from their prey.

Several small scorpion species of the genus *Centruroides* (family Buthidae) occur in North America. Those in the southeast are minimally toxic, but at least one species in the southwest is potentially lethal. **Anyone with a sensitivity to any insect venom should be extremely careful when working with scorpions**. Although most of the *Centruroides* are a dark smudged tan or gold color, those in southern Florida are larger and nearly all black.

Probably the most popular Old World scorpion is the emperor scorpion, genus *Pandinus*. Unlike many cannabalistic scorpions, the emperor scorpions can be kept if enough food is provided. Those housed together should be approxi-

This female emperor scorpion, Pandinus imperator, *is carrying a large clutch of neonates. The babies will soon molt and assume a dark color.*

mately the same size, and females carrying young should be housed separately. Despite their impressive 6- to 7-inch (15 to 18 cm) length, the sting of *Pandinus* has been likened to a bee sting; however, most seem reluctant to sting.

Provide a sand substrate for your scorpions, and pieces of bark to hide beneath. Although plants are not necessary in their terrarium, species from woodland areas could probably tolerate the extra moisture provided by plants. Desertland species need no extra moisture beyond their food insects (crickets) and a once or twice weekly gentle misting.

The Sonoran green toad, Bufo retiformis, *is a small and remarkably beautiful desert species.*

Desert Amphibia

Although some amphibians find suitably moist microhabitats for survival in the desert, it is difficult for most to adapt to life in a desert terrarium. We will mention only three aridland-adapted toads, and caution that none can survive in areas of absolute dryness. It is important that if you choose to keep amphibia in a desert terrarium, the lower layers of sand be kept moistened—trickle water through a standpipe—a shallow tray of fresh water be kept always available, and the entire terrarium be gently misted about twice a week.

Desert Toads

Most people immediately recognize toads as such, but few realize the considerable beauty of some of the desert species. As a group, toads are rather squat, variably warty, often with dry-appearing skin and protuberant eyes with wonderfully intricate designs of gold in the irises. Many toads have easily seen parotoid (shoulder) glands that produce an acrid-tasting toxin effective in deterring some predators but of little consequence to others.

Many species of toads seek water only for the purpose of breeding, although some seldom wander far from the environs of ponds or other water sources. None can withstand conditions of absolute dryness for long. Toads, like other amphibia, will dehydrate unless some moisture is available. Since toads absorb moisture, and the impurities it contains, through their skin, it is of paramount importance that both their water sources and the substrate are clean and chemical-free.

Two of the prettiest desert toads in the United States are the Sonoran and the common green, *Bufo retiformis* and *B. debilis* ssp., respectively. Both near 2 inches (5.1 cm) from snout to vent and have rather flattened bodies. Both live in irrigated regions and oases in the deserts of the Southwest. Both are very hardy, readily accepting small insects and arachnids. The Sonoran green toad is a protected species found only in Arizona and

adjacent Mexico, and is now seldom seen captive in collections, except in zoos. It has a complex black reticulate pattern separating the spots of green or goldish-green.

The Common Green Toad

This toad has an eastern (*B. d. debilis*) and a western (*B. d. insidior*) subspecies, remains quite common, and may occasionally be purchased at rather low prices. The eastern race has small, well-separated black spots on a green ground. The western form has many of the black spots connected, but not a fully reticulate pattern such as on the Sonoran green toad.

Both species of green toad have nasal, insectlike trills with fair carrying power and may be found actively breeding during the desert monsoons. They are nocturnal in their activity patterns, and an occasional heavy misting will induce them to emerge and actively forage for their insect repast. These seem to be long-lived little creatures. None currently are captive bred.

The Great Plains Toad

Bufo cognatus, a larger and duller species, is also a common denizen of aridland habitats in our central and southwestern states. It is also primarily nocturnal and has an overpoweringly loud, staccato, rivet-gun-like call. Great Plains toads look much like most of the other garden toads or hoptoads. Some specimens are prettily patterned with light-outlined, dark-edged spots that are, themselves, considerably darker than the normally light gray ground color. Other specimens may be quite pallid and show little pattern contrast. Great Plains toads may occasionally attain 3.5 inches (8.9 cm) in length and are very hardy in captivity.

Lizards

Eyelidded or Eublepharine Geckos

The geckos in the family Euble-pharidae vary in size, but are of similar appearance (see pages 43 to 46). They all have tiny scales and easily autotomized tails. They lack toe pads, and have well-developed and entirely functional eyelids. The Asian leopard gecko and the African fat-tailed gecko (see pages 44 to 46) are the two species most readily available in the pet trade. The several banded geckos are occasionally available in the pet trade, and two species may be collected in the deserts and aridlands of the southwestern United States.

Description: The tails of some of these attractive and hardy geckos are proportionately slender, those of others, heavy. The caudal scales of all eublepharines are arranged in distinct whorls. The tails of all are easily broken, those of the slender-tailed species especially so, and, like the tails of other lizards, the regenerated tail, often fat and bulbous, differs from the original in shape and scalation.

Since they are rather slow-moving, most eublepharines can be moved by shepherding them into the palm of one hand with the other, then cupping them with the free hand to prevent them from falling.

Behavior: Some of the larger species are capable of overpowering and eating newly hatched nestlings of small ground-nesting birds and rodents. Captives adapt well to a varied diet of crickets, common and giant mealworms, butterworms, spiders, and other commonly available arthropods. Limit the number of waxworms offered; these have an unhealthy calcium-to-phosphorus ratio. Newborn (pinky) mice are also eagerly accepted by many, if not most, of the larger geckos. Although eublepharines are capable of eating comparatively large prey items, food offered should be kept within reason. If you're fortunate enough to have access to an insecticide-free yard or garden, an even more variable diet can be offered to your lizards. Not only are sow bugs and hairless caterpillars a welcome change, but, because of their more varied diet, wild insects generally contain more nutrition than domestically raised ones. Occasionally dust the insects with a calcium/multivitamin additive that is high in D_3 before feeding them to your geckos. They may also enjoy soft, ripe, pulpy fruit such as papaya, skinless mango, and kiwi. Supplemental calcium and vitamin D_3 is especially important to gravid females and rapidly growing juveniles.

Breeding: Some well-fed eublepharine geckos may attain sexual maturity in slightly less than a year. Adult eublepharines may be easily sexed by comparing the areas immediately anterior and posterior to the vent (anus). Males, especially those that are sexually active, can be distinguished from the females by their bulbous tail base, containing the hemipenes, and, on many but *not* all species, by a vaguely chevron-shaped arrangement of enlarged preanal pores. Females that are incubated at very high temperatures often have malelike preanal pores. Males of some eublepharine species are slightly larger than females.

As with many other lizards, the sex of eublepharine geckos is determined by incubation temperature rather than genetic arrangement. This is referred to as *temperature-induced sex determination* and commonly designated by the acronym TSD. To produce both sexes, incubation temperatures should range from 84° to 87°F (29° to 30.5°C). If cooler than 84°F (29°C), the sex ratio of the hatchlings will favor females; if warmer than 87°F (30.5°C), a preponderance of males will develop. If for

some reason incubation temperatures drift upward into the mid-90°s F (34° to 36°C), females are again produced, but many embryos will die in the egg. Excessively warm incubation temperatures may result in skeletal deformities or other aberrations, among which are extraordinarily light colors—some bordering on a leucistic appearance.

Adult male eublepharine geckos are highly territorial and only one should be kept to a cage. Several females may be housed with him.

Although winter cooling may not be a mandatory prelude to successful breeding of many eublepharines, cooling and shortening the photoperiod will measurably enhance your likelihood of success.

A healthy female eublepharine gecko should produce several clutches of two eggs each over the seven- or eight-month breeding season. Incubation duration varies somewhat with temperature, but will probably average about 55 days.

Being soft-shelled, eublepharine eggs are quite moisture-permeable, which makes the level of moisture in the incubation medium critical. Keep the medium moist by adding small amounts of dechlorinated water daily or as needed.

Namibian Sand Gecko; Genus *Chondrodactylus*

This is one of the large number of geckos without eyelids. The Namibian is a robust gecko of the southern and southwest African deserts and savannas. It is an

Chondrodactylus angulifer, *Namibian sand gecko, is a fearsome predator on large desert insects.*

entirely terrestrial species that is adult at a length of about 6 inches (15 cm). Of this length less than half is tail length.

The Namibian sand gecko, *C. angulifer*, is active during the warmer months of the year. It may become less so during the austral (southern hemispheric) winter. Captive specimens reproduce better when cooled somewhat during our shorter winter days and nights. Actual hibernation does not seem to be necessary either for the well-being of the lizards or to assure fertility.

Males are capable of producing clicking vocalizations. These are most frequently heard during territorial disputes or when the gecko is restrained.

This is a sexually dimorphic species. The males are somewhat the larger of the sexes and bear from one to several pairs of dark-bordered white eye-shaped ocelli along their back. The females lack the ocelli, having instead several posteriorly

directed dark dorsal chevrons. Females have a more prominently banded tail than males. The overall color scheme varies from buff to reddish, blending quite well with the sands on which these lizards live. The heads of both male and female are large and a fringe of serrate scales is found beneath the toes. The large eyes are partially shaded and protected by a flange of enlarged scales.

Namibian sand geckos are quick to utilize the vacated burrows of other desert animals. In the terrarium they readily accept rock caves or other such areas of seclusion. This gecko species habitually stands tall at the mouth of its burrow, its legs nearly fully straightened. It seems alert and is ever ready to retreat back into the burrow if danger threatens. *Chondrodactylus* is, itself, a fearsome predator, easily overcoming insects, arachnids, and even smaller lizards. As captives, most adults will readily accept pinky mice along with the more traditional invertebrate fare.

In captivity, the Namibian sand gecko is not an overly active species. A pair or a trio may be maintained in a 20-gallon (76 L)—long floor space 12 × 30 inches (30 × 76 cm)—terrarium. Either a desert or a dry savanna setup will suffice. Daytime temperatures of 88° to 92°F (31° to 33°C) should be provided for most of the year. Nighttime temperatures can be lowered by several degrees. A slight winter cooling for about two months, coinciding with the shortest natural photoperiod,

The web-footed sand gecko, Palmatogecko rangei, *prefers a diet of tiny insects.*

seems to heighten breeding success when temperatures are again raised.

Web-footed Sand Gecko; Genus *Palmatogecko*

This is a curious little—to 4 inches (10 cm)—gecko of slender stature and sand-swimming habits. It is one of the many reptile species endemic to the fog-shrouded Namib Desert of southwestern Africa. Like many other desert animals, this is a persistently nocturnal species. If conditions are suitable, it is active throughout the year.

The web-footed gecko is clad in finely granular scales similar in color to those of the sands on which it lives. Tans, buffs, and the palest of grays are the usual hues. The two most unusual external characteristics are the feet and the eyes of this

species. The toes are webbed to their tips with a thin pliable skin, giving the lizard the appearance of wearing snowshoes. The eyes are very large and protuberant. The iris of each is colored in dark and red pigments that are especially apparent in well-lit situations when the vertical pupils are tightly contracted. Males produce clicks and squeaks, both during territorial displays and when restrained.

Because of the proximity of cold austral ocean currents, the coastal Namibian desert is often shrouded in dense fog. The nearness of the ocean minimizes daytime/nighttime temperature fluctuations. Duplicating these conditions will take some work on your part.

Maintenance: As a result of the persistent fog, some moisture often

One of the prettiest recent reptilian introductions in the pet trade is the painted agama, Laudakia stellio brachydactyla, *from North Africa.*

lowed skeletons of cholla cactus can also be supplied but are not absolutely necessary. Web-footed geckos are burrow diggers and dwellers, both to escape the worst of the heat and to retain their own body moisture. Therefore, it's necessary to dampen the lower layers of the sand substrate in your terrarium. In the terrarium daytime sand surface temperatures of between 88° and 95°F (31° to 35°C) are suitable. The below-surface temperature should be somewhat cooler. Nighttime temperatures should be allowed to drop by only a few degrees, if at all. Web-footed geckos drink water from flat receptacles, and lap the droplets from the rocks in their terrarium if these are misted during their period of activity. They prefer prey insects of small size, and are especially fond of termites and baby crickets.

Web-footed geckos have a reputation of being delicate captives. While it is true that they prefer rather exact terrarium conditions, if these conditions are met, and if adequately small food insects are provided, the species is quite hardy. As with all geckos, to prevent aggression, no more than a single male should be kept in each terrarium. From one to several females may be housed with each male. This species is now being captive bred in small numbers by dedicated hobbyists. The hatchlings are tiny and initially require fruit flies and termites, prey items that even the adults enjoy.

exists beneath the surface of the sands. It is this layer of slight moisture that web-footed geckos seek when constructing their home burrows. You can provide the desired moisture gradient if you use several inches of sand substrate and a standpipe in one corner of the tank. The standpipe is simply a 1-inch (2.5 cm) piece of PVC pipe that extends from just above the top of the sand to the bottom layer. Water poured into the pipe will moisten the lower levels of sand while allowing the upper levels to remain dry.

Provide a few flat rocks, such as pieces of shale, and drought-tolerant plants (sansevierias or haworthias) for cage furniture. Pieces of corkbark and the bleached, hol-

The inland bearded dragon, Pogona vitticeps, *may just be America's favorite large lizard. It should be offered a diet high in vegetable matter.*

Painted Rock Agama

In recent years a colorful subspecies of the rough-scaled rock agama, *Laudakia stellio*, has been available to hobbyists. This, *L. s. brachydactyla*, has been dubbed the painted rock agama by dealers. Actually, the name is rather descriptive of this robust, spiny-scaled, desert rockland creature.

This foot-long (30 cm) agamid is one of the most brilliantly colored of the whorled-tailed agama species. When seen from above it is difficult to decide whether the ground color of a reproductively active male of this form is russet or turquoise, as bars of both are often present in nearly equal amounts. The sides are darker, the head is tan, and the tail is ringed in tan and blue. The color is somewhat duller when the lizards are not in breeding condition. This subspecies, which occurs in Saudi Arabia, the Sinai Desert, Israel, and Jordan, is referred to as the Hardun by the Moslems of North Africa. The flattened body form allows this lizard to take cover in fissures and exfoliations. It is an agile and alert lizard that enjoys hot temperatures and basks extensively. A night temperature of 70°F (21°C) can be raised to 85°F (29°C) during the day and the illuminated basking area can attain a temperature of 115°F (46°C). Multiple clutches of two or three up to a dozen eggs each, usually four to eight, are produced.

Hobbyists have found this to be a reasonably hardy lizard, and it is now being bred in captivity in small numbers.

Bearded Dragon

The inland bearded dragon, *Pogona vitticeps*, is currently one of America's favorite lizards. It is annually bred in captivity by the thousands and in recent years the price of these lizards has plummeted from $150 each to as little as $25. The inland bearded dragon, usually referred to in America simply as the bearded dragon, is a heavy-bodied, attractive, but subtly colored Australian agamid species. It is a quiet, confiding, omnivorous lizard that can become very responsive to its keeper.

The bearded dragon is a heat-tolerant basker. Body temperatures of basking lizards may exceed 95°F (35°C). When they are cold, they are reclusive and inactive. Although often seen on the ground, bearded dragons easily ascend fence posts, dead trees, anthills, and other such elevated positions to bask and display. In a terrarium, they enjoy elevating themselves on limbs and rocks and will use a brightly lit basking area having a surface temperature of 115°F (46°C). The most dominant males usually assume the most prominent positions. A curious armwaving (circumduction), used particularly often by subadult and adult female dragons, apparently acts as an appeasement gesture.

The beards consist of black, pointed scales and are distended for territorial and breeding displays. The throats of the males darken noticeably as the breeding season nears. All bearded dragons are oviparous.

Diet: Captive dragons will readily eat vitamin/calcium enhanced crickets, mealworms, grasshoppers, and an occasional pinky mouse. Chopped greens, such as collards, mustard, kale, and romaine, grated vegetables, and some fruit should be regularly offered.

Bearded dragons seem prone to calcium metabolism disorders. Make sure that the calcium/phosphorus ratios are at least 2:1 in favor of calcium—the diet listed here meets this need—and that sufficient vitamin D_3 is provided to permit calcium absorption and metabolism. This is particularly important to fast-growing baby dragons and to ovulating females.

Breeding: Young sexually mature inland dragon females can be amazingly prolific. Large, well-fed females may produce over 100 eggs a year, occasionally more than 35 a clutch. Fecundity decreases after the lizards attain five or six years of age, and may virtually end late in life.

Spiny-tailed Agamids

The several species of the agamid lizard genus *Uromastyx* are variously known as spiny-tails, dabb lizards, and, most recently, by the diminutive of uro.

Of the more than 15 species in this genus, only 4 are found in the American pet trade with any regularity. Most are moderately sized lizards with the males attaining 13 to

16 inches (33 to 41 cm) and the females being considerably smaller.

Pudgy, unafraid lizards, if offered suitable diets and spacious quarters with deep substrate, and a basking area that has a surface temperature of 115°F (46°C), the spiny-tailed agamids will do well in captivity. A low cage humidity is important. Although the spiny-tails are occasionally available in neighborhood pet stores, their exacting requirements will make them unsuitable candidates for all but very experienced collectors.

In their native habitat, the spiny-tailed lizards are accomplished tunnelers, at times constructing home burrows of 10 feet (3 m) or more in length. The burrows are often begun among rocks or near the root mass of a low shrub. When the lizards are "at home," they often plug the burrow with loose earth to help prevent moisture loss inside the burrow.

In the wild, the majority of the water required by these lizards is metabolized from the vegetation they consume. Water needs are also met when body fat reserves are metabolized during lean times. Captive uros will learn to drink from a flat dish, but if you live in a humid climate, it may be necessary to offer the water dish for only limited time periods during the week to control humidity.

Diet: Surprisingly, the preferred diet of wild spiny-tails is not soft, succulent, moist vegetation but rather hard and dry leaves, blos-

When in reproductive readiness, adult males of the ornate spiny-tailed agama, Uromastyx ocellatus ornatus, are beautifully colored in tans and blues.

soms, and other bits of vegetation. The leaves and blossoms of *Artemesia* and related composites, such as wormwood, cudweed, or tarragon, are among those most relished. Captive spiny-tailed agamids should be provided with a basic herbivorous lizard diet to which is added fresh and dried peas, pelleted alfalfa, fresh beans of all types, wild birdseed, and millet. Other seeds may also be consumed. Chick starter mash, available in most farm feed stores, has proven an excellent dietary supplement. The vegetables offered should consist of kale, various greens—no spinach or swiss chard; they interfere with the metabolism of calcium—grated vegetables, some fruit, and suitable blossoms when available. The blossoms and leaves

The chuckwalla, Sauromalus o. obesus, *is a vegetarian lizard of the America deserts. These lizards are strongly dimorphic, with males being the much larger and more colorful sex.*

of the common dandelion, hibiscus, and nasturtium are relished.

Although most spiny-tails show great interest in and will readily consume crickets and other insects, these should be provided as a treat *only*, not a regular component of the diet.

Comments: The ground color and intensity of pattern of spiny-tailed agamids is altered by temperature. When cool the lizards are the dullest and darkest, the better to absorb the warmth of the sun. As the lizards warm, their colors lighten.

One of the most variably—and beautifully—colored of the spiny-tailed lizards is the North African *U. acanthinurus*. It is also one of the hardiest and is the only species being bred with any regularity in captivity. Like all members of the genus, it is oviparous. Darkest on the head and the tail, when this species is suitably warm, much of its body is suffused with tans, reds, yellows, and greens. These are long-lived animals; a pair kept indoors in Miami survived for more than 20 years.

A very few of the Arabian *U. benti* are occasionally imported to America. This is another moderately sized species with a sandy ground color and prominent dorsal barring.

At present, two races of the very attractive *U. ocellatus* are rather regularly imported to both America and Europe. These are *U. o. ocellatus*, the ocellated, and *U. o. ornatus*, the ornate, spiny-tails. The females of both are of a sandy hue, often with dorsal and lateral barring and ocellations. The males of both are colorful, but healthy, optimally warmed males of the aptly named ornate spiny-tail are spectacularly so. These are suffused with intensely bright turquoises and russets and are among the world's most beautifully colored lizards. This lizard is currently present in fairly large numbers in several captive breeding facilities in the southwestern United States and in smaller numbers in indoor facilities in Europe.

Chuckwallas;
Genus Sauromalus

S. obesus, the chuckwalla, an iguanid lizard of the deserts of the southwestern United States, is a big, waddling, herbivorous lizard that is restricted to areas of jumbled boulders and rocky escarpments. It is represented in the United States by at least three subspecies.

It is the western chuckwalla, *S. o. obesus,* that is most often seen in the pet trade. This race has a tremendous range and is geographically variable in color. Males are the larger and more colorful sex, being blackish anteriorly, cream to brick red centrally, and dark around the rear limbs. The tail may be reddish to cream. Females and young tend to be broadly banded with dark and light gray, and to have a prominently banded tail.

Given low humidity, high temperatures, spacious quarters, and suitable diet, chuckwallas can and do thrive as captives. They are ideal species for advanced hobbyists and zoological institutions.

Chuckwallas have a relatively short annual activity period. As would be expected from a large lizard in a temperate climate, they emerge from hibernation rather late in the year (mid- to late April, depending on the temperature) and retire again well before the cold weather has truly set in. While up and about, chucks are active only during the warmest part of the day, when they may be seen—with binoculars—sitting and thermoregulating on top of rocky prominences. A body temperature of from 99° to 102°F (37° to 39°C) seems to be their operating optimum. At that temperature they are active, alert, wary, and even somewhat agile.

Diet: In the wild the range of the common chuckwalla, *S. obesus* ssp., is roughly analagous to that of the creosote bush, the leaves of which form an important food source for this lizard. Providing this food for captives is largely impossible. Chucks also consume considerable amounts of flowers, especially dandelions, leaves, and seeds of many desert plants. Some insects are also eaten. In captivity, to avoid gout, they should be treated as an herbivorous species.

Breeding: Chucks are oviparous lizards, the females laying a single clutch consisting of from a few to nearly a dozen large eggs. Many wild females may clutch (lay eggs) only every second year. Captive females, traditionally better fed and having a somewhat longer annual activity period than their wild counterparts, may reproduce annually.

Desert Iguana;
Genus *Dipsosaurus*

Like the range of the chuckwalla, that of the desert iguana follows that of its major food plant, the creosote bush. Unlike the chuckwalla, however, which is a denizen of boulder-strewn regions, the desert iguana inhabits open sandy deserts, and seeks refuge in burrows of its own making, in thickets of creosote bush, and in the warrens of desert mammals such as kangaroo rats.

The desert iguana is an attractive and active lizard that should be provided a comparatively large cage. While heavy-bodied, it is not obese. It has a short head with a rounded snout, stout limbs and a tapering tail that is about equal in length to that of the head and body. Except for the low vertebral crest, the body scales are small while those of the tail are large and arranged in prominent whorls.

While the ground color of *Dipsosaurus* varies somewhat, approximating the color of the sand in any given area, overall this is a foot-long (30 cm) tan lizard. The ground color is sandy gray and overlain on the sides with a blush of brown or brownish red. Light ocelli are present anteriorly, wavy lines posteriorly.

Diet: Besides the leaves and blossoms of the creosote bush, desert iguanas also eat other desert leaves and blooms and a few insects. An excess of insects in the diet may result in visceral gout in later years. Desert iguanas should be considered an herbivorous species.

Maintenance: Given ample warmth, low humidity, brightly lit, UV-enhanced facilities, and a suitable diet, captive desert iguanas will thrive. A brilliantly illuminated hot spot of up to 115°F (46°C) should be provided. Some captive desert iguanas have neared 15 years in captivity, and there is every reason to believe that, as we learn more about these lizards, a time span of 20 years or more can be attained. Much remains to be learned about the breeding biology of these interesting aridland lizards.

Swifts and Relatives

The xeric-dwelling swifts—also referred to as fence lizards, canyon lizards, and spiny lizards—are quite popular with hobbyists. Indeed, these are often the lizards first noticed and kept by young enthusiasts.

Unfortunately, because wild-collected specimens remain so inexpensive, few American enthusiasts attempt to breed any. European hobbyists have a much better track record in captive breeding both the oviparous and ovoviviparous species.

Spiny lizards make hardy captives, feeding avidly upon mealworms, crickets, grubs, flies, moths, and locusts. They also may eat some fruit and an occasional dandelion or other blossoms. If kept indoors, both full-spectrum lighting and superwarmed basking areas need to be provided. A low relative humidity environment is important. If kept outdoors, the enclosure must be in full sun, sheltered from heavy rains, and well drained. Drainage is especially important in humid areas. Excess moisture will produce a difficult to cure fungal disease that will eventually be fatal to the affected lizards. Both nighttime cooling and a natural photoperiod are probably necessary to induce breeding and the production of viable eggs. The largest species near 14 inches (36 cm) in overall length, while the smallest species are barely a third that size.

Granite spiny lizard: Perhaps the most beautiful member of the genus *Sceloporus* in the United States is the granite spiny lizard, *S. orcutti*. Males attain a total length of 10.5 inches (27 cm), of which about one half is tail length. Females are somewhat smaller.

Light-phase adult male *S. orcutti* may vary in ground color from copper to charcoal. A dark wedge, often obscured in darker males, is present on each shoulder. Dorsally, scales are marked with black, turquoise, and yellow-green. The entire venter and throat is brilliant blue. Light-phase males often have a broad stripe of intense purple for the entire length of the dorsum. Females tend more toward a coppery ground color, are often prominently banded, and have the purple dorsal area less well defined. The venter is whitish or faintly washed with blue. Juveniles are prominently crossbanded.

Orcutti is an oviparous species. Each clutch contains from 6 to 15 eggs. Deposition occurs in early or midsummer. Incubation takes about two months. The hatchlings readily consume small crickets.

Few lizards can equal the beauty of a male purple phase granite spiny lizard, Sceloporus orcutti.

The scales of the neck, sides, posterior dorsum, and tail are heavily keeled and spinose. Scales of the anterior dorsum are rounded posteriorly and decidedly less keeled and spinose.

Common spiny lizard: In one or another of its many subspecies, the common spiny lizard, *S. undulatus*, is the most widely distributed of the

North American swifts. In the East it is a species of the pine oak woodlands and is particularly common in clearings where there are many fallen trees and even on the fence rails that surround pastures.

Prairie lizard: The western subspecies of *S. undulatus* are known as prairie lizards. They are more apt to frequent rocky outcrops than trees. Most, like *S. u. garmani*, are very strongly marked with longitudinal bands rather than crossbars. The males, often having chestnut lateral areas striped with straw yellow, are the more richly colored.

Blue spiny lizard: At 14.25 inches (36 cm), *S. serrifer cyanogenys*, the blue spiny lizard, is the largest North American member of this genus. The black collar against a steel blue to rather bright blue ground combines to make this a beautiful lizard. This, too, is a rock-dwelling species of southern Texas and adjacent Mexico. It is easily confused with the slightly smaller crevice spiny lizard, *S. poinsetti*, a species from slightly further west in Texas and Mexico. The tail of the blue spiny lizard is not prominently banded while that of the crevice spiny lizard is. Most crevice spiny lizards are also grayer than the blue spiny lizard, but there is much variability. Both of these species bear live young.

Desert spiny lizard: One of the commonly seen larger species is *S. magister* ssp., the desert spiny lizard. It ranges widely through much of the Southwest and is found in trees, cactus jumbles, or on rocky prominences. It is not brilliantly colored, but often has dark shoulder spots or a poorly defined collar. The gray back has paired dark spots and males have black-edged turquoise ventral and throat patches. Although it is usually smaller, occasional specimens may exceed 12 inches (30 cm) in total length. It is an oviparous species, producing one or more clutches of 10 to 15 eggs.

Tree lizards and Side-blotched lizards: The tree and side-blotched lizards are small—to about 5.5 inches (14 cm)—relatives of the swifts. The tree lizards are contained in the genus *Urosaurus* and the side-blotched lizards in the genus *Uta*. The very arboreal tree lizards have large scales scattered among the small on the back, and prominent longitudinal lateral skin folds. Males have spectacular patches of brilliant blue on the venter and throat. The predominantly terrestrial side-blotched lizard is abundant in rocky areas. The dorsum is clad in sandy hues and the belly patches are pale blue. The dorsal scales are larger than the lateral scales.

Unfortunately, in America the lizards of these genera are more eagerly sought as a food source for hatchling milksnakes than for the terrarium qualities of the lizards themselves. This is unfortunate, for with reasonable care both the side-blotched and the tree lizards can be both hardy and long lived. Both genera are oviparous. These lizards feed upon small insects and other arthropods, most of which are found in bark crevices or dead wood in the trees, or among the rocks where the lizards abound. Like the males of many lizards, those of these genera are brilliantly colored during the breeding season.

Collared lizards: The members of the genus *Crotaphytus* stand out for two reasons. They are fast runners, resorting to bipedal locomotion in the wild, and they are among the the most beautifully colored of any American squamates. Both sexes are at their brightest during the breeding and egg deposition season, with the males being the brighter. When gravid, females of all species bear lateral bars or spots of orange.

The collared lizards are big headed and squatty, and, if hungry, will prey on smaller cagemates. Insects such as grasshoppers, crickets, beetles, flies, moths, and their larvae are eagerly accepted.

Stressed lizards, such as newly captured specimens or those kept in less than ideal conditions, are more apt to suffer adversely from parasite infestations. An emaciated or dehydrated appearance often accompanies parasite overloads.

Collared lizards will learn to drink from a water dish. Until acclimated, they may prefer lapping up droplets of water sprinkled on the stones in their enclosures.

A hot spot—up to 115°F (46°C)—for basking, a cooler resting area, and full-spectrum lighting are

With its big head and bipedal gait, the eastern collared lizard, Crotaphytus c. collaris, *looks like our favorite interpretation of* Tyranosaurus rex.

imperative. Night temperatures may drop into the 60°s F (16–21°C) with no ill effects to the lizards.

Most crotaphytines hibernate to a greater or lesser degree. The duration of dormancy is considerably less in the South than in the more northerly areas. It is probable that a lengthy period of dormancy is necessary to trigger the physiological changes that culminate in successful reproductive activity. All crotaphytines are oviparous. From a few to as many as a dozen eggs are produced annually. Although dependent on temperature, incubation durations may vary from 55 to 90 days. Hatchlings are from 2.75 to 3.5 inches (7 to 10.8 cm) in overall length. Incubation in a low-humidity incubator seems to most reliably result in hatchlings.

Although the least colorful of the curly-tailed lizards, this species, Leiocephalus carinatus armouri, *is the most readily available in the pet trade.*

Crotaphytine lizards will thrive as captives if healthy when received and if offered proper quarters. Low relative humidity and a spacious cage with a substrate of several inches of dry sand are necessary. Rocks will be both appreciated and used extensively.

The common name is derived from the double, prominent, but dorsally interrupted black collars. The brownish head, bright yellow throat, and green body identify the eastern collared lizard, *C. c. collaris*. All the eastern collared lizard subspecies have dark, often black, mouth linings.

The males in breeding color of the western race, *C. c. baileyi*, are walking advertisements in greens and yellows. The dorsal surface of

the head is more yellow than that of its eastern counterpart, and the throat may be either solid or striated blue or yellow.

The somewhat less colorful desert collared lizard, *C. bicinctores,* is a familiar sight through much of the far West. The body is tan and the mouth lining is light.

When they are cornered, collared lizards are essentially fearless, and will leap up to a foot off the ground to firmly bite their aggressor. Therefore, checking the color of the mouth lining is not as hard as it sounds. Merely peer inside while the lizard is biting your finger!

Curly-tailed lizards: The curly-tailed lizards resemble a robust swift or spiny lizard, and, like these, are in the family Iguanidae. Curly-tailed lizards lack the femoral pores—enlarged scales beneath the rear legs—that are prominent on the swifts and spiny lizards. None of the curly-tails is clad in truly brilliant colors—reds and dark greens are incorporated into the color schemes of some; others are of various hues of grays and browns—but all are alert and attractive. Only 3 of the 20 or more species of these West Indian lizards are available with any regularity to American hobbyists, and only one, the northern curly-tail, *Leiocephalus carinatus armouri*, a species that is now firmly established in Florida, is readily so. When startled or when coming to rest after a period of activity, many curl the distal two thirds or more of their tails upward in a half circle. Although some of the smaller species are adult at about 6 inches (15 cm) in total length, some larger species may exceed 10 inches (25 cm). Tail length accounts for considerably more than half the total length.

A prominent but low vertebral crest is characteristic of lizards of this genus.

These primarily terrestrial lizards are most often seen among rock piles or in cracked seawalls.

Female curly-tails are smaller, and often less colorful, than the males.

Curly-tails feed upon insects and other arthropods as well as some vegetation, and are remarkably hardy as captives. They require a dry terrarium with a sandy substrate into which they will burrow when fright-

ened or cool. They are adept at darting around on rock surfaces and horizontal logs. Their terrarium should be decorated accordingly. All will drink water from a shallow dish.

Small Desert Skinks

Although many of the world's skinks are desert dwellers, comparatively few of these species appear in the American pet trade. Most, if kept properly, are hardy. The species we discuss here are primarily insectivorous, but most will lap at a fruit-honey mixture or eat an occasional piece of sweet fruit.

Ocellated or barrel skink: The European ocellated skink, *Chalcides ocellatus*, continues to gain popularity with American hobbyists. Those currently available are wild-collected specimens, but the species is being captive bred with increasing regularity. This skink is named for the rather regularly arranged ocelli present on both its back and its sides.

At its largest, the ocellated skink may attain nearly 1 foot (30 cm) in length. Most, however, are adult at a length of 5 to 6 inches (13 to 15 cm). The legs are proportionately short but are fully functional and used when the skink is moving slowly. Ocellated skinks occur in very diverse, well-drained habitats. This skink may be very abundant just beneath surface debris or vegetation in semideserts and on rocky plains. The ocellated skink is alert and quickly seeks shelter when startled. It is also quite adept at sand swimming. *C. ocellatus* is

At a record length of 13.5 inches, the Great Plains skink, Eumeces obsoletus, *is the largest skink of North America.*

viviparous. Clutches may number from 4 to more than 10 babies. Besides southern Europe, the ocellated skink may be found in northern Africa and Southwest Asia.

This hardy species will thrive in both desert or dry savanna setups. The sand substrate should be dry on top and dampened slightly on the bottom layers via a standpipe.

Remember that specimens from the more northerly part of the range will require somewhat lower temperatures and fewer hours of daylight during reproductive cycling than those from the South. Many European hobbyists fully hibernate ocellated skinks of European origin.

To lessen the draw on wild populations, we should do everything possible to promote successful captive propagation of this hardy lizard.

Great Plains skink: Though there are numerous species of aridland skinks native to North America, the wide-ranging Great Plains skink, *Eumeces obsoletus*, is the largest and prettiest species. It occurs in our central and western states and adjacent Mexico. Hatchlings are jet black except for white dots on the sides of the face and a royal blue tail. The adults vary from fawn to tan in ground color, may have poorly discernible stripes, and have black-edged dorsal and lateral scales. Adults have a yellowish venter. While most adults are in the 8- to 10-inch (20 to 25 cm) range, the record size is a hefty 13.75 inches (35 cm).

For our Great Plains skinks to cycle reproductively, they need to be hibernated for a two-month period. The food insects or pre-

The sandfish, Scincus scincus, *a specialized burrowing skink of North Africa and the Middle East, is a wonderful lizard that is now available to hobbyists.*

pared foods of gestating females should be enhanced with calcium-D_3 additives twice or thrice weekly. Fast-growing hatchlings may require the calcium-D_3 supplements daily. Large females may produce 20 or more eggs, but 8 to 12 is a more usual clutch size. Eggs produced by our females have hatched in from 50 to 60 days at a temperature of 80° to 86°F (27° to 30°C).

Schneider's skinks: Of the several subspecies, only the nominate race of the Schneider's skink, *Eumeces s. schneideri* is currently readily available to American hobbyists. The ground color of this 9- to 12-inch-long (23 to 30 cm) lizard varies from buff to pearl gray. The dorsum is spotted, or vaguely barred with orange. It is a beautiful, aggressive, and seldom-bred Asian lizard.

Schneider's skink is an oviparous species. Most are cold-tolerant, hence ideal for hobbyists in temperate climes. Besides the normal diet of insects, many of these skinks will readily accept prepared foods and some fruit.

These skinks will thrive in either desert or savanna terraria. We have also kept them outside in the large metal rings. Like most aridland and savanna lizards, these skinks thermoregulate frequently during their periods of activity. Those kept outside would bask on rocks having a surface temperature of more than 100°F (38°C). We provide them daytime thermal gradients in indoor terraria. During the summer, the nighttime temperature is about 70°F (21°C). The daytime temperature varies from about 80°F (27°C) (cool end) to a sand-surface temperature of 100° to 105°F (38° to 41°C) under the basking light.

Much work on the reproductive needs of these lizards remains to be done. The pet trade remains entirely dependent on wild-collected specimens.

Sandfish: Sandfish is the wonderfully descriptive common name applied to the sand-swimming skinks of the genus *Scincus*.

Members of this genus may be encountered in aridland, loose sand habitats, from eastern North Africa to Pakistan. Despite the fact that they are accomplished burrowers, there is no trend toward reduction in limb size; however, the toes are flattened and have serrate flanges on the trailing edges.

The eyelids are well developed and functional and the lower jaw is noticeably countersunk, a feature that prevents the loose sand from entering the lizard's mouth.

Sandfish should be provided with as large a terrarium as possible. The sand substrate should be between 6 and 12 inches (15 to 30 cm) in depth. Keep in mind the weight of the sand when designing a stand for the terrarium. The bottom layer of sand is kept barely moistened by trickling a little water down a vertical PVC standpipe.

Although they are probably more likely to seek their prey while walking on top of the sand, sandfish may approach it submarine fashion from below. They eagerly consume small beetles, particularly favoring small June beetles, tenebrionid (meal) beetles and their larvae, spiders, and other suitably sized arthropods. When conditions are favorable, sandfish can metabolize most of their moisture needs from their insect prey and the moist bottom layers of terrarium sand, but, when their terrarium is too dry, sandfish will drink from a low receptacle. The suggested sand-surface daytime temperature at the hot end of their tank is about 110°F (43°C). The cool end of the tank can be up to 15 degrees cooler. Nighttime temperatures of both the hot and cool end of the terrarium can be allowed to drop by another several degrees.

At present, despite the fact that they are apt to be secretive, sandfish are immensely popular in the reptile hobby. With some care they are long lived. Captive lifespans in excess of 10 years have been documented. These oviparous skinks are not yet captive bred with any regularity. From three to seven eggs are laid in each clutch.

Racerunner and Whiptailed Lizards

Although only a few species of these lacertilian speedsters are regularly available in the pet trade, many additional species occur across the continental United States and Latin America. Even where found in humid, rainy areas the racerunners and whiptails are usually associated with sunny, sandy, fast-draining glades, field edges, and other open habitats.

The lizards depend on their alertness and speed to avoid predators. At night, or during adverse weather conditions, racerunners and whiptails seclude themselves under man-made ground-surface litter such as sheets of plywood or tin, or under flat rocks and other such moisture-shedding natural ground cover. They are also accomplished burrowers. In captivity, racerunners and whiptails fare best in savanna and desert terraria.

For captives, a brightly illuminated basking spot of 105° to 110°F (41° to 43°C) should be provided, and the ambient cage temperature should grade downward to 85° to 92°F (29° to 33°C). Besides warmth, they should be provided with full-spectrum lighting, absolute dryness in the top levels of their substrate, sufficient and varied food, and several hiding areas. Their quarters should be spacious and uncrowded, with no more than a single male of the same—or a closely related—species per enclosure.

Breeding: Racerunners and whiptails are oviparous. Certain of them are parthenogenic. All have relatively few, proportionately large eggs. For instance, six-lined racerunners (northern populations of which may also require winter cooling to cycle them for breeding) normally produce from three to six eggs. The egg clutches of the ameivas seldom exceed five eggs. Clutches of the rainbow racerunner are often no more than three eggs. Healthy, fully adult females with sufficient fat reserves may double or even triple clutch.

Incubation durations can vary tremendously. At 90°F (32°C) the incubation of rainbow racerunner eggs took about 52 days. At 86°F (30°C) the hatching percentage was lessened and incubation was increased to 73 days.

Diet: Racerunners and whiptails are very adept at finding prey insects. They fully utilize not only visual, but tactile and chemosensory techniques as well. It seems likely that auditory cues also play a part in prey location. These lizards are able to unerringly unearth burrowing beetle larvae that seem to be making no visible signs on the surface. A rapid scratching with the front feet is used to uncover subterranean prey once it is located. A similar motion, but this time without the foot coming in contact with the surface of the ground, is used to indicate unease or aggressive intent.

Several species in these genera are known to be unisexual (=parthenogenic), all-female forms. Others are unisexual in certain areas of their range and bisexual in others. Egg development is stimulated in the unisexual populations by pseudo-courtship displays.

Rainbow lizards; Genus *Cnemidophorus*

The various racerunners vary in color from pretty to spectacular. Many are various shades of tans and

The rainbow racerunner (or whiptail), Cnemidophorus lemniscatus, *is a neotropical species that is collected from the wild for the pet trade. It is now established in Florida, and can be bred in captivity.*

browns, all overlain with light and/or dark stripes, spots, or a combination of both. They range from a slender, active 8 inches (22 cm) to about 1 foot (30 cm) in overall length. They traditionally rest in an alert posture, the head held well away from the ground. All members of this genus are primarily insectivorous, but some, if not most, opportunistically consume fresh blossoms.

At least 15 species of whiptails are found in the arid and semiarid areas of the United States.

Two native species that are occasionally seen in captivity are the eastern six-lined racerunner, *Cnemidophorus sexlineatus* ssp., and the western checkered whiptail, *C. tesselatus* ssp.

The former is sexually dimorphic, with the females lacking the pale blue to turquoise belly of the male.

Both sexes are prominently and precisely patterned dorsally with six bright yellow longitudinal stripes that extend from the sides of the face to well onto the tail. Some specimens display a rather well-defined vertebral stripe, as well, which results in seven rather than six lines. The very beautiful subspecies known as the prairie racerunner, *C. s. viridis*, has less-well-defined lines and is suffused with pale to bright green on the face, sides and anterior back.

The variably spotted checkered whiptail is a unisexual species that is patterned with tiny to large spots and/or bars of black on a tawny ground color.

Ridge-tailed Monitors

Once truly a rarity in the United States, the Australian ridge-tailed monitor, *Varanus acanthurus*, is now the species most frequently bred. Despite this, prices for this saxicolous desert species remain very high in North America.

The ridge-tailed monitor is a beautiful spiny-tailed species that occasionally attains an adult size of 28 inches (71 cm) but most seen in herpetoculture are well under that length. In fact, comparatively few specimens attain 20 inches (51 cm) in total length. The tail of *V. acanthurus* is rather short, approximately 1.5 times the snout vent length, heavy, and prominently whorled with spiny, keeled scales. The ground color of the lizard is olive brown to terra-cotta. There are light longitudinal stripes on the nape and sides of the neck. Irregularly arranged light ocelli or eye-shaped spots on the trunk cause intricate reticulations of the dark pigment. Light rings alternate with dark on the tail. The rings are best defined on the basal three-fifths of the tail length.

This species is found over much of the arid and semiarid northern half of Australia in deeply creviced escarpments and on stony plains. It is a proficient burrower.

This monitor employs tripodal posturing, using its tail as a support to enable it to see a greater distance.

Despite being quite cold-tolerant, spiny-tailed monitors are worshippers of warmth and sunlight. During the summer months, daytime highs of 88° to 94°F (31° to 34°C)—with a warmed basking spot of 106° to

Once only rarely available, the ridge-tailed monitor, Varanus acanthurus, *is a prolific breeder in captivity.*

110°F (41° to 43°C)—are suggested. Nighttime temperatures may be allowed to drop to 70° to 74°F (21° to 23°C). Ambient winter temperatures may be a few degrees cooler, but the superheated daytime basking area should be retained.

Breeding groups of one male and several females work well.

It appears that egg size and egg quantity may vary with the size of the female monitor. Maximum clutch size is often quoted as five, and the hatchlings are said to be tiny with a total length of 2.5 inches (6 cm). However, we have had clutches from large females number up to eight eggs and the hatchlings are somewhat more than 4 inches (10 cm) in total length. Admittedly, this is still less than the size of the even smaller Storr's monitor, but it is larger than often reported.

Eggs may be incubated in slightly dampened sphagnum moss, and will hatch in 81 to 90 days at so-called room temperature (82° to 90°F [28° to 32°C]). Hatchlings begin eating suitably sized insects within 24 hours. A diet of commercially procured crickets, mealworms, wax-worms, and butterworms was augmented with field plankton.

Storr's Monitor

Although certainly not yet a commonly seen species, the attractive little spiny-tailed Storr's monitor, *V. storri*, has been bred in small numbers in the United States for more than 15 years. It is a rather common monitor in two disjunct areas of Australia.

Storr's monitor is reddish tan with a fine but vague pattern of darker reticulations. The spiny-tail of *V. storri* is unpatterned.

Storr's monitors are tiny—reportedly to 12 inches (30cm), but most are smaller—rock-dwelling monitors with a tail somewhat greater in length than the combined head and body length. They are hardy and easily kept.

These monitors will dig long tunnels, enlarged at the end to permit the lizard to reverse its position. The interactions between members of the group we observed were interesting. The males were somewhat, but not persistently, territorial, usually satisfying themselves with posturing and threats rather than actual skirmishes. Threats and feints involving inflating or flattening the body, extending the legs, inflating the throat (gular) area, and craning the neck were utilized.

Our males frequently assumed a tripodal stance but we have not seen females do so.

Indoor summer daytime terrarium temperatures should vary from 88° to 94°F (31° to 34°C), with a brightly illuminated basking area of from 106° to 110°F (41° to 43°C). Night-time temperatures can drop into the low 70°s F (21° to 23°C). Winter temperatures a few degrees cooler may assist in reproductive cycling. The superwarmed daytime basking area should be retained. Photoperiods should also be lessened somewhat during the months of winter. A natural photoperiod seems best.

Up to six eggs are laid. If incubated in barely dampened sphagnum, at a temperature of from 82° to 90°F (28° to 32°C), hatching occurs in about 80 days.

Hatchlings measure about 5 inches (13 cm) in overall length, and are precisely like the adults in coloration and pattern. They usually begin feeding within a day of hatching.

Although the adults of Storr's monitors were primarily insectivorous, eating crickets, caterpillars, grasshoppers, waxworms, and June beetles, they would readily consume the occasional pinky mice offered them. They also lapped eagerly at a honey-pureed fruit mixture that was periodically offered. Storr's monitors drink readily from water dishes.

Unfortunately, the price of these tiny monitors remains quite high and is apt to remain so until the lizards are captive bred on a larger scale.

Desert Snakes

Not all the snakes mentioned in this section are commercially available on a routine basis. If not offered commercially, however, most are easily found within proper habitats and ranges on rainy spring or summer nights as they cross roadways or are active in their natural habitat.

While the juveniles of such large snakes as gopher and bull snakes (*Pituophis*), racers and whipsnakes (*Coluber* and *Masticophis*), and some garter snakes (*Thamnophis*) are suitable candidates for inclusion in a desert terrarium, they all quickly outgrow most terraria. Because as adults they are often nervous and can quickly rearrange or destroy terrarium plantings and furniture, we have mentioned these species in the applicable cage sections, but there are many small or placid species that lend themselves well to desert setups.

Although some desert snakes are diurnally active above ground, most are secretive or adapted either to burrowing or nocturnal activity. Of the desert snakes, some are beautifully, variably, and intricately colored, while others are quite dull. Many of the smallest species feed on invertebrates and of these some are spider specialists, others are generalists, and one or two feed primarily on scorpions. Many of the large adult snakes eat the traditional rodent prey.

All of the species mentioned here, except the Spotted Python, are in

Despite its propensity for burrowing, the Kenyan sand boa, Eryx colubrinus loveridgei, is a favorite of hobbyists.

the family Colubrindae. The python is assigned to the family Boidae.

Although the hog-nosed snakes seldom bite and are considered harmless snakes, bites have occasionally resulted in edema and intense itching. These snakes should be handled with caution. The night snake is considered a mildly venomous species, but almost never bites.

Kenyan Sand Boa

The Kenyan (East African) sand boa, *Eryx colubrinus loveridgei*, is a pretty, hardy, and readily bred species.

Dorsally, this 18- to 22-inch-long (46 to 56 cm) snake has a pattern of orange, buff, or yellow against a brown or olive brown background color. The venter is off-white. Males have a tendency to be more brilliantly colored and smaller than females. Albino and anerythristic strains are now being captive bred. The albinos are patterned yellow or cream on white, while the anerythristic strain is patterned with black against a light gray-blue ground color. Although both of these morphs are in demand by hobbyists, we continue to prefer the more commonly seen and far less costly normal phases.

Males may be identified by their proportionately longer and stouter tail and the larger cloacal spurs. These sand boas tend to bite when disturbed. Once in hand they usually become quiet. Neonates are about 8 inches (20 cm) long at birth and entirely ready to bite upon emergence from the amniotic sac.

The Kenyan sand boa is an easily bred species. It requires nothing more than moderate cooling to cycle reproductively. To do this, simply offer a greater daytime thermal gradient and drop the nighttime temperature a few degrees for up to 90 days during the winter months. Couple this with a reduction in photoperiod. Our snakes are cooled during the months of December, January, and February. As we do throughout the year, we continue to provide the normal seasonally variable hours of daylight. During this time the daytime highs do not usually rise above the low 80°s F (26° to 29°C) and nighttime lows may drop into the mid-60°s F (18°C). It is not unusual for the boas to refuse most or all food during cooling. Since this is normally a very robust and hardy species, this seldom causes

any problems. Breeding begins soon after the springtime elevation of the cage temperature.

These snakes do well in trios—one male, two females. Young are produced annually. Parturition occurs about four to five months after breeding, in late summer or early fall.

Gravid females should be provided with a heating pad, with the setting on low—sand temperature of 92° to 96°F (33° to 36°C)—under one half of the terrarium and run around the clock.

Clutch size may vary from 3 to 22—usually 10 to 16—rather hefty babies. Although a few of the neonates may insist on lizards for their first meal, the vast majority will accept newborn mice. Even the lizard eaters will soon switch over to mice, especially if the pinkies are scented with lizard odor. Several of our neonates have eaten crickets that accidentally got into their cage, but we can find no reference to insects being included in the diet of wild specimens. One of the Kenyans that accepted several crickets was a neonate that had refused to eat anything we offered. After eating several crickets, the little snake ate a cricket-scented pinky mouse and then readily began accepting normal, unscented, pinkies. (See Scenting Food Items, page 100.)

We found that a terrarium made from a 20-gallon (76 L) long aquarium was ideally sized for a trio of these small boids. The substrate was of 3 to 5 inches (7.6 to 13 cm) of dry builder's sand.

Note: Sand is a very heavy medium. Be certain that your terrarium's stand can hold the weight.

A small untippable dish of clean water should be present in the cage.

Summer daytime temperatures ranging from the mid-80°s F (29°C) to the mid-90°s F (35°C) are ideal. A heating pad or a heat tape under one end of the terrarium will provide a thermal gradient. This can drop at night to the mid- to low-70°s F (21° to 24°C) (see above caution for gravid females).

Like other erycine species, much of the Kenyans' moisture requirements are apparently obtained from food animals. Adult snakes are usually ravenous feeders on lab mice and/or rat pups.

Spotted Python

Though this dry forestland and aridland resident of northeastern Australia attains a moderate size—commonly to 36 inches (91 cm)—it is a rather quiet snake that does well in a desert terrarium provided fresh drinking water is in constant supply. It is known scientifically as *Antaresia (Liasis) maculosa*.

This small python has a ground color of light to dark olive against which the very irregular brownish to reddish brown dorsal and lateral blotches contrast strongly. Hatchlings are often more strongly patterned than old adults.

The spotted python is an easily bred species that lays clutches of from 2 to 12 fairly large eggs. Reproductive cycling seems most assured

The spotted python, Antaresia (Liasis) maculosa, *of Australia is one of the smallest of the true pythons.*

if a regimen of nighttime cooling and a lessened photoperiod are implemented for the winter months.

At 85° to 90°F (29° to 32°C), the eggs hatch following about two months of incubation. The hatchlings usually feed readily on pinky mice but a few may initially insist on lizards. Adults voraciously accept mice and newborn rats.

The spotted python is very hardy and is quite temperature-tolerant. By day it should be provided with a warmed basking spot having a temperature of about 95°F (35°C). A temperature of 78° to 88° F (26° to 31°C) is suitable for the rest of the cage. Winter temperatures can be cooler, with daytime highs in the upper 70°s F (24° to 26°C) and nighttime lows in the mid-60°s F (18°C). The small python's diminutive size allows a pair, a trio, or, since males

There are many small burrowing snakes that feed on invertebrates. The banded sand snake, Chilomeniscus cinctus, *from the deserts of the American Southwest and Mexico, is a pretty example.*

The banded sand snake is a stubby little species—to 10 inches (25 cm)—with numerous dark bands on a yellowish, pinkish, or reddish ground color. The body rings do not involve the belly, but those on the tail usually completely encircle it. The dark band on the head is broad and has straight to convex edges.

The western shovel-nosed snake has a flattened snout and is more variable in coloration. It may be black- and yellow-banded, or have partial red bands in the center of each, or some, yellow bands. Some bands may encircle the body. The first dark crescent-shaped band on the head usually has a concave anterior edge and a convex posterior edge.

Both of these snakes eat invertebrates including spiders, centipedes, small beetles and their larvae and, perhaps, some species of ants and their pupae.

Both are oviparous, but neither is bred with any regularity in captivity.

Leaf-nosed Snakes

There are two species of pretty little snakes with greatly developed, free-edged, wraparound, rostral scales, found in the southwestern United States. These are the spotted (*Phyllorhynchus decurtatus* ssp.) and the saddled (*P. browni*) leaf-nosed snakes. Although both occasionally may attain a length of 18 inches (46 cm), most adults are between 12 and 16 inches (30 to 41 cm) in length. Both can be feisty,

are not particularly territorial, two pairs to be kept in a 30- to 75-gallon (114 to 284 L) terrarium.

Sand and Shovel-nosed Snakes

Two tiny burrowing species, the banded sand snake, *Chilomeniscus cinctus*, and the western shovel-nosed snake, *Chionactis occipitalis* ssp., are common denizens of our western aridlands. Although both are so secretive that they will seldom be seen, both are very prettily colored and, if properly provided for, will live for a considerable time in the desert terrarium. Both are sand swimmers—snakes that wriggle quickly through yielding sands by using a forceful side-to-side motion.

drawing back into an S and striking animatedly at a provoker. With handling, both soon become calm, however. Both species of leaf-nosed snakes feed on lizards and their eggs and are particularly fond of banded geckos, but may accept anoles and other smooth-scaled lizards as well.

Both of the leaf-nosed snakes have a ground that blends well with the color of the soil on which they are found. The spotted leaf-nose is busily patterned with a series of large, vaguely darker-edged, dorsal spots and alternating smaller lateral spots. There is often a dark bar from the jawline, upward through the eye, and over the top of the head. However, some specimens, especially very pallid ones from the far West, may lack the bar across the top of the head. The pupils are vertically elliptical.

The saddled leaf-nosed snake is much more precisely and less busily patterned. It has fewer, larger, and darker markings that extend well down onto the sides. The lateral markings are little more than slightly darkened smudges.

Although the leaf-nosed snakes can and do burrow, they are as likely to seek seclusion by secreting themselves among jumbles of boulders, cactus skeletons, or in the burrows or surface nests of small rodents. They should be provided with ample cover in the terrarium.

Both species of leaf-nosed snakes are oviparous, having up to six eggs per clutch. They are captive bred only sparingly.

The saddled leaf-nosed snake, Phyllorhynchus browni, *is a secretive North American snake that feeds on geckos and their eggs.*

Ground Snake

The ground snake, *Sonora semi-annulata*, a small—to 15 inches (38 cm)—secretive insectivore, is the most variably colored (polymorphic) snake species to be discussed here. Among other colors and pattern variations, ground snakes may be a solid pale gray, gray with a darker head, gray with a precisely delineated russet vertebral line, yellowish gray on the sides and a black-banded russet dorsally, or pinkish gray with prominent slate-colored bands.

The ground snake is widely distributed in western North America, and is often seen crossing roadways at night, or under brush, rocks, and debris when land is being cleared. It is capable of burrowing in yielding soils, but seems to prefer being at the soil surface, but under natural or human-generated debris.

Prey items of this easily maintained, nonaggressive, aridland snake include insects and other arachnids.

Female ground snakes lay from two to six eggs. The species is not being captive bred.

Hog-nosed Snakes

The most desert-adapted of the three species of hog-nosed snakes is the western, *Heterodon nasicus* ssp., a form with three difficult to differentiate subspecies. This is a snake of the central United States, including the Chihuahuan Desert region, and of northern Mexico.

Care should be used when handling this species. Although it is considered a harmless snake, the western hog-nose has enlarged teeth in the rear of its upper jaw, and since some of the rare bites have resulted in signs of weak envenomation, the snake quite probably has some toxic components in its saliva.

H. nasicus has a dorsal ground color of sandy brown to olive gray. The top of the head is dark with an intricate pattern of elongate dark blotches extending to the upper lip and onto the sides of the neck. Dark dorsal saddles extend from the nape to the tail and well-defined alternating dark blotches are present along the upper sides. The belly is largely to all black. The nose is prominently upturned.

Besides being the most arid-adapted of the hog-nosed snakes,

H. nasicus also has the broadest diet. In addition to toads, frogs, salamanders, and lizards, western hog-nosed snakes rather routinely include small rodents in their diet. This, of course, makes them somewhat easier to keep than the eastern and southern hog-noses that are largely toad specialists. We suggest, though, that mice not be used as the exclusive diet of captive western hog-nosed snakes. We feel very strongly that a broader diet is better.

Seldom more than 28 inches (71 cm) in length, some western hog-nosed snakes of 36 inches (91 cm) have been recorded.

This is an oviparous species that lays up to about 20 eggs in each clutch. All three subspecies—*nasicus*, the Plains hog-nose; *gloydi*, the dusty hog-nose; and *kennerlyi*, the Mexican hog-nose—are bred extensively in captivity. Most breeders believe that a period of winter dormancy heightens the possibility of breeding success.

Night Snake

About six subspecies of the tiny nocturnal *Hypsiglena torquata* may be found in various areas of our southwestern and Pacific states. Most examples are under 18 inches (46 cm) in length when adult, but occasional specimens may near a slender 2 feet (61 cm) in total length. Although it is classified as a mildly venomous species, it is too small to be of danger to humans.

This is a snake with a variably gray ground color, and brown to olive brown dorsal spots. It is usually easily identified by the presence of a large neck blotch on each side; these may be joined or separated vertebrally. A dark postorbital bar (dark marking behind the eye) is also apparent. The pupils are vertical.

Although night snakes occur in areas devoid of rocks and boulders, they are most common where either natural or human-generated litter is abundant. They emerge from their lairs at night and search the aridlands for small lizard and amphibian prey. Once seized, the prey is often held, sometimes for long periods, until it is at least partially overcome by the weak venom.

No efforts have been made to breed this oviparous species in captivity. Between two and six eggs are laid in each clutch.

Turtles and Tortoises

Although adults of virtually all species of turtles and tortoises will quickly rearrange the decorations and plantings in even a large terrarium, baby and juvenile specimens are both attractive and entertaining. As these shelled reptiles grow, it will become necessary to move them into larger cages and place them outside if feasible.

Turtles and tortoises require fair amounts of B carotene as well as vitamin D_3 and calcium in their diet. The latter two supplements are especially important during periods of rapid growth, and, if lacking, will result in a softened and/or malformed shell and bones. Excessive amounts of protein and/or unduly hastened growth can result in pyramiding, a condition where the center of each carapacial scute raises well above the growth areas at the edge of each scute.

Recent assessments have shown that preformed vitamin A should not be fed. Rather, sources of B carotene, such as orange-yellow vegetables, should be included in these turtles' and tortoises' balanced diet, so that the animals can make their own vitamin A from the bioconversion of B carotene.

Scenting Food Items

What does the term "scenting" mean when used in conjunction with food presentation to reptiles, and why and when is scenting important?

Many reptiles, and some amphibians, identify prey by olfactory cues. Among these are some species that have evolved preferences for a certain kind of prey.

A few examples of these species (not all are discussed in this book) and their preferred prey are shown in the box on the next page.

Reptile	Prey
Ball pythons, *Python regius*	gerbils/jirds
Eastern hog-nosed snakes, *Heterodon sp.*	toads
Gray-banded kingsnakes, *Lampropeltis alterna*	lizards
Leopard rat snake, *Elaphe situla*	wild rodents
Water snakes, *Natrix* sp. and *Nerodia* sp.	fish, frogs
Pink-tongued skinks, *Hemisphaerodon gerrardi*	slugs, snails

To these species, if it doesn't smell right, it isn't food. (Captive bred reptiles are often somewhat less selective in their prey animals.)

Is it a viable alternative to induce a reptile to accept a prey item that it doesn't naturally recognize?

While we advocate *normal and natural* diets, we have found that certain substitutions are entirely justified.

Food Substitutions: Food substitutions are acceptable if they remain similar; that is, if one type of mammal is substituted for another type of mammal, for example, if you were to substitute a mouse for a gerbil.

A food substitution is not justified if the reptile is induced to eat, solely for the convenience of the keeper, unnatural food items, such as an easily procured mouse rather than a less easily obtainable toad or fish.

Using the ball python as an example, let's look at the first case—a mouse for a gerbil. As a source of nutrition, a rodent raised on a diet of lab blocks is *very* different from a rodent that has eaten a natural diet all of its life. Despite their external similarities, a laboratory white mouse is about as different

from a wild white-footed mouse as you can get and still remain in the realm of mousedom! A comparable nutritional difference holds true in a baby hatchery chick and a wild quail, and probably even in a long-term captive toad fed a diet of fattened crickets compared with a wild toad eating a natural diet. Domestically produced rodents and hatchery birds also *smell* very different from their wild counterparts, and herps that recognize prey by smell may not even consider a lab produced animal edible. But lab mice are readily available, whereas wild mice seldom are, and certain populations of wild mice carry viral diseases that can be transmitted to humans. Captive bred gerbils (of one species) are available, but they're comparatively expensive. Lab mice are, therefore, the food rodents of choice—for us, the keepers. But it is sometimes necessary to convince the herps—our charges—that we know better than they—and, often, we don't! An important part of the convincing will revolve around "scenting"—making a readily available creature that is initially olfactorily unacceptable to the herp smell acceptable.

Ball pythons, a west and tropical African savanna snake, have evolved where gerbils and jirds, a gerbil-like little jumping or scuttling savanna rodent, are abundant. Like many herps, ball pythons rely strongly on the scent of their prey as a recognition factor. If it doesn't smell like a gerbil or jird, it probably isn't edible. So, to tempt a wild-caught ball python to eat, we may need to make a lab mouse smell like a gerbil. One way of doing this is to house the mouse intended as food with a gerbil. After a few hours in close proximity, the mouse may acquire enough gerbil scent to become acceptable to the python. With time, as your ball python becomes used to captivity, and with the inevitable mingling of scents and tastes of a scented prey animal, you will be able to phase out the scenting procedure.

This same method may be used for scenting lab mice with the odor of wild mice, or even for scenting mouse pups, which are more easily digestible than larger mice, with toad, frog, fish, or lizard.

To give a mouse the scent of a fish, frog or toad, simply rub the mouse against the other animal. If a large number of scented mice are necessary, some breeders sacrifice a toad, frog, or fish, dice it into a freezer container, add some water, and dip the mouse in a small amount of thawed concoction when desired. The serum and blood from a lizard's autotomized tail can also be used.

Nature's Own Foods: Is the use of warm-blooded prey items, such as mice, in place of cold-blooded prey, such as toads or fish, an acceptable practice?

We don't think so, in most cases.

The nutritional content and digestibility of mice is very different from those of fish, frogs, or toads. While some herps (eastern and southern hog-nosed snakes and some garter and water snakes) can be tricked into eating a scented mouse pup, regurgitation of the mice is not infrequent, and what seems to be an unreasonably high mortality of those herps that do not normally include mice in their diet has been noted.

On the other hand, for herps such as western hog-nosed snakes, the various western garter snakes long-nosed snakes, and glossy snakes that normally include an occasional baby mouse in their toad, frog, or lizard diet, feeding mouse pups is far more acceptable.

Chopping a prekilled slug or snail into fish-flavored catfood will work well for a lizard such as the pink-tongued skink. Usually, within a few meals, the slug or snail can be left out, and the lizards will thrive on the catfood alone.

Although there are many tricks that can be successfully used to change or augment your pet's diet, we strongly feel that the more natural a diet is, the better it is. Consider carefully available diet when you're choosing your pet reptile or amphibian.

Only a few snakes can be maintained in the aquatic terrarium. Here a tentacled snake, Erpeton tentaculatum, *anchors itself in an Amazon swordplant.*

Chapter Six
Water Terraria

Water-holding setups or aquariums are also types of terraria. Some are wholly aquatic, while some offer both a land and a water area. In the design of both types you can allow your creativity free rein, incorporating plantings, driftwood barriers and hides, rock ledges, and virtually any other decorations you choose. Make certain you secure the logs and rocks so that they cannot shift and injure the inhabitants.

The Aquatic Terrarium or Aquarium

The aquarium for your aquatic caecilians, aquatic frogs and toads, and most aquatic baby turtles should be set up and maintained in precisely the same manner as an aquarium for fish. Water quality, including the removal of chlorine and chloramine and the prevention of buildup of nitrates, nitrites, and ammonia, is critical. If large or many amphibians or reptiles are kept in a small water volume, maintaining water quality will be a real challenge. We suggest the use of a biological filter as well as frequent partial water changes.

Remember, at all times, the substantial weight of a water and gravel substrate-filled aquarium. Be sure to use an aquarium stand or other very sturdy, level surface. If your tank is not adequately supported all around the bottom frame, the weight and pressure of the water and gravel will break the panels of glass. Proper bottom support of show or high tanks is especially critical. It may even be necessary to consider and ascertain the total weight the floor of your house can support before setting up an aquarium of 200 gallons (757 L) or more.

The final appearance and size of your aquarium will necessarily be dictated by the kinds of reptiles and amphibians that you intend to house. Live plants may grow well and provide a lush appearance in a tank of small species such as newts, dwarf underwater frogs, or oriental fire-bellied toads, but would be quickly uprooted by the boisterous activities of such larger species as

The Aquatic Terrarium

Materials Needed
- Aquarium and stand
- Silicone sealant
- Substrate materials
- Filters and air pumps
- Heater
- Glass partition (if applicable)
- Plants
- Tank furniture
- Water conditioner
- Top
- Lighting

Setup Procedure

1 Place the aquarium on its stand in the spot chosen. Consider the load-bearing ability of your floor if you are using a very large aquarium.

2 Thoroughly wash the inside of your aquarium, and all substrate, rocks, driftwood, and other furniture in fresh, clean water. Be sure all dirt and dust is washed from the gravel/river rock.

3 Secure rocks or other ornamentation—tank furniture—with a nontoxic sealant if necessary. Allow the sealant to cure for a minimum of 24 hours.

4 Once the sealant has cured, place the washed substrate in the tank to the desired depth.

5 Now is the time to put your partition in place and anchor it suitably, if applicable. Clips to hold tank dividers in place are available in aquarium stores.

6 Half fill the aquarium with dechlorinated or aged water or dechlorinate the water after filling.

7 Push nonanchored driftwood or other accessories into the gravel as desired.

8 Plant rooted plants to their crown in the gravel as desired.

9 Add the rest of the water, pouring it slowly into a cup or a cupped hand to avoid disturbing the gravel and uprooting the plants. Dechlorinate.

10 Arrange heaters and filters as desired.

11 Add mats of floating plants and cork or other haulouts.

12 Arrange lights as necessary and be sure that the top fits fully and tightly.

Following setting up, we like to allow about 24 hours for tank stabilization before adding the animals. This is not mandatory, but we feel it preferable.

Filtration

Among the most important things to remember when

keeping aquatic reptiles, amphibians, or insects is that *clear water* does not necessarily equate to healthy water. In all but the most newly set up aquatic terrarium, dissolved wastes will be present in the water. Not even the best of the mechanical filters can remove these dissolved pollutants, and biological filters large and efficient enough to do the job are not feasible for most hobbyists.

We have always adhered to the theory that the easier the maintenance of any terrarium, be it large or small, simple or complex, the better the overall setup becomes, and the more likely it is that the necessary maintenance practices will be adhered to.

We rely on the presence of healthy, growing aquatic plants (even the presence of algae can assist), filtration, and periodic partial water changes. While the latter can be easily accomplished with small aquatic terraria, water changes become somewhat more burdensome when your setup is of 50-gallon (190 L) size or more. We rely on siphoning to remove the necessary water. The siphoned water is either run into a floor drain (easy), into pails to be carried elsewhere and emptied (tedious), or out of a window into our garden (easy). Do not start a siphon with your mouth!

The replaced water must be the same temperature as that still in the terrarium. The water may be replaced by filling pails

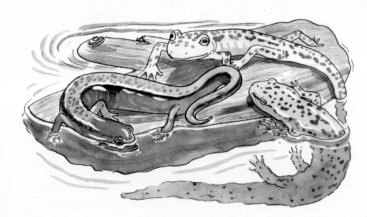

from your faucet and carrying them to the setup (tedious), by running a trickling garden hose into the terrarium through the window (easy, weather and water temperature permitting), or by running a plant watering hose from the nearest indoor tap into the tank (easy).

We add a commercial chloramine and ammonia removal solution (such as Kordon's Amquel) as the water is entering the tank.

Since we enjoy naturalistic setups, we take pride in the Amazon swordplants and various other growing aquatics that thrive in our tanks. The plants help remove the dissolved wastes and provide oxygen.

In keeping with our Easier is Better theme, our filters are large sponge cylinders supported on plastic inserts and topped by powerheads that are tightly seated, suitably sized, and flow adjustable. We may or

may not use the tube attachment to provide injected air. The sponges quickly become bacterial filters, thus assisting us even more in the quest for suitable water quality. One such unit per tank is sufficient for terraria of up to 120 gallons (454 L) in size, but we use two units for terraria larger than 120 gallons. The powerhead draws so much particulate-bearing water into the sponge that the latter requires cleaning about every second day. To do this, we merely unseat the powerhead, lift the sponge out into a pail, and rinse it clean (kneading it firmly) in nonchlorinated water (chlorine kills the desirable bacteria).

Although undergravel filters are certainly an option, we have found them unsuitable for our needs. Should you decide on these, we urge that their efficiency be enhanced by the addition of powerheads.

This aquatic terrarium is home to tentacled snakes and small turtles.

African clawed frogs, Suriname toads, and aquatic turtles. Some aquatic turtles eat most varieties of aquatic plants. Innocuous though they may appear, aquatic caecilians, amphiumas, and sirens are persistent burrowers that uproot even firmly anchored plants.

With large herps, we keep the tank decorations either light in weight or large and immovable. Often, we provide only floating plants and driftwood pieces that will not break the aquarium glass if brought sharply in contact by the maneuverings and kickings of the inhabitants. Keep the glass breakage factor in mind if using rocks for decoration. They must be either so large that the frogs and turtles can't move them, or, if small, anchored

with silicone aquarium sealant to the bottom or back of the tank. Even a small rock, when shoved by powerful hindlegs, can have a devastating effect on panels of aquarium glass.

Although dwarf underwater frogs, newts, or baby turtles will thrive in a tank of only 5 or 10 gallons (19 to 38 L), an adult Suriname toad, mudpuppy, or larger turtle will require five or more times that space.

Substrate

We prefer 2 inches (5 cm) or more of smooth, pea-sized river gravel and, when the inhabitants allow, intricate arrangements of submerged driftwood and rocks and a profusion of live aquatic plants. The finished product often allows the inhabitants to be seen only when they choose to be.

The substrate can be sloped, although slopes are often quickly unsloped through the antics of the inhabitants, or tiered, a much more reliable method. Tiers can be easily made from strong glass strips secured with silicone sealant. To facilitate proper viewing, the lowest tier should be at the front of the tank.

Heating

Heating can be provided by either a standard or a submersible aquarium heater, but make sure the glass sheath of an electric heater cannot be broken by the activities of large specimens. Anchor the heaters *very* securely and check the anchors frequently. If a heater is broken, unplug the heater *before* putting your hands or any other implement in the water. We have found that heat from undertank heaters is not dispersed well through the thick gravel substrate, so we do not use these. Heat for a haulout area provided for baby turtles may be provided by an over-tank light.

Filtration

Several types of filtration systems are available. Standard foam cartridge corner filters, which operate from an equally standard vibrator pump, are efficient, as are outside filters. We have found that a standard, large-sized foam cartridge with an attached submersible power head works very well, is very adaptable, and provides both mechanical and biological filtration. Coupled with periodic partial water changes, filters of these types are useful for small

aquaria or on profusely planted, sparsely inhabited, larger aquaria.

We suggest that you discuss the availability and efficiency of biological filters with your aquarium store. Biological filters are very efficient at removing both particulates and ammonia buildups and should be considered by any hobbyists maintaining large aquaria populated with large numbers or large-sized herps.

Lighting

Adequate and proper lighting is essential when you are growing live plants in your aquarium. We usually utilize at least two tank-length fluorescent plant-grow bulbs in a reflector top. If you keep small animals such as fire-bellied toads, paradox frogs, or turtles, you may wish to use a BL-type blacklight tube as well. In the case of the tank housing our fully aquatic tentacled snakes—a mildly venomous rear-fanged species—which often lie on top of floating *anacharis*, we also supply directed-beam —spotlights—incandescent lighting under which the snakes can bask if they choose. They often do so.

Haulouts

Aquatic frogs and newts, some turtles, and a very few snakes thrive in an aquarium setup; however, you must provide a surface-level or above-water haulout area for them to use if they desire.

In the case of the various fire-bellied toads, newts, and baby aquatic turtles, floating corkbark, projecting anchored driftwood, and mats of growing, floating aquarium plants will provide ideal, easily accessed haulouts. At least one of the cork or driftwood haulouts should be illuminated and warmed by a directed-beam incandescent lamp, and be high enough and big enough so the turtle can get completely out of the water.

Haulouts are not needed for fully aquatic species such as the various dwarf underwater frogs, African clawed frogs, or Suriname toads.

Tops

No matter what kind of aquatic amphibian or reptile you maintain, a full, *tight-fitting* top is essential. Newts, other aquatic salamanders, and aquatic caecilians are adept at finding and escaping through even the smallest opening—often around an air hose or electric cord. Although fully aquatic, Suriname toads and clawed frogs may occasionally propel themselves upward and out of an uncovered tank. Baby turtles are less adept than many other species at escaping, but even these may wedge themselves between a heater tube or a filter stem and work their way upward and out of an aquarium. A complete but easily manipulated cover is one of the most important parts of any setup containing any species of herps.

Variations

There is no denying that live plants add a dimension of beauty and naturalness to any aquatic terrarium. When separated from boisterous or marauding herps, plants can be grown as a background in any properly lighted aquarium. The plants will need to be planted along the back glass, and then a thin pane of upright glass, extending from the bottom glass to the top of the upper frame of the aquarium, is inserted in front of the plants. To allow the plants a chance to grow and spread, we suggest that they be allowed a space of at least 6 inches (15 cm) from the back glass. There is no need to devote this space only to plants. Interesting fish or smaller, nonobtrusive herp species can be housed with the plants. One such 50-gallon (189 L) setup of which we are particularly fond had Suriname toads in the front section and highly predaceous Amazonian leaf fish, *Monocirrhus polyacanthus*, which would have become the prey of the toads if housed together, in the planted section. When a full tank divider is used, it is necessary to provide filtration to both sections.

An aquarium filled only partially is ideal for some turtles that are aquatic yet weak swimmers. Such species as matamatas and alligator snapping turtles do best when they can stretch their necks and noses upward from where they are sitting to the water's surface, rather than swimming. Despite the fact that they are strong swimmers, soft-shelled turtles prefer a water depth that allows them to breathe while buried in the substrate. Most of the softshell species become stressed and prone to fast-growing shell diseases if not allowed to conceal themselves in the substrate.

Because their shells are easily damaged, we suggest that soft-shelled turtles be provided with a substrate of smooth sand, not sharp silica.

Aquarium Plants

Aquarium plants of many kinds are available at aquarium stores and in the wild. (Check laws before taking plants from the wild.) Many aquarists decry the use of wild-collected plants, stating the possible introduction of insect or other pests as the principal reason. The truth is that many, if not most, of the plants available in aquarium shops have been collected from the wild. They just have gone through two additional steps, collector and wholesaler, before becoming available to the aquarist or terrarist.

Two genera of eelgrasses, *Vallisneria* and *Sagittaria*, are among the most widely sought and adaptable of the inexpensive plants. In the wild, plants of these genera are also mainstays in the diet of many turtles. Turtles will eat these plants as avidly in the aquarium as in nature. If grown in proper light, all commonly seen aquarium species of these plants will thrive, multiply by runners, and, occasionally, flower.

Amazon sword plants (genus *Echinodorus*) of several varieties, from dwarf to typical, are readily available and are among the easiest of the submerged plants to grow. Enough light and a little time will result in deep green, fast-growing foliage, rapid-multiplying, by runners,

and occasional flowers. Despite a brittleness at the leaf bases, these are fairly sturdy plants that do not seem especially palatable to most aquarium inhabitants. Once established, the roots are long and pervasive, making these among the most stable of the aquarium plants.

Several plants are available as unrooted bunches. Among these are *Elodea (Anacharis), Cabomba* (fanworts), and *Myriophyllum* (milfoil). If the stems are separated and planted in the gravel, these plants will root and grow profusely. *Anacharis* and *Myriophyllum* also grow well as floating plants in high-light conditions. Hornwort (*Ceratophyllum*) is a pretty but brittle plant that usually does better as a floating plant than when rooted.

A great many other plants, among them a dozen or more species of *Cryptocoryne* (cryps) and *Aponogeton* (lace plants and relatives) are available and are variably prolific. Many of the Cryptocorynes are adaptable to relatively low-light conditions. Of these plants, because of a period of dormancy and the propensity of the leaf apertures to become filled with algae, the lace plant is the most difficult, but its great beauty and exotic appearance make it worth the effort.

Water Creatures

Aquatic Caecilians

Only two species belonging to a single neotropical family, the

Typhlonectes natans, *an aquatic neotropical caecilian, is readily available in many pet stores where it is sold under the name of "Sicilian eel" or "rubber eel."*

In their native South America the typhlonectines live in silted quiet waters, and burrow avidly through the mud and mulm of the substrate. Apparently, they are able to burrow even deeper and so avoid desiccation when water levels fall during the dry season.

Typhlonectine caecilians live well as captives, and have been bred several times. They can be sexed with some difficulty by ascertaining cloacal shape. It might be better to simply purchase a group of a half dozen or so and trust to luck that both sexes are present; they usually are. These caecilians prefer soft, somewhat acidic water and a substrate in which they can easily burrow and hide. We have provided ours with several inches of milled sphagnum moss—a nonabrasive cover that provides excellent security, helps to acidify the water, and will eventually sink to the bottom of the aquarium.

It is almost impossible to grow aquatic plants in such a yielding substrate, and we beautify the aquarium by placing one or more pothos or philodendrons on plastic aquarium-pump supports hanging from the back of the tank. The tendrils lie on and in the water, providing a tropical look. Additionally, such floating plants as Riccia and hornwort are used. Lighting for these burrowing creatures is optional, but must be used if live plants are included in the setup. Caecilians eat bloodworms, tubifex worms, and small earthworms, and will accept

Typhlonectidae, are currently seen in the American pet trade. These are *Typhlonectes natans* and *T. compressicauda*. Both are of similar appearance, and both require identical care.

The typhlonectine caecilians are often seen in pet stores, where they are most often referred to as rubber eels or Sicilian [sic] eels. They may attain 2 feet (61 cm) in total length, but most seen in the pet trade are between 10 and 15 inches (25 to 38 cm) in length. When adult, the aquatic caecilians have no external gills, but neonates—these creatures birth live young—have huge, flattened gill membranes that are attached by a slender stalk. They lack functional eyes, have virtually no tail, and have a short, retractible, tactile tentacle near the nostril. The overall color is dark gray to charcoal.

Dwarf sirens are interesting, tiny, salamanders of aquatic habitats in the southeastern United States. Pictured is a narrow-striped dwarf siren, Pseudobranchus axanthus.

some prepared, pelleted fish foods. Despite lacking sight, their olfactory sense is acute, and these amphibians are quick to realize when food has been provided and animatedly seek it out.

Dwarf Sirens

These tiny creatures—to 6.5 inches (16.5 cm)—are attenuate salamanders that will thrive in captivity when provided with aquarium conditions such as those described for the aquatic caecilians. Dwarf sirens are native to coastal plain habitats in the southeastern United States.

Despite their belonging to the same family (the Sirenidae) as the larger sirens, the two species of dwarf sirens, *Pseudobranchus axanthus* and *P. striatus*, are far more delicate. These interesting salaman-

ders have three pairs of external gills, tiny forelimbs with three toes on each hand, and no rear limbs. They are clad in a ground color of muddy gray, olive, or brown, with light stripes, variable by both species and subspecies, along their back and upper sides. Like the caecilians, dwarf sirens burrow persistently and especially utilize a thick mat of submerged plant material—we provide an inch or more of milled sphagnum—over a substrate of fine washed sand. Mats of floating plants also seem to be appreciated. These are shy, retiring salamanders. Although they do not do well in most community setups, they don't seem to squabble among themselves. Fish, if added to the siren's aquarium, often pick at the salamanders' exposed gill filaments, causing the little amphibians severe distress. We have, however, found dwarf underwater frogs (*Hymenochirus* species) to be acceptable and benign tankmates. Captive breeding has been accomplished only once or twice, and then, seemingly, more by accident than by design. The eggs seem at least semiadhesive, and are scattered in floating plants. Lighting is optional, but if provided, need only be subdued for the salamanders, yet bright enough to sustain life and growth of the plants in the tank. Dwarf sirens require bloodworms, whiteworms, tubifex worms, daphnia, or other such tiny invertebrates as food. Some specimens will accept certain prepared foods, but others seem not to. A temperature of from 70° to 80°F (21° to 27°C) seems acceptable to these salamanders. It is possible that a period of winter cooling with water temperature dropping to the low- to mid-60°s F (16° to 18°C), and with reduced photoperiod, might stimulate reproductive cycling.

Dwarf Underwater Frogs

These frogs are often available in pet stores around the world. They are captive bred in huge numbers, and there is no longer a significant draw on wild populations for the pet trade.

These tiny frogs (*Hymenochirus curtipes*) are members of the tongueless frog family, the Pipidae. They are olive to olive brown in color, usually with numerous small dark spots dorsally. The skin is granular and the lidless eyes are situated laterally. Besides having fully webbed hindfeet, the forefeet are extensively webbed. Reproductively active males develop a small but visible postaxillary gland immediately posterior to the apex of the forelimbs. During periods of reproductive activity, males make faint clicking sounds.

Water temperatures of between 72° and 85°F (22° to 29°C) seem suitable for these very undemanding frogs. They particularly relish small live foods such as white, tubifex, and bloodworms, a little washed brine shrimp, or daphnia. They will also eat many prepared fish foods and most frozen fish foods.

Oviposition can be stimulated by briefly chilling the aquarium water slightly, then increasing the temperature about 5 degrees and keeping it there for a few days. This can be done by adding cold dechlorinated tap water, then raising the aquarium heater's thermostat. Males grasp the gravid females by the waist and the pair indulges in a series of vertical looping or half loop runs through the water. The eggs, often numbering a total of many hundreds, are laid in small numbers while the pair is upside down at the water's surface. The eggs develop quickly and the tadpoles are easily raised on infusoria, cyclops, daphnia, and washed, newly hatched brine shrimp.

The African Clawed Frog, *Xenopus laevis*

This is a larger relative of the dwarf underwater frogs. Its larger size—to 4 inches (10 cm)—allows the clawed frog to be a more efficient and voracious predator. Adults eat tadpoles and fishes, as well as the more typical frog fare of worms, insects, and small crustaceans. The keeping and sale of the African clawed frog is banned by several states.

Breeding: Clawed frogs are bred in captivity by the tens of thousands. Breeding activities are initiated by deepened and cooled water, which would occur in nature during heavy rains. The several hundred adhesive eggs are laid singly, often attached to submerged aquatic plants, or to the sides of the aquarium or the substrate. The tadpoles, which hover in midwater, have a tentacle at each side of the mouth and a tailtip filament, and feed by filtering suspended algae and finely pulverized flake foods from the water.

The normal coloration of the clawed frog is olive to olive brown with vaguely outlined mottlings and reticulations. Leucistic—white with black eyes—and albino—white with red eyes—phases are now more popular than the normal coloration in the pet trade. More rarely, yellowish and piebald clawed frogs are offered.

Clawed frogs have a smooth, slimy skin and are very difficult to grasp by hand. They lack webbing on their fingers, have protuberant, dorsally situated, lidless eyes, and well-defined lateral lines of short, well-separated, vertically oriented "stitchmarks."

The large size of adult clawed frogs necessitates that they be pro-

The African clawed frog, Xenopus laevis, *is now available in normal, albino (shown here), leucistic, and piebald phases.*

vided with a fairly large and a well-filtered aquarium. Because of the well-developed predatory tendencies of these frogs, it is also necessary to choose tankmates carefully. The tankmates must be large enough so that the frogs don't regard them as potential prey. If grabbed by a clawed frog, spiny or armored fishes, such as talking and related catfishes, can become lodged in its mouth or throat and cause the frog's death. Although an attenuate tankmate, such as a moderately sized caecilian, fire eel, or siren, may be too large to swallow at one time, a clawed frog will often engulf the head, thus killing the fish or amphibian, and from that point on, swallow the remainder a bit at a time.

Suriname Toads

There are several species of Suriname toads, but two, the dwarf

(*Pipa parva*) and the common (*Pipa pipa*), are the species seen most frequently in the pet trade. These are neotropical relatives of the Old World clawed and dwarf underwater frogs. All are in the family Pipidae, the tongueless frogs.

The common Suriname toad is a grotesquely flattened, large—to 6.5 inches (16.5 cm)—pipid with an even more flattened head. The eyes are tiny and lidless, situated anteriorly, and oriented dorsally. The webless front toes are directed forward, and each is bifurcate at the tip. The heavily muscled hind limbs are powerful organs of propulsion, and the huge feet are fully-webbed. Lateral and dorsolateral lines of short, elevated, stitchlike, sensory organs are well developed, but are not always easy to see. Suriname toads are clad in skin the color of mud, often somewhat lighter on the sides and venter. The common Suriname toad has a dark T on the venter, the top extending across the chest. When removed from the water, Suriname toads move clumsily but are far from helpless.

Diet: These toads prey upon tadpoles, fish, worms, and aquatic insects. Food items are unceremoniously shoveled into the tongueless mouth with the aid of the forelimbs. The toads have prodigious appetites, and correspondingly prodigious amounts of body waste. Use biological filtration and make frequent water changes.

Breeding: Suriname toads of all species have complex and interesting breeding methods. Breeding and ovulation seem stimulated by deepened water levels, temperature changes—primarily a rapid cooling such as would occur in nature at the onset of the rainy season—and photoperiod. Similar to other pipid frogs, male Suriname toads amplex the females inguinally. The pair goes through several loops, or partial loops, and at the apex of each, the female expels several eggs. Motions of the male seem instrumental in pushing the eggs forward onto the back of the female where they adhere. The glandular dorsal skin of the female thickens and encloses, or mostly encloses, each egg. Incubation occurs in the individual dorsal pockets. As in some other species, the hatchlings emerge as tadpoles. Alternatively, some species, such as the common Suriname toad, retain the eggs until metamorphosis is complete and the young emerge as miniatures of the adults. We have had Suriname toads breed in water of only a foot (30 cm) in depth, but depths of 18 inches (46 cm) or more are preferred.

Fire-bellied Toads, Asiatic Floating Frogs, and Paradox Frogs

Although of rather similar habits, these three frogs are not closely related. In fact, they belong to three very different families: the Discoglossidae, fire-bellied toads; the Ranidae, floating frogs; and Pseudidae, paradox frogs.

The oriental fire-bellied toad, Bombina orientalis, *is a common and beautifully colored pet trade species that may lose its trademark belly color in captivity.*

Of the half dozen species of fire-bellied toads, only the oriental fire-belly, *Bombina orientalis*, appears with any regularity in the American pet trade. The European fire-bellied toad, *B. bombina*, and the yellow-bellied toad, *B. variegata*, are often encountered in the European pet trade. All are mottled black on gray, or green with a black and red or yellow reticulated belly. It seems probable that the intense reds and yellows seen on the bellies of wild-collected specimens are caused and retained by the ingestion of pigments contained in their natural insect diets. While fire-bellied toads are easily bred in captivity, the diet of gray crickets and mealworms that is most often given frequently produces frogs with bellies of black reticulated gray or muted orange. Perhaps if

feed insects were given a diet high in B carotene and other carotenoids, the ventral colors from which the frogs have taken their common names would prevail. Dietary experimentation is necessary.

Although fire-bellied toads are bred with increasing regularity in captivity, the pet trade remains more or less dependent on wild-collected specimens.

The Asian floating frog, *Occidozyga lima*: This is a robust, inch-long (2.5 cm) species with eyes directed somewhat more dorsally than those of most common frogs. Its pupils are diamond shaped. It floats happily on the surface of the aquarium water, especially if there are small mats of floating vegetation, and dives readily if frightened. The roughened dorsum is olive gray, olive brown, or olive green, there is usually a brighter green vertebral line, and the nose is often bright green also. A more or less well-defined gray lateral stripe may be present. The yellowish belly is liberally dusted with black. The legs are comparatively short and each thigh bears a black posterioventral stripe.

The Paradox Frog, *Pseudis paradoxa*

This frog is a South American species that is occasionally seen in the pet trade. With its corpulent build and dorsolaterally oriented eyes, the paradox frog looks much like the floating frog, but has much longer hind limbs that lack the black ventral thigh stripe. Dark mottlings and yellow and black bars mark the rear inside thigh and femur. The dorsal color is usually an olive green, with or without darker mottlings. A dark bar is usually visible behind the eye and covers the area of the eardrum. Another dark spot is often visible at the anterior apex of the forelimbs. Pseudid frogs have an added phalanx on each of their digits and an opposable thumb.

Both common and scientific names of this frog are derived from the fact that immediately before metamorphosis, its tadpoles can be 8 or more inches (20 cm) in length and the maximum length of the adult frog is only about 3 inches (7.6 cm). Thus, paradoxically, the adults are substantially smaller than the larvae.

Because of their smooth, slimy skin, paradox frogs are difficult to grasp. They are much easier to net than to catch by hand. Be sure to cover the top of the net or the frog will quickly jump free. This frog has not yet been been bred in captivity.

Providing that water quality and reasonable temperatures are maintained, all these frogs are among the easily kept species. All are perfectly at home in the aquaterrarium among mats of floating plants or where leaves and stems of rooted plants bend over and lie on the surface. Floating or stationary corkbark islands, favored by fire-bellied toads, will probably be shunned by floating and paradox frogs.

Diet: Small gut-loaded crickets will be eagerly accepted by all these frogs. Because these insects will walk around on the plant mats and cork for an hour or two, they are often offered as food. Since mealworms will fall to the bottom of the water and drown, they must be fed to the frogs from forceps. We prefer to use small sections of nightcrawlers, also presented to the frogs on forceps. If the food is offered slowly, the frogs will usually readily accept forceps-presented insects and worms.

Amphiumas, Greater and Lesser Sirens, and Mudpuppies/Waterdogs

Here we again have three families represented. The amphiumas belong to the family Amphiumidae, the sirens to the family Sirenidae, and the mudpuppies-waterdogs to the family Proteidae. All of these salamanders are permanently aquatic. All have lidless eyes.

The mud-colored amphiumas look superficially like eels, but lack fins. All amphiuma have two pairs of legs, so minute that they may be overlooked. Amphiumas lack external gills but have a gill opening visible on each side of the head. Of the three species, the two larger ones, the two-toed, *Amphiuma means*, and the three-toed amphiuma, *A. tridactylum*, are often available from reptile dealers, and occasionally from pet stores. Although usually smaller, these can exceed 30 inches (76 cm) in total length. Amphiuma can and will bite if carelessly restrained.

Both greater sirens, *Siren lacertina*, and lesser sirens, *S. intermedia* ssp., are also available from reptile dealers and pet stores. These unusual salamanders have three pairs of (usually) bushy external gills and a pair of well-developed forelimbs that may be partially hidden by the gills, but no rear limbs.

The greater siren is a heavy-bodied, 2- to 3-foot-long (61 to 91 cm) salamander. The sides of its mud-colored body are usually flecked with gold or silver specks that appear metallic. The original, nondamaged tailfin is rather bluntly rounded.

The lesser siren, nearly as long, is somewhat slimmer. Nonmetallic light spots may be present on the sides of the head and the snout may be almost white. If body spots are present, they are usually darker than the

The four legs of the two-toed amphiuma, Amphiuma means, *are so small that they can hardly be seen. This North American salamander can and will bite if carelessly restrained.*

ground color. Nondamaged tailfins are lance-shaped.

Mudpuppies and waterdogs of the family Proteidae have only four toes on each of their four feet. The legs are short but well developed. Three pairs of variably bushy gills are always present. Most species have prominent dark spots on their sides and a dark stripe through the eye. These interesting creatures vary from the 6-inch (15 cm) total length of the dwarf waterdog, *Necturus punctatus*, to the foot or more (30 cm plus) of the common mudpuppy, *N. maculosus* ssp.

All these salamanders will thrive in waters 70° to 78°F (21° to 26°C). Common mudpuppies would perfer the lower end of this temperature

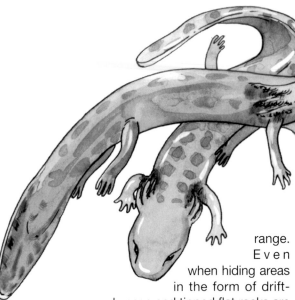

range. Even when hiding areas in the form of driftwood snags and tipped flat rocks are provided, amphiumas and sirens are persistent burrowers. They will usually dislodge even the most firmly rooted plants. Mudpuppies do not burrow and will use thickets of rooted plants as hiding areas.

Diet: All of these salamanders eat worms, glass (grass) shrimp, small fish, small crayfish, and aquatic insects. In many cases, numbers of these can simply be kept in the aquarium, allowing the salamanders to feed at will. Watch any fish left in the tank to make sure that they are not picking on gill filaments.

None of the sirens, amphiumas, or mudpuppies has been captive bred, and the reproductive biology of many species is poorly understood. External means of sexing these amphibians are lacking. It is possible that, if both sexes are present, winter cooling, coupled with seasonally

Axolotls and Waterdogs

As used here, these designations both refer to salamanders of the family Ambystomatidae. Pet dealers often incorrectly use the terms interchangeably. In the pet industry, the term axolotl should be reserved for the permanently larval Mexican *Ambystoma mexicanum*. If the term waterdog is to be used at all when referring to these salamanders (waterdog is the accepted common name for the very different salamanders of the familiy Proteidae mentioned earlier in this chapter), it should be used only for the larval North American tiger salamanders, *A. tigrinum* ssp., that are periodically available. These salamanders would be better referred to, at all stages of their life, as tiger salamanders.

The axolotl is readily bred in captivity. It is now available in leucistic (white or gold with black eyes), albino (white with pink or red eyes), normal (olive gray), and piebald (gray and white) phases.

For several reasons the axolotl (pronounced "axe-oh-lotl" with the accent on the axe) is the better choice of these two for the aquavivarium. Firstly, all axolotls available in the pet trade are bred in captivity, hence there is no depletion of wild populations, and secondly, they are permanent larvae, and suitable

Mudpuppies, **Necturus maculosus,** *may attain a foot in length and like cool to cold water. They thrive in well planted aquaria.*

aquavivarium—wholly aquatic terrariums—inhabitants throughout their long lives.

On the other hand, the larval tiger salamanders currently available in the pet trade are all collected from wild populations. Several races, which, as adults, vary widely in color and pattern, are sold. Larval tiger salamanders nearly always metamorphose and leave the water within a year. When adult they are perfect and very long-lived candidates for either the semiaquatic or the woodland terrarium.

Both the tiger salamander and the axolotl can be differentiated from the true waterdogs by the presence of five toes on each hind foot. Fish are poor companions for both of these gilled creatures.

Over most of their range, tiger salamanders live a normal life, as aquatic larvae and terrestrial—actually burrowing—adults. Where terrestrial conditions are untenable, however, or where water quality inhibits the normal thyroid activity that promotes metamorphosis, as in the axolotl, tiger salamanders may remain in the larval stage for extended periods, or even for their entire life. This condition is referred to as *neoteny,* and neotenic tiger salamanders attain sexual maturity while still larvae. The conditions necessary to breed tiger salamanders in captivity are not yet known with certainty, but a reduced winter photoperiod and a winter chilling, when temperature drops to the 50°s F (10° to 15°C) or very low 60°s F (16° to 17°C) for 90

Despite their beauty and popularity as aquarium pets, most newts produce very toxic skin secretions. This is a male Japanese fire-bellied newt, Cynops pyrrhogaster, *in breeding colors.*

days, may provide the necessary cycling process.

Eastern American Newts and Japanese Fire-bellied Newt

Newts around the world, whether small or large, aquatic or terrestrial, all belong to the family Salamandridae. The western American, and other more terrestrial, newts are discussed in the section on semi-aquatic terraria, pages 133 to 162.

Of the tailed amphibians available to the pet trade, the newts are most frequently seen. Newts occur over much of the temperate world, and are particularly diverse in Europe and Asia. Two genera containing six species are found in North America. Because of noxious skin secretions that protect them from many preda-

tors, newts are usually less retiring than many other salamanders.

Eastern newts: Our eastern newts are members of the genus *Notophthalmus.* Those seen in the pet trade are the four subspecies of the red-spotted newt, *N. viridescens.* Of these, two subspecies, the red-spotted and the broken-striped newts are, respectively, attractively adorned with a row of black-edged vermilion spots or stripes along both sides of their dorsa. The remaining two subspecies, the pleasantly colored central, and the particularly drab peninsula newts, usually lack red.

The eastern newts are small creatures. The largest race, the red-spotted form, reaches a mere 5.5 inches (14 cm) in total length. All four subspecies of the eastern newt have quite a complex life cycle. Eggs are deposited in water and hatch into prominently gilled larvae. After a period of time, if conditions are right, the larvae resorb their gills and transform into rough-skinned, often brightly colored, terrestrial-dwelling subadults. At this stage of their lives, the creatures are often referred to as *efts*. In the Northeast, central region, and some areas of the South, efts are red or red-orange. Those in the Deep South are often only slightly, if at all, brighter than the adults.

The eft stage lasts from one to several years, but is foregone entirely in some newt populations or if terrestrial conditions are unfavorable. After completing this stage, eastern newts return to the water, fade in coloration from red to olive green, with black-spotted yellow bellies, and, there, complete their lives.

Adult eastern newts are often sold as oddities for aquaria. Slow-moving, they are compatible with most community tank fish, but will prey upon fish eggs or freshly dead baby livebearers. Adult washed brine shrimp, bloodworms and whiteworms, and chopped earthworms are relished by newts. Some prepared fish foods are also consumed. Their skin secretions usually protect them from the occasional aggressive tankmates.

Japanese fire-bellied newt, *Cynops pyrrhogaster:* This is a beautiful, hardy, readily available, moderately sized species. Fire-bellied newts are proportionately stout and attain a length of about 5 inches (13 cm). They are rich brown dorsally and rich brown marbled with vermilion ventrally. Fire-bellies will thrive for a decade or more in an aquarium or in a semiaquatic terrarium if kept cool, clean, and well fed.

Newts are palearctic in distribution. At the southerly extremes of their range, most are found in cool water at high altitudes. These red-spotted newts are active, even feeding in waters with temperatures in the high 30°s F (2.8° to 4°C). They have been seen indulging in breeding activities as early as late February.

Breeding: To condition newts for captive breeding it is usually necessary to cool them—to 48° to 55°F (9° to 13°C)—and reduce the hours of light for a period of from 45 to 60 days. Most will continue feeding during the period of cooling. Begin feeding your newts more heavily as their waters are gradually warmed—to 68° to 75°F (20° to 24°C). Coupled with lengthening hours of daylight, this will stimulate your newts to begin their courtship activities. These may range from simple to complex, but all are interesting to observe.

Of the Asiatic newt species, only the Japanese fire-bellied is captive bred with any degree of regularity. A quiet water species, the courtship involves several procedures. Pheromones, which play a part in sexual receptivity, are produced in the male's chin glands. By rubbing the female with his chin, the male brings these stimulants into play. He also indulges in elaborate body positioning and tail fanning. The tail fanning is another way of dispersing the pheromones. During courtship the male produces a spermato-phore, the sperm-bearing cap of which is picked up by the female with her cloaca. After accepting the sperm packet, the female lays her eggs singly among floating plants or on the leaves of rooted plants. The adhesive eggs are positioned with her hind legs.

Eggs and adults should be separated after deposition is completed, for newts *will* eat their own eggs. The development of newt eggs can be a lengthy process. Within a few days after hatching, the babies will be looking for food. We use washed brine shrimp, daphnia, and finely chopped earthworms initially. With increased growth, the shrimp and daphnia are discontinued and the worm pieces increased in size. Bloodworms and white worms, both mainstays in the aquarium industry, are also offered. Incubation in the aquarium can take up to six weeks. Three to six months are required for the larvae to metamorphose.

Metamorphosis: Metamorphosis can be a critical time for newts. Besides altering epidermal structure, they change from external gills to functional lungs. At that time, drowning is most likely. To forestall that possibility, it is best to reduce the depth of the water and offer more surface plants or other easily accessible resting places on which the young may crawl. Once metamorphosis is complete, remove the juveniles of the terrestrial forms to a terrestrial or semi-aquatic tank. From that point on, growth will be rapid for most newts.

Tentacled Snake

The tentacled snake, *Erpeton tentaculatum*, is a two- to three-foot (60 to 90 cm) long, fully aquatic snake species from Southeast Asia. It is a member of the rear-fanged subfamily Homolopsinae. The homolopsines are a grouping within the immense, and taxonomically unwieldy, snake family Colubridae. Collectively, the colubrine snakes are often referred to as the harmless snakes. However, this is an entirely inaccurate designation for some colubrines, including the tentacled snake. These creatures have enlarged teeth in the rear upper jaw and a venom-producing apparatus. Although tentacled snakes are reluctant to bite, the virulence of their venom is unknown and they should be handled with caution. Still, many states that have sanctions against the private ownership of venomous snakes have no such regulations against *Erpeton*, so we include them here.

The depressed body of the tentacled snake is clad in keeled scales that vary, specimen by specimen, from mud-brown to mud-gray, with blotched and striped phases. Blotched tentacled snakes have dorsal blotches alternating with lateral blotches. The lateral blotches terminate ventrally in a whitish dot. These whitish ventrolateral dots are usually the most conspicuous markings on the entire snake. The ventral scutes are not greatly enlarged. A tentacle is located on each side of the nose. The tentacles, which protrude anteriorly when the submerged snake is quiescent, may dangle downward or fold back against the sides of the snout when the snake's nose is above water. It is speculated that the tentacles of *Erpeton* are innervated and sensory in function. Because in nature these snakes occur in often silted waters where vision may be obscured, this theory makes sense.

Tentacled snakes are stiff and ungainly on land. Even though fully aquatic they are not particularly agile swimmers. This species prefers to rely on cryptic coloration and rigid twig-like camouflaged appearance rather than actual escape mechanisms. Rarely do tentacled snakes make any attempt to flee.

While several babies of these placid snakes are comfortable in a 10-gallon (38 L) tank, a 75-gallon (284 L) tank is best for a group of adults. The setup contains several submerged manzanita twigs, tangles of floating plants, and large Amazon sword plants rooted in the substrate of small rounded river rocks, as well as filtration and lighting.

If healthy when procured, tentacled snakes are not difficult captives. In fact, they are remarkably hardy, and captive lifespans of more than a decade have been achieved. Water quality (within reason) doesn't seem to matter much, but maintaining a temperature of between 78° and 85°F (26° to 29°F) is important.

Merely keeping both sexes of tentacled snakes together has resulted in occasional breeding success. Tentacled snakes are livebearers, having from as few as 2 to as many as 15 babies per clutch. The babies are diminutives of the adults and may begin foraging even before the post-natal shed.

Usually, tentacled snakes orient themselves vertically or diagonally, tails wrapped loosely around the sunken manzanita branches. With their tails holding them in position, the snakes may twine loosely together, support themselves by lying across or against the stems of submerged vegetation, or merely allow their bodies to float free in the gentle current. When they are resting, their dorsally situated nostrils are usually just above the water line. When looking for food, the snake tips its head downward in an inverted "J" with its neck on the surface of the water. In this position, the snake is ready to grasp any fish that approaches, but seems especially aware of those that swim into the crook of the J. Another frequently assumed hunting position is with the back touching the bottom of a horizontal branch beneath which fish are likely to travel. *Erpeton* grasps its piscine prey— wild-collected fish and baitstore minnows—with a lightning-quick sideways snap. Orienting the prey into a headfirst position and swallowing are also accomplished with amazing speed.

Our tentacled snakes are kept in groups. As often as not all will be in contact with each other. The point of

Although fully aquatic, the neotropical matamata, Chelus *fimbriatus, should be able to stretch its neck upward and breathe without swimming.*

contact may be only the tail, or it may be along virtually the entire length of the snake except for the head. When finally one snake moves away from the group, it is usually soon followed by one or more of its tankmates. We find it interesting that seldom does one of these supposedly asocial animals remain alone for long.

Matamata

Whether a hatchling, or a 15-inch-long (38 cm) adult, this neotropical turtle is of spectacular appearance. It is contained in the family Chelidae and, because it folds its head and neck laterally under the anterior overhang of the carapace, is referred to as a side-necked turtle.

The matamata, *Chelus fimbriatus*, has a narrow carapace with three pronounced keels. The head is flattened and triangular, and the nose is a cylindrical tube. Sensory skin fringes and flaps adorn the chin and neck. Juveniles often have a wash of strawberry or rose on the underside of the neck.

Although fully aquatic, the matamata, a species of the Amazon and Orinoco drainages, is not a strong swimmer. We suggest that they not be kept in water deeper than the distance they reach when stretching their long necks and snorkel-like noses upward to breathe. In other words, have the water shallow so the turtles don't have to swim to get air.

Matamatas seem quite hardy at each end of the size spectrum, but many with a carapace length of between 3.5 and 5 inches (9 to 13 cm) inexplicably die. This is true even of specimens that have been captive raised from hatchling size. In fact, specimens collected from the wild at this seemingly critical intermediate size seem less prone to problems than captive raised matamatas.

The matamata has comparatively weak jaws, and feeds by expanding its throat and literally vacuuming passing fish into its mouth. The turtle then contracts its throat, expelling excess water, but retaining and swallowing the fish in a series of very visible gulps.

The vast majority of the matamata turtles in the pet trade are wild-collected. This species has been captive bred only a few times. Because of its large size at adulthood, it is more easily bred in a pond setup in a tropical greenhouse than in an aquarium. Like all turtles, female matamatas need an area of warmed, dampened soil in which to dig their nest and lay their eggs. Unless the conditions in the greenhouse are ideal and can be maintained for the entire lengthy incubation period—more than 200 days—the eggs should be moved to a high humidity incubator set at 84°F (29°C).

Snapping Turtles

Both the alligator snapping turtle and the common snapping turtles belong to the family Chelydridae. They are both highly aquatic and are suitable for most home collections only when small. Carefully consider this before acquiring these turtles since release of large, difficult specimens should not be considered an option, and finding a zoo or other public collection that will accept them is usually difficult.

The Alligator Snapping Turtle, *Macrochelys temminckii*

This turtle is found in large river systems, and their associated lakes and oxbows, of the southeastern coastal plain and the Mississippi River drainages. It is the largest species of freshwater turtle found in the United States. Adult males may weigh more than 150 pounds (68 kg) and measure more than 20 inches (51 cm) in shell length. The females are much the smaller of the sexes.

This turtle has a roughened, mud brown carapace, a tiny plastron, a grossly oversized head, correspondingly powerful, hooked jaws, and a roughened tail that is nearly as long as the carapace. Dermal tubercles and projections are abundant on the sides of the head, chin, and neck. The forelimbs are heavily scaled.

The young of this species have even more wrinkles than the adults. The carapace is concave on its front margin, roughly parallel on the sides, and both convex and heavily serrate posteriorly. Once past the vulnerable juvenile stage, the alligator snappers have few enemies other than humans.

Breeding: Female alligator snappers probably leave the water only for the purpose of egg laying; males may never do so. Females lay one clutch annually and egg count can be from half a dozen to more than four dozen. The smooth-shelled, nonglossy eggs are roughly the size and shape of Ping-Pong balls. The emerging hatchlings measure about 1.5 inches (4 cm) in straight carapace length. Natural incubation probably takes from three to four months. In captivity, at a consistent 86°F (30°C) incubation lasts about 82 days. The babies were once heavily collected for the pet trade but they are now protected by law in most of the states in which they occur.

Although the diet of many hatchling alligator snappers seems to center largely on fish, they also eat worms, crayfish, and insects.

The ability of the alligator snapper to fish with its lure-like tongue is always of interest. When not in use, the gray tongue is hidden, even when the turtle's mouth is open. Within one or two twitches, however, the double-ended tongue becomes engorged with blood, and pink to red in color.

Macroclemys depends mostly on wait-and-ambush techniques for procuring prey, while specimens of *Chelydra* more actively seek out their prey.

The Common Snapping Turtle

When adult, this turtle may exceed a 15-inch (38 cm) shell length and weigh more than 65 pounds (29 kg). It is the same mud brown as the alligator snapper and is darker when young. When viewed from above, the dorsolaterally directed eyes of the common snapper are easily visible; the more laterally directed eyes of the alligator snapper, less easily so. The record size of the common snapper is 19⅜ inches (49 cm) in carapace length.

When submerged, the attitude of the common snapper (*Chelydra serpentina* ssp.) seems benign, but when this turtle is out of the water, either forceably or voluntarily, the trait from which it takes its common name is best observed. Its long neck enables it to reach a target a considerable distance away. When molested, common snappers will snap repeatedly, at times lunging with such force that the whole turtle may skid forward.

Common snappers may inhabit nearly any pond, lake, pothole, river, or water-filled depression that holds water, even temporarily. They are even active at very low water temperatures.

Common snappers actively forage for fish, amphibians, reptiles (including smaller turtles), carrion, small mammals and birds. Mollusks, crustaceans, worms, other aquatic organisms, and some plants are also consumed. It was long thought that the plants were merely a peripheral, ingested with the snails, shrimp and other aquatic invertebrates that live among them, but it is now known that common snappers willingly eat fruit and vegetable matter.

These turtles are less persistently aquatic than the larger alligator snappers. They sun on emergent snags and stumps, banks, sandbars, and leaning treetrunks. Snappers often float at the water's surface where their dark color quickly absorbs heat.

Breeding: Common snappers usually lay one egg clutch annually. Clutch size varies from 8 to more than 30 eggs. Depending on temperature, the incubation time can be as short as 50 days or more than twice that.

The hatchlings have a shell length of about 1 inch (2.5 cm). The carapace has three distinct keels. Hatchlings are very cryptic, blending in easily with the background.

Map and Sawback Turtles

The map turtle derives both the common and generic names *Graptemys* from the intricate carapacial markings. These light lines, forming circles, blotches, and reticulations, are best defined on the hatchlings, juveniles, and males.

Of the 12 or so species of map turtles, only three are seen with regularity in the pet trade. All are extremely sensitive to unclean water conditions. The importance of clean filtered water to the relative health of the map turtles cannot be over-emphasized. Without nearly absolute cleanliness, map turtles are very prone to disfiguring and potentially fatal shell lesions. All are wary turtles with variably distinct vertebral keels and strongly serrate rear margin on the carapace. Adult males are usually only half or less the size of adult females. These

Hatchling map turtles require scrupulously clean aquarium water and attention to diet, but are beautiful and hardy if cared for properly. Pictured is a hatchling Mississippi map turtle, **Graptemys pseudogeographica kohnii.**

turtles are associated with river systems and are most diverse in the southeastern United States. The yellow-blotched is considered an endangered species, and most other species are also protected.

Map turtles are often divided into the narrow-headed and the broad-headed species. The females of the broad-headed species often eat molluscs and crustaceans, while the smaller males of these and of the narrow-headed species eat worms and aquatic insects.

Adult female common, false, Alabama, Barbour's, Escambia, and Pascagoula maps develop conspicuously enlarged heads, strengthened jaw muscles, and flattened crushing (alveolar) plates behind the mandibles. A bite by an adult female of any of these forms would be unpleasant.

Map turtles, as a group, are highly aquatic and extremely wary. Map turtles prefer to bask on protruding snags and brush as well as on sandbars that are insular or peninsular.

Mississippi Map Turtle

The most commonly offered baby map turtle is the Mississippi map (*G. pseudogeographica kohni*), a species with a plastron more prominently and intricately patterned than its carapace. Mississippi map turtles are best identified by the presence of a big yellow, sometimes fragmented crescent behind each eye. Even if incomplete, no other head stripes extend past it to the eye.

False Map Turtle

The very similar false map turtle, *G. p. pseudogeographica*, is also frequently seen in the pet trade. Rather than a crescent, the false map turtle has an often transverse elongate spot or two behind its eye, but some of the lower head stripes reach the eye. There are no prominent light spots on the mandibles of either of these map turtles.

The above map turtles all have a low but well-defined vertebral keel.

Black-knobbed Sawback

Of the sawbacks, only the black-knobbed sawback, *G. nigrinoda* ssp.—represented by two races—has not yet been provided federal protection. It is regularly seen in the pet trade each spring and summer. This small and beautiful turtle is restricted in distribution to three river systems in southern Alabama.

Females of all of these species attain about 7.5 inches (19 cm) in shell length, and the males about half that.

The black vertebral projections, from which this species takes its name, are large and bluntly rounded. The ringed sawback is considered an endangered species.

Breeding programs are now in place for two Texas species of *Graptemys*. These are the very pretty Cagle's map, *G. caglei*, and the somewhat less brilliantly colored Texas map turtle, *G. versa*. Both are narrow-headed insect eaters.

Diet: While most turtles of this genus will readily accept prepared foods, they become truly animated when live food such as crickets is occasionally provided. Although certainly very different in food value than the larvae of the caddis and mayflies for which these turtles would usually forage, gut-loaded crickets that have been fed chicken starter mash or a mixture of fruit and vegetables seem to be a welcome addition to a balanced diet that includes trout, catfish and reptile chows.

Aquatic Insects and Spiders

If you want to keep insects in your aquatic terrarium, there is a wide variety to choose from. Keep in mind that most aquatic insects have a shorter life span than reptiles or amphibians, and may be aquatic only in their larval stage, as is the dragonfly nymph. When they mature, they become land dwelling insects, and frequently winged insects to boot. Before you acquire any larval aquatic insect, find out what the adult form looks like, and plan on where you will turn the adult loose outdoors. Obviously, you're a step ahead if you select only local, native insect species for your aquatic terrarium. You can't set free nonnative species either legally or ethically.

To acquire your native aquatic insects, spend some time wielding a dip net and bucket in a stream or pond. We found that the ponds on the local city-owned golf course were a good way to find residents for our aquarium, and nighttime was the best time to go looking. If you venture out, be certain to have permission before you go onto someone else's property.

Once you have a few specimens netted and placed in your bucket of water, take a moment to look at what you've found. A single pass through the vegetation at water's edge may yield water-diving beetles, water scorpions, tiny red water mites and a dragonfly nymph. Return most of these items to the pond; the water mite is too tiny to see easily and it will be difficult to find enough tiny prey items for it. The dragonfly nymph is attractive, certainly, but if it metamorphoses while you're at work, you may not find the adult in time to turn it loose. Water scorpions, water spiders, and diving beetles are already adults and are fairly easy to keep and to see. They are all carnivorous, feeding on tiny insects or fish. You'll need to drop the surface of the water about three inches below the tank edge to enable them to display normal hunting behaviors. Most adult water insects bear wings, and although they may be clumsy fliers, a secure top on the tank is necessary to prevent their escape.

Diving Beetles, Family Dytiscidae

Like other aquatic insects such as the whirligigs, water boatmen, and back swimmer, the diving beetles have a modified pair of legs used as oars for swimming. These are flattened, ovoid beetles that feed on insect prey. Most are dark brown to black in color. A few have contrasting spots or stippling.

Diving beetles range from ⅜ inch to 1⅝ inches (0.8 to 3.8cm). They are found in quiet ponds during the summer months across the United States and in Canada. Large groups may swarm to bright lights. Some species are extremely cold tolerant and can be seen swimming about in the winter under ice.

They insert their eggs into vegetation stems in the water, and the larvae feed on tiny insects, leeches, and other larvae. Like the adults, larvae must come to the surface to breathe. Larvae emerge to pupate in the mud near the pond. The adults trap air under their elytra or wing-covers and utilize this trapped air when submerged. Both adults and larvae may burrow into mud to survive dry periods.

Dragonfly nymphs are well camouflaged predators that may be found in nearly any body of permanent water. They are immensely interesting insects.

In the aquarium, the diving beetles need quiet water 2 to 12 inches (5.1 to 30 cm) deep, with 3 inches (7.6 cm) or so between the top of the tank and the water's surface.

Insects, such as this yellow-spotted diving beetle, are active and pretty, though predatory, aquarium inhabitants.

Aquatic plants provide an egg deposition site and something to cling to when submerged; a floating clump will give them a resting spot at the surface. Be sure the top of the tank is tight. To feed diving beetles, provide a few pinhead crickets sprinkled on the water's surface several days a week, small fishes, and tiny tadpoles.

Water Scorpion

Superficially, water scorpions (family Nepidae) look like stick insects or slender mantids, with elongate bodies .75 inch to 1.75 inches (1.9 to 4.4 cm) long and paired grasping forelegs. Like stick insects, they may sway back and forth in a slight current. They easily can be identified by the paired breathing tubes protruding from the tip of the abdomen. They have piercing mouthparts that are quite capable of penetrating human skin if carelessly handled. Their saliva is both an anesthetic and digestant for their prey, which means their bite is likely to itch. Three pairs of oval disks below the abdomen are called false spiracles, and are used to gauge water depth and compensate for changes in water pressure.

Water scorpions, which despite their name, are insects, feed on worms, water mites, small fish, tadpoles and other insects, and wait for their prey in vegetation at the water's edge or in shallow water. They place their eggs inside the stems of aquatic vegetation. Nymphs emerge in three weeks and mature in five weeks.

These insects will do well in fairly shallow water from three to eight inches deep, with vegetation to hide in. Don't crowd them; when found in the wild, there's usually at least a foot of space between examples. Water should be room temperature and can drop slightly at night.

Fishing Spiders

Called swamp spiders in England (family Pisauridae), they are up to 3 inches (7.6 cm) across the outspread legs and hunt in the woods or near the water. The six-spotted fishing spider (*Dolomedes triton*) is greenish brown with white stripes along the cephalothorax and abdomen; there are six pairs of spots on the abdomen. The brownish-gray fishing spider (*Dolomedes tenebrosus*) of New England and Canada bears darker crossbars over its legs and abdomen.

They wait for their prey at water's edge or on a large leaf or lily pad, keeping three or four legs lightly poised atop the water, to read the changes in the surface tension that signal the movement of other spiders or potential prey. During the breeding season, fishing spiders tap the surface of the water with their legs, sending messages to potential mates about their location and availability. Diet is largely insects, with a few tadpoles, small fish, and tiny frogs.

Fishing spiders are found in Canada, the eastern United States, and, rarely, in the Rockies. They hunt in and near slow-moving

Water scorpions are abundant in many ponds. They look like a bit of waterlogged stick.

streams. When threatened, they may submerge and remain underwater for half an hour or longer. Evidently, the air trapped in the hair on the body is utilized for oxygen. Females spin a silken egg sac for their eggs, usually in late summer, and remain near the sac or carry it until the spiderlings hatch and disperse.

In the aquatic or semiaquatic terrarium, fishing spiders need a waterside perch. They will feed on almost any water-going insect you net and place in the tank, or on tiny guppies or minnows. Crickets are also a good food source, particularly if there is a land area of the tank. Fishing spiders can be seen during the day, but those observed in southern Florida seemed to be most actively hunting at night.

Pothos, Epipremnum aureum, *are ideal terrarium plants that thrive in conditions of humidity and moderately low light.*

Ferns of various kinds make wonderful accent plants.

Chapter Seven
Semiaquatic Terraria

Although semiaquatic terraria are immensely versatile, and can be pleasing to the eye, these setups are often high-maintenance enclosures that require steady monitoring to keep clean. Maintaining a suitably low relative humidity can be equally challenging. Three principal designs can be readily adapted. In most cases, bigger really is better; when properly set up, containing fully compatible plants and animals, large terraria are usually easier to maintain than small ones.

Plants for Semiaquatic Terraria

Syngonium

This is also referred to as arrowleaf philodendron. Young potted plants have simple arrow-shaped leaves; with growth, this plant vines extensively but usually retains the simple arrowhead-shaped leaves. If the vines begin ascending a tree, holding tightly with adventitious roots that form at the leaf nodes, the leaves enlarge and develop a five-pronged hand shape. Old plants can cover entire trees. The adult is not necessarily what you are looking for in a terrarium plant, but newly potted ones are one of the more ideal plants. Syngoniums are as easy to grow as philodendrons and pothos, but the leaves are held erect on longer stems. They are available in a normal green and in several variegated forms. These plants can tolerate relatively low light, very high humidity, and even lengthy total submersion. When they become too leggy, they tolerate sharp pruning well.

Philodendrons

Philodendrons occur in two forms—basically terrestrial, self-heading varieties such as *P. selloum*, and vining climbers, such as *P. oxycardium* and *P. micans*. *P. selloum* is a common landscaping plant in Florida and southern Texas that attains an immense size, and pups easily. It is suitable only in its smallest sizes in only the largest terraria. Like Syngonium, until the stems begin climbing, the leaves of

Philodendrons, such as P. micans, *are lush additions to the semiaquatic terrarium.*

the various vining species of Philodendron remain small and the growth habit is compact. Most of the common cultivars are immensely versatile plants that grow well under normal terrarium conditions. These plants can withstand close pruning, grow hydroponically or in soil, clamber strongly over moist land areas, and even grow along the surface of the water section. With its reddish leaves, *P. micans* is a particularly beautiful plant that is eagerly sought by many terrarists.

Pothos

This plant is one of the most commonly grown and hardiest of plants. It has been placed in the genera *Pothos*, from which it gets its common name, *Scindapsus*, and now resides in the genus *Epipremnum.* As a houseplant, the leaves remain small and the vining growth habit compact. Where native, or when planted outside in tropical settings or in a conservatory, the plant becomes a climber and develops leaves that may exceed 2 feet (61 cm) in length. Pothos is an ideal terrarium plant, tolerating low light and high humidity with equanimity. It occurs in all-green, variegated, and several marbled forms, the latter of which are somewhat less hardy then the green and variegated forms. This plant will grow in soil, hydroponically, or, for a time, partially submerged, can be sharply pruned, and will root readily from leaf nodes.

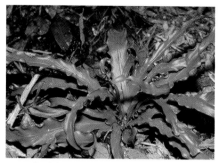

Marbled pothos, Epipremnun aureum (left), is a wonderfully adaptable vine that tolerates low-light conditions. Some cultivars of the large Boston fern, Nephrolepis species are so small that a 10-gallon (38 L) terrarium provides them ample room.

Ferns

There are several species of small terrestrial tropical ferns well adapted to the humidity provided in a semiaquatic terrarium. Among these are *Davallia* sp., the rabbit's-foot ferns, *Hemionitus* sp., palmate ferns, and small specimens of *Asplenium*, birdsnest ferns, and *Nephrolepis*, Boston or sword ferns. All grow well in rich, damp, but not wet, soil and care should be taken that their roots are not perpetually sodden. Two aquatic ferns are also ideal subjects for the aquatic section. These are *Ceratopteris thalictroides*, the water sprite, and *C. pteridoides*, the water fern. All, whether terrestrial or aquatic, require reasonably intense lighting and will reproduce asexually as well as by spores.

Tropical Selaginellas

These are brilliant green, occasionally burgundy, fern-relative ground covers that add beauty, color, and a look of the tropics to semiaquatic and woodland/rainforest terraria. These plants thrive in an atmosphere of humidity and moderate lighting. Many species of selaginellas are available from specialty nurseries, and a few of the standard types are often available from local nurseries across the country.

Fittonias

Provided their roots are not submerged, there are hardly any plants more ideal for a life of beautifying a terrarium than the white-veined and the red-veined fittonias, *Fittonia argyoneura* and *F. verschaffeltii*, respectively. These spreading plants provide a wonderful ground cover, and are strong enough to support the bodies of small frog, salamander, and lizard inhabitants of a terrarium. These plants are available in many nurseries, and dwarf cultivars have been produced.

Prayer Plants

The habit of closing up the leaves during periods of drought and at night have earned the various members of *Maranta* and related genera the common name of prayer plants. Although often offered for sale, even the most common of these is not overly hardy under normal home conditions; however, prayer plants thrive in the greenhouse-like humidity of a cool—68° to 76°F (20° to 24°C)—terrarium. There are several forms and phases, some of which remain small enough to permanently decorate 10- and 15-gallon (38 to 57 L) terraria. The soil surrounding the roots should be moist, but not wet.

Begonias

Begonias of many species and growth habits are abundantly available but we suggest that you steer clear of the various Rex and tuberous begonias, both of which need an exacting regimen of care. The fibrous rooted species, however, including those most often offered as bedding plants in tropical regions, have beautifully colored, waxy-appearing foliage and small attractive flowers, and are easily grown in well-lit, not necessarily sunny, terraria. They can withstand many mistakes on our part, and will often rebound with considerable vigor, even after a period of almost total neglect. If they appear leggy and unattractive, discard and replace them. The soil in which they grow should be moist, but not sodden.

Freckled Lily

Provided a well-drained area is available, the pretty little bulbous plant often referred to erroneously as the freckled orchid, *Ledebouria*

(Squilla) violacea, can be easily grown. The upper surfaces of this small lily's foliage are flecked with dark green against a ground of silvery gray-green and the undersurfaces of the leaves are violet. Tiny greenish flowers are borne periodically. This plant grows best when well-lit, but sunlight is not mandatory.

English Ivy

Hedera helix in its various cultivars is a popular, but not recommended, terrarium plant. Ivy requires bright light with some sunshine preferred, and many forms do best if provided in winter with less water and cool temperatures that induce a period of semidormancy. In their favor, ivies have many foliage forms and colors, and can be inexpensively replaced when necessary.

Tradescantia and Zebrina (Inch Plant or Wandering Jew)

These plants are often suggested as terrarium plants; however, to thrive, these plants need brilliant lighting, including several hours of full-spectrum lighting or natural sunlight each day. They are beautiful plants, grown more for their variably green, white, yellow, and reddish foliage than for the small pink and white flowers many produce. They grow well in moderately moist soil and warm, humid conditions, but will lose foliage color in poor light. Even under ideal conditions leaves die, leaving the fleshy stems leggy and relatively unattractive. These plants can be easily propagated from stem-tip cuttings and will become full and bushy if the growing tips of the long stems are regularly nipped back.

Orchids, Bromeliads, and Staghorn Ferns

These are coveted groupings of plants that often find their way into terraria. While smaller and more tolerant species and cultivars of the orchids and bromeliads or very young staghorn ferns may do well in terraria, most are best suited to life in airy outside cages or brilliantly lit, well-ventilated, room-sized vivaria, or better yet, greenhouses. Some of the smaller orchids such as Pothos, Encyclias, and Oncidiums may be placed temporarily in indoor terraria during blooming, then moved again to better growing conditions such as a greenhouse or outdoors when the blooms are spent. All are interesting plants that will often do particularly well in herp greenhouse conditions.

Cryptocorynes

Cryptocorynes of several species are often offered by aquarium stores. Many are robust growers, even under conditions of relatively low light. All prefer a rich growing medium and somewhat acidic water. Despite their normally submerged growth habit, many of the "cryps," as they are called, grow well in shallow water and will extend leaves and inflorescences well above the water line. Unless you have a deep layer of gravel mixed with peat covering the bottom of the water area, cryps are probably best grown in shallow pots with a gravel/peat/potting soil mixture. Since cryps vary in size by species, choose what you buy wisely. If there are only a few inches of water in your aquatic section, choose a small cryp such as *C. chordata* or *C. willisii*. If deeper water is available, species such as *C. ciliata* or *C. griffithii,* which develop leaves 8 to 12 inches (20 to 30 cm) in length, may be entirely suitable.

Vallisneria

This is often referred to as eelgrass, or in one of its forms, corkscrew val. The name eelgrass is descriptive of many vals—long, slender, bright green grasslike aquatics. While not particularly suited for shallow water, in water several inches or more deep, val makes a pretty green carpet of waving leaves. The form named corkscrew, *V. spiralis*, has an interesting, gently spiraled, leaf structure. To succeed with the various species in this genus, it is important that only the roots are buried and that adequate light is provided.

Sagittaria

This is a coarser plant than val, but like the latter, has a grasslike appearance. It is a common marsh plant in many areas of the eastern United States, and can grow emerged as easily as submerged. There are dwarf varieties (*S. microfolia*) for shallow water, and larger forms such as the very common *S. natans* for deeper water.

It is more difficult to maintain absolute cleanliness in a semiaquatic terrarium than in an aquarium, but the beauty that can be built into a semiaquatic arrangement makes the extra effort well worthwhile. There are at least three simple and effective ways to construct semiaquatic enclosures.

1 Land section situated on top of a contoured platform of pea-sized river rock.

2 A piece of glass, held in place by aquarium sealant, to separate the land section from the water section.

3 Water section contained in a heavy plastic receptacle.

For land area of any type, a base layer of activated charcoal is optional. Whether or not the charcoal is used, we have found virtually no difference in the serviceability of the terrarium. If you use charcoal, place air-conditioner filter material or heavy plastic screening on top of the river rock gravel to keep the gravel separate from the soil.

The cleaning of the land section is made much easier if the tank has bottom drain holes and the land area is over the drain holes. Purchase a tank with these drain holes in place.

You'll need these supplies to set up any of the three terraria:

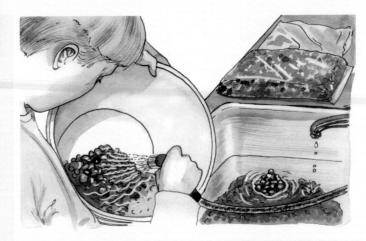

Wash the river rock thouroughly.

Materials Needed

- Terrarium and stand
- Sealant
- Chosen substrates
- Air-conditioning material or screen
- Plants (both terrestrial and aquatic)
- Filter*
- Tank furniture
- Lights and top
*Filter is optional for Style 3.

Setup Procedure

1 Place the chosen terrarium on its stand.

2 Decide on the amount of space that will be used for the land area.

3 Thoroughly wash the river rock you intend to use.

4 **Style 1.** For this first method, add enough thoroughly washed, pea-size river rock to

design the desired bottom contour. Somewhat more than half the bottom area, built up to a depth of about 5 inches (13 cm) is sufficient. This will be the land section of the tank. The remaining section, which will hold the water, has a gravel covering only .5 inch (13 mm) or so in depth. The gravel slopes gently from one to the other.

Style 2. After deciding the amount of space to be devoted to land, affix the glass divider, sloping the top toward the land area, along both sides and the bottom with silicone aquarium sealant. The upper side of the sloped glass should be thinly coated with silicone sealant over which a fine dusting of sand is strewn before the sealant dries. This will allow a toehold for the terrarium inhabitants.

After allowing 24 hours for the sealant to dry, test the dividing panel for watertightness by filling the water area to the desired depth.

If the panel is fully watertight, drain and add the river rock substrate to the desired depth in both the water and the land area. If you find leaks, dry the aquarium, reseal the panel, retest, then continue.

A twofold benefit of using the sealed glass partitioning is the ability to adjust water level and, as gravel depths are reduced in the water area, overall terrarium weight is reduced as well.

Style 3. Place substrate in the tank to a depth of 2 to 3 inches (5.1 to 8 cm). Choose, clean, and place a plastic reservoir in the terrarium, sinking it to its rim in extensive land section. Add water in the water reservoir and plants to the land area.

Dust sand on sloping glass divider.

5 Arrange all heavy tank furniture such as rocks, logs, and so on, setting them firmly in place on top of the pebble substrate or affixing them in place with aquarium sealant if it appears that the herp inhabitants will be able to move these and trap themselves.

6 Add the topsoil, further contouring the land surface if desired. From 1 inch (2.5 cm) to several inches may be desired.

7 Add plants and plantings. These may be as simple as several stems of a vining pothos or philodendron placed on top of the soil, or may involve the use of such exotic moisture-tolerant terrarium plants as Fitto-

nia, *Maranta*, and various small ferns. Plantings can be sparse or profuse.

If kept humid, the stems of pothos and philodendron will quickly root from the leaf and stem nodes and will soon, if lighting is adequate, form a jungle. Other rooted plants may be planted directly into the terrarium soil, or sunk in their pots to the rim in the gravel and soil. If you are using terrarium Style One, be certain that the roots of the potted plants are above the water level. Mossy logs and stones can be easily and artistically incorporated into the design. Additional water cleanliness can be assured by placing a layer of woodland mosses over the potting soil.

8 Add water and filtration. With the current availability of submersible power heads,

not only can the water supply be kept clean, clear and circulating, but riverine and waterfall tanks may be easily designed. There are even terraria available with tough plastic inserts that allow you to design and plant a mossy woodland stream bank or seepage area.

9 Add aquatic or emergent plants to the water area, as desired. Sagittaria and other hardy emergents are readily available, and submerged types such as cryptocorynes and Vallisneria will thrive in well-lighted pond areas.

10 Add top and lighting. The kind of lighting will vary greatly according to its purpose. If the terrarium is housing only amphibians, fluorescent fullspectrum lighting may be all that is necessary. Reptiles of most kinds will require one or more

Terrarium cross section: Substrate, topsoil, furniture, plants, water, aquatic plants, top, and lighting.

ium may choose to have solid tops, while an open screen top may better suit a terrarium being maintained in humid areas such as the Southeast or in fogbelts.

Comments on Cleaning

Cleaning Style 1 entirely is relatively easy; it requires only pouring water onto the land area. As the water percolates down through the gravel, it will carry with it a little topsoil and many of the impurities present. Then, after moving a little gravel in a corner of the water section to expose the glass bottom of the tank, you may easily siphon the water from the terrarium. It is best to run from 5 to 10 gallons (19 to 38 L) of water through in this manner before finally adding the water that will remain. Flushing and cleaning the land area always carries into the water some soil and/or discoloration, but we consider this a very normal and therefore not unattractive part of this style terrarium. The water used, both for the cleaning process and as the final refilling, *must* have had the chlorine and chloramines removed. Both reptiles and amphibians can be nearly as sensitive as fish to these additives.

hot spots for basking. To provide optimum conditions, it may be necessary to provide one basking spot on land and another on a limb or rock protruding from the water. The latter arrangement will be especially impotant when basking turtles are involved.

It should be noted that the more tightly closed the terrarium, the more humidity it will retain. Thus, in arid areas of the country, keepers of a semiaquatic terrar-

The cleaning of the water and land areas of terrarium Styles 2 and 3 must be accomplished separately. Cleaning the water of Style 2 merely involves siphoning the water out, cleaning the glass of the water area, and then replacing the water. Cleaning the water

Terrarium with river insert.

area of Style 3 is even easier. You simply lift the receptacle from the tank, empty the water, sterilize the container, replace the receptacle, and refill it.

Unless there is a drain hole in the bottom glass of the land area of Styles 2 and 3, which would then allow a periodic flushing, cleaning the terrestrial portion will involve entirely removing the substrate, sterilizing the glass, then cleaning and replacing the pebbles and renewing the topsoil. This can be very time-consuming. Depending on the size of the terrarium and the number of reptiles and amphibians it contains, cleaning and replacing the soil should be done from every few weeks to every few months. Unfortunately, there is no set formula for determining when cleaning is necessary, and it is always better to err on the side of safety. However, if flushing is possible, it will dramatically reduce the frequency with which soil removal and replacing is required.

The River Terrarium

The concept of a river terrarium was brought to fruition a few years ago with the availability of a commercially available river terrarium kit. This consists primarily of a simple, molded, three-dimensional plastic insert, made in several sizes, that slips lengthwise into standard aquarium tanks. Built into the insert are pockets for moisture-tolerant plants, a stream bed over which a circulating pump can direct a bubbling stream of water, and other features that were once only available to hobbyists who had the ability to work with fiberglass. The insert is textured to look superficially like the mud and stones of an emergent stream or riverbank.

While this offers an opportunity to many who would otherwise not be able to construct a semiaquatic river tank, it is not a particularly elegant compromise. Hobbyists who can work efficiently with fiberglass can fashion wonderfully intricate designs. Such arrangements as a tanktop waterfall dropping first into a series of small descending pools and finally into a meandering tank bottom stream are possible. If you do not feel personally competent to mix and form the fiberglass resin, perhaps you know a creative home handyman who could help you.

The river terrarium concept need not be restricted to small indoor terraria. It can be adapted on a grand scale to garden settings for turtles and tortoises, or to greenhouse settings in which reptiles such as iguanas, basilisks, water dragons, or tree boas are housed.

The intricacy of your home-built terraria is limited only by your imagination and available funds.

Semiaquatic Creatures

Green and Gray Tree Frogs

The green tree frog, *Hyla cinerea*, is a slender, smooth-skinned hylid of the eastern United States. It's one of the world's prettiest tree frogs. Its dorsal coloration is typically light to dark green. Cold, dry, or otherwise stressed specimens may assume an olive brown to brown coloration. Most specimens have a broad, enamel white lateral line extending from beneath the eye to the groin. The line may be shorter or even absent in some specimens. Green tree frogs may attain a length of nearly 2.5 inches (6 cm). The breeding calls of this species are frequently repeated nasal honks.

Rather than just a single species, there are two American gray tree frogs that are genetically different, but morphologically identical. Their composite range covers the eastern United States. Unless the specimens are males, and are chorusing at identical temperatures, it is impossible to differentiate them in the field. The relatively slow trill, or pulse, rate of the more northerly of these two sibling species, the gray tree frog, *Hyla versicolor*, produces a beautiful musical fluting. At the same temperature, the much faster pulse rate of the more southerly Cope's gray tree frog, *H. chrysoscelis*, produces a rather harsh stacatto.

Although these tree frogs may vary between chalk white and lime green at some point, if left to rest quietly at agreeable temperatures, their dorsal (back) color will eventually assume a shade of gray. An irregular, darker figure, rather like a vaguely star-shaped piece of lichen, adorns the back of both species and both have a light spot reaching from the edge of the upper lip to the eye. The dorsal skin of the 2.25 inch (5.7 cm) gray treefrogs is roughened, but not nearly as warty as that of a toad. The concealed surfaces of the hind limbs and the groin are a black reticulated golden orange to rich orange.

Although they are easily maintained on diets of vitamin-enhanced insects, and live long lives as captives, little effort has been made by hobbyists to breed these tree frogs. Perhaps this is because wild-collected specimens remain so readily available and inexpensive. Should you wish to try breeding them, coolness—lows in the high 40's F (8° to 9°C) and low 50's F (10° to 12°C)—and reduced photoperiod during the winter months—seem among the most important aspects of any cycling attempts.

Red-eyed Tree Frogs

The red-eyed tree frog. This is a beautiful phyllomedusine hylid that occurs over much of Mexico and Central America. Although it has been periodically imported in large numbers, it is only recently that captive-breeding success with red-eyed tree frogs has occurred.

Red-eyed tree frogs, *Agalychnis callidryas*, are one of the neotropical leaf frogs. The egg clusters are deposited by the females on leaves or lianas overhanging the water. Rather than the foam nest so often associated with this type of egglaying, a gelatinous outer coating contains the arboreal egg masses of this species. The tensile strength of this coating deteriorates over time, and the hatchlings wriggle free, dropping into the water.

Females, the larger sex, attain a length of only about 3 inches (7.6 cm). Males are nearly 1 inch (2.5 cm) smaller.

The body coloration of red-eyed tree frogs is variable. The coloration of distressed examples—and, more rarely, entirely contented ones—may be some shade of brown. More usually, however, the body color is leaf green. White dorsal spots may be profuse, few, or none. The amount of blue on the flanks can vary considerably from population to population. In the frogs most extensively marked, the blue can begin at and involve the apices of the forelimbs, the upper arm itself, then extend back to the groin and anterior femur. It may be robin's egg, through sky, to deep purplish blue. The white barring in the blue flanks can be even more variable. Some of the variability seems related to the location from which the frogs have come; some seems individual. The venter, underlimbs,

The red-eyed tree frog, Agalychnis callidryas *(top), remains a terrarium favorite. A second species, the maroon-eyed leaf frog,* A. litodryas *(bottom), is less colorful but equally hardy.*

and toes are suffused with a variable amount of golden-yellow.

Maroon-eyed Leaf Frog

The other neotropical green tree frog with reddish eyes is the pink-sided maroon-eyed leaf frog, *A. litodryas*. This frog is more pallid, often yellowish dorsally *and* laterally, and has deep maroon eyes. A relative newcomer to the American pet market, it requires a regimen of care identical to that given its red-eyed cousin.

Like the red-eyed tree frog, it is a quiet, nocturnal frog that spends the day hunkered down, eyes closed, legs drawn tightly against its body. In the evening, however, especially if the terrarium is liberally misted at dusk, it becomes active. It is then the angular grace of the tree frogs can be truly appreciated.

These forest species prefer lushly planted terraria in which high relative humidity is retained. Proper ventilation must also be addressed, however. Do not have the tank so humid that droplets of water form and run down the sides. A slight hazing of the glass by moisture is better, especially when you are attempting to stimulate breeding behavior. Continued high relative humidity and misting induce both normal activity patterns and reproductive behavior, all the more so if the misting occurs at dusk.

Breeding: Greatest breeding success seems to occur when several males are maintained with a single female, although communal breeding involving a dozen or so males to several females is certainly also productive.

Seasonal cyclings seem necessary to induce breeding. A summer high of about 16 hours of illumina-tion, and 85° to 88°F (29° to 31°C) temperatures, are acceptable. Winter reductions in relative humidity, temperature, and photoperiod are recommended. It is also recommended that this winter regimen be for a period of 60 to 90 days. During this, daytime highs in the low 70°s F (21° to 23°C) and nightime lows in the low 60°s F (16° to 17°C) are recommended. With slower metabolisms, the frogs will not require as great an amount of food as usual during their weeks of cooling. During this time, reduce the size of the individual feed insects.

Following these reductions, an increase of temperature, relative humidity, and misting frequency will induce greater activity, ovulation, and spermatogenesis within a week or two.

Neither the red-eyed tree frog nor the maroon-eyed leaf frog is easily sexed. Most adult females are larger than adult males. Reproductively active males develop horny, dark nuptial excrescences on their thumbs. The males vocalize, in coarse single-syllabled notes, which do not differ greatly, if at all, from territoriality calls. The notes are regularly, but not rapidly, repeated. Receptive females are drawn to the calls of the males. When the males see the females, they often cease calling and approach them. Amplexus is axillary; the male grasps the female immediately behind the forearms. The female carries the quiescent male on her back from site to site, and may sit for lengthy periods in the water between depositions to replenish the water in her bladder. Adequate water is necessary to assure the proper consistency of the jellylike outer egg casing. The glutinous jelly is clear; the eggs themselves are greenish.

Clutches contain approximately 20 to 75 eggs and are typically glued to the leaves of plants that overhang the water. Captive females often choose a spot several inches above the water on the aquarium glass for a deposition site. This has proven precarious, for because of condensation on the glass, the eggs often dislodge, fall into the water, and die. To prevent this, gently remove the eggs laid on the glass and place them on a leaf or other support a few inches above the water. Keep in mind that the very tiny newly hatching tadpoles will need to be able to either drop directly into the water or reach the water within a few flips of their bodies after hatching. Tadpoles denied access to the water after hatching will die. Often three or four clutches of eggs may be deposited in a single night by a female.

The time taken for the development of the eggs and growth and metamorphosis of the tadpoles will be largely dependent on temperature—78° to 85°F (26° to 29°C)—seems ideal. Hatching can occur in as little as 5 or as long as 11 days. The tadpole stage can last from 40 to 60 days.

The newly metamorphosed tree froglets have round rather than vertically elliptical pupils and yellow irides (irises). It may take nearly three weeks for the elliptical pupils and red or maroon irides to develop.

Within a few days after hatching, the metamorphs will have developed an almost insatiable appetite. Due to a rapid growth rate the metamorphs are especially prone to metabolic bone disease (MBD) at this stage of their lives. Feed them frequently, and a lot, and dust all food items with a good quality D_3/calcium mixture.

Waxy Monkey Frog

The big-eyed *Phyllomedusa sauvagei* is a leaf frog from middle South America. It has an ornately patterned leaf green on white belly and is usually referred to as the waxy monkey frog.

The common name refers to the waxy antidessicant exuded from the skin pores. Waxy monkey frogs are well able to withstand conditions of drought that would be fatal to most other frogs. In fact, one of the surest ways to kill captives is to keep the cage too moist! This species has been found sitting on branches exposed to the sun during the low humidity of the Paraguayan dry season where temperatures were 115°F (46°C).

As with other members of this subfamily, this species deposits its adhesive eggs on foliage overhanging the breeding ponds and usually folds the foliage around the egg cluster. If the female becomes dehydrated during amplexus or egg

Waxy monkey frog is the wonderfully descriptive name coined for the colorful Phyllomedusa sauvagei *of interior South America.*

deposition, she will descend to the water, rehydrate, then again ascend to the deposition site, all the while carrying one or more amplexing males on her back.

The males of this 2.5- to 3.5-inch-long (6 to 8.9 cm) species have a nuptial pad that bears a noticeably roughened surface during the breeding season. The males are smaller than the females and seem to have a darker throat skin as well. When healthy and at least reasonably content, both sexes are bright enamel green dorsally during the day, but may dull to brown at night. A deeper brown is assumed if cage conditions become unfavorable.

This species produces up to 700 eggs in each clutch. Captive-hatched babies are now readily available.

Horned Frogs

These frogs derive their common name from the fleshy supraocular projection, a horn, if you will, present on each upper eyelid. The horns may vary in size from the barely discernable nubbins of the ornate horned frog, *C. ornata*, to the prominent projections borne on the eyelids of the Suriname horned frog, *C. cornuta*.

In 1985 the ornate horned frog was only beginning to become a popular pet species and the Chaco horned frog was barely known. Today these two frog species, together sold by pet stores as "Pac-Man" frogs, have already become the all-time favorites of hobbyists. Not only are both species almost invariably available, but now both designer-colored hybrids between the two as well as albino Chaco horned frogs have been developed.

Ornate Horned Frog

Adult females of the ornate horned frog, *Ceratophrys ornata*, are among the largest members of this genus, some exceeding salad plate size. Normally, they are even broader than they are long. Males are significantly smaller, often less than half the size of the females. Sexually mature males have a suffusion of dark pigment on the throat.

Ornate horned frogs are usually strongly patterned with green or terra-cotta against a lighter ground color.

Most hobbyists acquire their horned frogs as newly metamorphosed, or slightly larger, froglets. At that stage in their lives they are about 1 inch (2.5 cm) in length, big headed, but of rather slender body proportions. Little then indicates the ultimate size that this frog will attain but one thing is similar in either juveniles or adults—temperament—and this is usually bad.

In their native South America, horned frogs are surrounded by myth. Tales relating to the ferocity of these frogs are widely spread, further enhanced in the telling.

As one might expect from their appearance, speed and agility are lacking in horned frogs. They have, instead, perfected bluff and actual aggression to dissuade potential predators from carrying out their intentions. They huff, puff, open their capacious mouths in threat, and actually jump forward and bite. A bite from the highly developed jaws of this large predatory frog is both disconcerting and uncomfortable. To add to the unpleasantness, these, and many other predacious frog species, have sharp jawbones studded with a number of small teeth as well as larger cusplike projections on their lower jaws. These latter, called *odontoid structures,* prevent prey animals—often other frogs—and sometimes even their keepers from escaping once grasped.

The Chaco, or Cranwell's Horned Frog, *C. cranwelli*

This is the second most frequently seen horned frog species. Like the ornate, it is produced in large numbers in captive breeding

A frog that bites? Careless handling of the predaceous ornate horned frog, Ceratophrys ornata, *can quickly and painfully prove this is so!*

programs. Although many wild-caught specimens are of rather dull coloration, color enhancement through selective breeding has now produced some very attractive animals. Albino specimens are readily available.

Suriname Horned Frog

Although at present it is only sporadically available, the prettily colored little Suriname horned frog, *C. cornuta,* occasionally appears on the pet market. Unfortunately, this is a species that prefers other frogs as prey. Only the occasional imported wild adult will voluntarily accept insects or earthworms as prey items. Fortunately, though, a few specimens have now been captive bred and the babies seem somewhat more amenable to captive conditions than the imported adults. Most females of the Suriname horned frog are adult at less than a 3-inch (7.6 cm) body length. The males are smaller. This species is predominantly tan or buff in coloration and has a broad vertebral stripe of similar color. The sides and legs are patterned with darker blotches and stripes. Occasional specimens have some lime green incorporated into the color scheme. These latter, usually males, are very attractive. Males also have a suffusion of dusky pigment on the skin of their throats. The horns of this species are very well developed—in fact, better so than those of any other member of the genus.

Diet: Horned frogs are voracious feeders. When attempting to catch live, unrestrained rodents or insects, the frogs often ingest significant amounts of their substrate. Fatal impactions have occured.

Two things can be done to reduce the possibility of intestinal impactions: First, feed your frog from forceps. In this way, the food can be brought directly to the frog. This will dramatically lessen the chance of your frog ingesting gravel, dirt, and plants. Second, choose with care the substrate, if any, used in your horned frog's container.

Because of their high fat content, laboratory mice should be fed only sparingly to these frogs. Blindness, characterized by corneal lipid deposits, has been traced to high-fat diets.

Baby frogs should be fed a cricket or a guppy every day or two. The frogs' growth will be rapid. To help guard against decalcification of the skeleton, food insects should be gut loaded or dusted with calcium at least once a week. Adult frogs require less dietary enhancement.

Comments: The necessity of absolute cleanliness in the terrarium cannot be overemphasized. Amphibia retain the necessary level of body moisture by almost constantly absorbing water through the skin, as well as intaking it through the cloaca. If the moist surfaces with which they are in contact are allowed to foul, the water being absorbed will be bacteria- and fungus-laden and soon cause disease.

Tomato Frogs and Kin

Guinet's tomato frog is flame orange in color, 4 inches (10 cm) in length, and as robust as any toad. It is designated by taxonomists as *Dyscophis guineti* and occurs only in northeastern Madagascar. If you look a little more closely you will see that the orange of the back is distinctively stippled with brighter red, or that a variably discernable dark rhomboid is present.

The tomato frogs are microhylids, members of the narrow-mouthed toad group.

It is particularly important that we learn the secrets of breeding these frogs through several generations.

Although there is little problem in breeding the wild-collected, naturally cycled adult frogs in captivity, beyond that success is sparse.

The few programs that have succeeded with these frogs have depended on typical cycling, including the use of a high-humidity caging system called a rain/hydration chamber, coupled with hormonal augmentation.

Guinet's tomato frog adults are sexually dimorphic. Females are nearly one third larger than the males, attaining a length of 3.5 inches (8.9 cm).

Despite references in literature to tomato frogs being denizens of roadside ditches, this is probably their habitat only during the breeding season. It is understandable that so many records of all the tomato frogs refer to ditches, for it is when they are in these habitats that the males are the most vocal. The calls are considered raucous by some observers, disharmonious by others. After completing breeding, these interesting microhylids disperse into nearby woodlands and become quite fossorial. They apparently emerge to feed during rainy weather. Captive tomato frogs are quite hardy, readily accepting suitably sized insects, earthworms, and, if the frogs are large enough, even pinky mice. They are quite temperature-tolerant, having sustained periodic temperatures of from 50° to 95°F (10° to 35°C) with no signs of discomfort.

Dyscophus guineti is the Madagascan tomato frog now seen in the pet trade. These are hardy frogs of variable colors.

Malayan Painted Frog

The microhylid most commonly seen in the American pet trade is the Malayan painted frog, *Kaloula pulchra*. As indicated by its alternate common name of "chubby frog," the 2.5-inch-long (6 cm) *Kaloula* is of robust build. Despite its name, the painted frog is clad in earthen hues. The dark dorsum is broadly edged with a well-defined but irregular fawn-colored dorsolateral band. Below the band the sides are darker.

If a pattern of typical cycling is followed, painted frogs can be bred easily. The floating eggs are strongly adhesive. *Kaloula pulchra* has one of the shortest-known metamorphosis spans. Under ideal conditions tadpoles can metamorphose in about two weeks.

Toads and Toadlets

Throughout the years, toads have caught the eyes of youngsters more often than those of herpetoculturists. Herpetoculturists often concentrate their efforts on brightly colored or rare species, types with immediate resale value if breeding efforts are successful. Youngsters, on the other hand, require no such incentive to channel their interests. To them, as it was long ago to us, a toad is one of the most wondrous of creatures.

Most toads are rather dull in color, primarily terrestrial, and seek water only for the purpose of breeding. A few, however, such as the two species we mention here, are divergent in either habits or color (see also Desert Terrarium, pages 68–69).

Because of one or more poorly understood factors, many species or subspecies of our "common" hop-toads are no longer common. Some are rare, some actually teetering on the brink of extinction. Before continuing, therefore, we must urge that before even picking one up, you check state and federal laws. Many species and subspecies are now entirely protected. It will require appropriate permits, to legally possess these.

The Malayan Climbing Toad, *Pedostibes hosei*

One of only a very few climbing species, this interesting toad, a species of the primary forests, is occasionally available in the pet trade. It is an angular 2.5 to 3.5 inches long (6 to 8.8 cm). Males and many females are a uniform rich brown in color but some females are nearly black, profusely spotted with orange tubercles and spots. The fingers are partially webbed and the toes are extensively webbed. Although less agile than most tree frogs, climbing toads can be set up in a similar manner, but with sturdier limbs. Despite a natural diet that is proportionately high in ants, if in good condition when received—many are not—the climbing toads can be maintained for varying periods in captivity but they cannot be called truly hardy. The food insects provided captives should be relatively small and should include termites. The call of the males, often voiced from arboreal sites, is a harsh two-part note with a rising inflection. This species is a streamedge breeder and lays strings of eggs in quiet waters.

Black and yellow on top, red and black below—the Argentine flame-bellied toadlet, Melanophryniscus stelzneri, *thrives on a diet of termites, fruitflies, and baby mealworms.*

larger variety of food than many other salamander species. Worms, pieces of calcium-dusted beef heart, and even pinky mice are avidly accepted.

Gravid female tiger salamanders captured from the wild have hatched eggs in captivity, and the larvae have been raised to adulthood. Actual captive breeding has occurred sparingly, if at all. Winter darkness and cold temperatures may help cycle tiger salamanders to reproductive readiness.

Although big and strikingly pretty, the eastern tiger salamander, Ambystoma t. tigrinum, *is a persistent burrower.*

Young Basilisks and Water Dragons

Although these lizards require large cages when they become adults, it should be mentioned that small examples of both make good semiaquatic terrarium inhabitants.

The hatchlings of these two are very different, but convergent lizards are quite similar in appearance. Both the basilisks and the water dragons have brown and green species. The adults of both attain a length of more than 2 feet (61 cm).

The basilisks (family Iguanidae) are neotropical; the water dragons (family Agamidae) are Old World. Both groups are lightly built with long limbs. All are agile climbers. All bask frequently, often for long periods. When moving rapidly, all are bipedal but the brown basilisks take this to an extreme. Their rear toes

are adorned with a flange of scales that provide a comparatively great surface area. Due to this modified toe scalation, the young, and to a lesser degree, some larger specimens, basilisks are capable of running across the surface film of quiet waters, but if they slow, or stop, they sink.

When frightened, both the water dragons and the basilisks either dive into the water or rely on a headlong flight to escape. They are fast and wary.

As babies, these lizards are almost entirely insectivorous. Gut-loaded or vitamin-dusted crickets, mealworms, and other insects are eagerly accepted. Canned cat food or reptile diet may be accepted. As adults, they often accept green leafy vegetables and flowers. Growth of the lizards can be very rapid. Tropical temperatures—80° to 90°F (27° to 32°C)—and high humidity are needed.

The green members of these genera—the green basilisk, *B. plumifrons,* and the green water dragon, *Physignathus cocincinus*—are the hobbyist favorites.

The Green Basilisk and Green Water Dragon

As they grow, males of the green basilisk develop finlike crests on the back and tail and a double crest on the head. It is from the narrow, plumelike anterior cranial crest that the plumed basilisk and specific name of plumifrons are derived. Males of the green water dragon have a high serrate vertebral crest. Both of these green lizards are bred extensively in captivity.

The Northern Brown Basilisk

This is the most commonly seen and the most easily bred of the brown-colored basilisks and several

The neotropical scorpion mud turtle, Kinosternon scorpioides, *varies in color geographically. It is among the largest mud turtles.*

breeding programs are now in place for the brown water dragon, *P. leseueri.*

Males of the northern brown basilisk have only a triangular head crest. There is no additional finnage. Male brown water dragons develop high, serrate, vertebral finnage.

Captive-produced hatchlings of all these lizards are quieter and more easily handled than wild-caught specimens. Invariably, males are more nervous than females. Secure, stress-free quarters will help you attain initial success with all these lizards.

In captivity, the young will do best in large quarters adorned with many sturdy, elevated basking limbs. The water must be kept scrupulously clean, a challenge since the lizards often defecate in their water receptacle.

Mud and Musk Turtles

Most mud and musk turtles are small enough, even when adult, to be kept in a large semiaquatic terrarium. Juvenile specimens are actually ideally suited for such setups. All are classified in the family Kinosternidae. The fact that the kinosternids can be aggressive to other turtles should always be kept in mind.

Most mud and musk turtles undergo moderate ontogenetic changes, having rugose, strongly keeled carapaces when small, and being smoothly rounded when adult. Some, however, such as the razor-backed musk turtle, *Sternotherus carinatus*, retain the juvenile keeling throughout their lives. These turtles are highly aquatic, but may, at times, wander far afield. Their shells are often covered with algae.

Both *Sternotherus*, the musk turtles, and *Kinosternon*, the mud turtles, are found in the United States. The musk turtles are typified by a reduced bottom shell (plastron) that has a single poorly developed hinge. The plastron of the mud turtles is proportionately larger and has two hinges.

No musk or mud turtle can be called brightly colored. Most are mud-colored throughout their life, with whatever contrasting colors they may have restricted to cheek or facial markings. The closest that any can come to brilliance would be the salmon plastron of the hatchlings of the riverine loggerhead musk turtles, *Sternotherus minor* ssp., or the reddish cheek patch of the red-cheeked mud turtle, *Kinosternon scorpioides cruentatum*. The 5-inch-long (13 cm) yellow mud turtle, *Kinosternon flavescens* ssp., is characterized by an olive yellow to olive green carapace and a bright yellow throat. For a mud turtle, this is brilliant indeed.

Several of the musk and mud turtles may have prominent yellow stripes on their faces when young (common musk turtle, *Sternotherus odoratus*, and striped mud turtle, *K.*

While certainly not brightly colored, the yellow mud turtle is adaptable and hardy.

baurii, among them) but these stripes usually fade and often fragment as the turtles age. Besides facial stripes, the striped mud turtle also has three well to obscurely defined yellowish carapacial stripes. These are usually brightest on juvenile specimens.

The sedentary mud and musk turtles are amenable to life in captivity. Although not overt baskers, mud and musk turtles will often lie quietly in sun-warmed shallows. Some may actually climb clear of the water on mudbars, protruding snags, or floating debris.

Although they are initially shy, musk and mud turtles soon come to recognize that the presence of a person often means an offering of food. If it is given to them, a submerged rock cave will usually be used extensively. These turtles are primarily carnivorous. They eagerly accept worms, aquatic insects, crickets, and pieces of raw meat and fish, as well as prepared trout, catfish, and cat chows.

Remember also the propensity of these turtles for climbing. You must be certain that they cannot escape by clambering up a filter stem, air hose, or by reaching the top rim of the tank from their basking platform.

Baby Basking Turtles

Back in the 1940s and 1950s, when we had almost no idea of how to care for them, baby basking turtles were routinely sold in almost every five-and-ten-cent store in the country. Most of those available were red-eared sliders, Mississippi maps, southern painted turtles, and river cooters, and they succumbed to inappropriate diets and abysmal caging conditions. Today, after decades of delving into the private lives of reptiles and amphibians, we have the knowledge to keep baby turtles well, but the babies are no longer legally commercially available to any but researchers. This is because of Public Health Service regulations that, citing the possibility of the transmittal of *Salmonella,* now prohibit the sale of any turtles of less than 4 inches (10 cm) shell length; yet, baby turtles are still one of America's most abundant reptile pets. Many are found and collected from the wild by hikers, campers, and fishermen. Others, bred by hobbyists and researchers, are exchanged as gifts. Whatever the method, baby turtles are ideal temporary inhabitants of the semi-aquatic terrarium.

Slider and Cooter

Hatchlings of the red-eared slider, *Trachemys scripta elegans*, have a busily patterned green carapace, a yellow plastron bearing prominent dark ocelli, and typically a broad red stripe behind each eye. The yellow-bellied slider, *T. s. scripta*, has a bright yellow blotch behind each eye. This striking marking is brightest in juveniles and female specimens, but is an excellent field mark when present. The plastron of the hatchling yellow-bellieds bear ocelli anteriorly but are usually immaculate posteriorly. The hieroglyphic river cooter, *Pseudemys concinna hieroglyphica*, is the most commonly seen of the non-red-eared green turtles. It has a carapacial pattern of dark rings, variable yellow markings on head, neck, and limbs, a reddish plastron on which are seen dark markings following the scute seams. The most constant carapacial marking is a well-defined letter C on the second carapacial scute.

Florida Red-bellied Turtle and Mississippi Map Turtles

One of the prettiest of turtles to be offered in the pet trade is the Florida red-bellied turtle, *Pseudemys*

The distinctive yellow crescent behind the eye of the Mississippi map turtle is a good field mark—if you can get close enough to the wary creature.

nelsoni. The babies are green, with head stripes that are less numerous than those of their congeners. The shaft of a yellow arrowlike marking lies between the eyes, with the point on the snout. The plastron of the babies is usually a shade of orange, rarely more yellow than orange.

The Mississippi map turtle, *Graptemys pseudogeographica kohni*, has a gray carapace, a yellow plastron with a dark central figure, and a yellow crescent behind the eye.

These are all highly aquatic basking turtles. (See pages 127–128). They forage and swallow while in the water, using both sight and smell to find food. In captivity, babies eat worms, crickets, snails, and small fish, plus trout, catfish, dog, cat, and turtle chows, and some vegetables such as romaine, escarole, and kale. Iceberg lettuce is of no benefit to these or any other turtle.

Basking is both psychologically and physiologically important to turtles in these genera. Provide a brightly illuminated, warmed basking spot on a snag protruding from the water *and* another directed low on the bank.

Keep in mind that unless the semiaquatic terrarium is huge, these turtles will be suitable inhabitants only as babies. Be prepared to move them to the greenhouse or a garden pool as they grow.

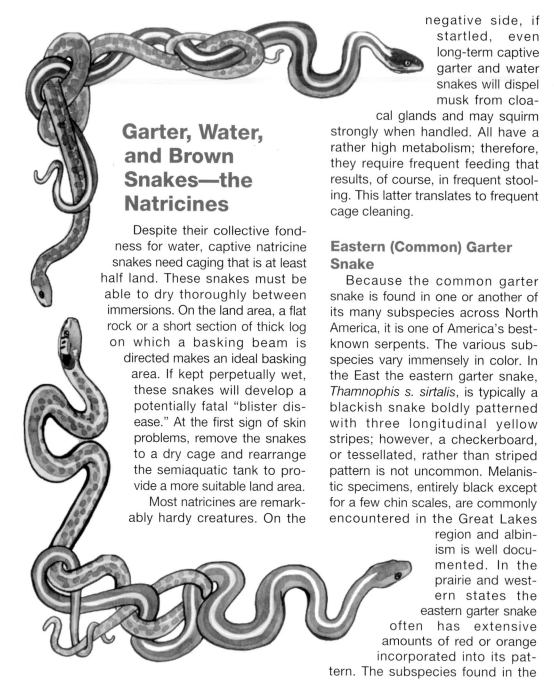

Garter, Water, and Brown Snakes—the Natricines

Despite their collective fondness for water, captive natricine snakes need caging that is at least half land. These snakes must be able to dry thoroughly between immersions. On the land area, a flat rock or a short section of thick log on which a basking beam is directed makes an ideal basking area. If kept perpetually wet, these snakes will develop a potentially fatal "blister disease." At the first sign of skin problems, remove the snakes to a dry cage and rearrange the semiaquatic tank to provide a more suitable land area.

Most natricines are remarkably hardy creatures. On the negative side, if startled, even long-term captive garter and water snakes will dispel musk from cloacal glands and may squirm strongly when handled. All have a rather high metabolism; therefore, they require frequent feeding that results, of course, in frequent stooling. This latter translates to frequent cage cleaning.

Eastern (Common) Garter Snake

Because the common garter snake is found in one or another of its many subspecies across North America, it is one of America's best-known serpents. The various subspecies vary immensely in color. In the East the eastern garter snake, *Thamnophis s. sirtalis*, is typically a blackish snake boldly patterned with three longitudinal yellow stripes; however, a checkerboard, or tessellated, rather than striped pattern is not uncommon. Melanistic specimens, entirely black except for a few chin scales, are commonly encountered in the Great Lakes region and albinism is well documented. In the prairie and western states the eastern garter snake often has extensive amounts of red or orange incorporated into its pattern. The subspecies found in the

North Pacific coastal areas, the red-spotted garter snake, *T. s. concinnus*, is one of the prettiest forms.

Ribbon Snakes

Two species of garter snakes are particularly slender, and we call them ribbon snakes. These are the western, *Thamnophis proximus*, and the eastern, *T. sauritus*, ribbon snakes, each with four subspecies. The western races are restricted to the central United States southward to Costa Rica. The range of the eastern ribbon snake embraces all of the eastern third of the United States and extreme southern Ontario, Canada.

Both species of ribbon snake are of very similar appearance. On all, the stripes are precisely delineated. The eastern species has a dark ventrolateral stripe that involves the outermost tips of the ventral plates. Although present on the western species, the ventrolateral stripe is usually narrower, less well defined, and restricted to the body scales.

It is the western ribbon snake, *T. p. proximus*, that is most often offered for sale. This pretty, graceful snake usually has yellowish side stripes and an orange vertebral stripe. It may reach more than 3 feet (91 cm) in total length, but most adults are several inches shorter.

Water Snakes

Hobbyists often pass by water snakes despite the fact that many are brightly colored as juveniles and are inexpensive. Of the several species usually offered by specialist dealers, two are particularly pretty. These are the Florida banded water snake, *Nerodia fasciata pictiventris,* and the red-bellied water snake, *N. e. erythrogaster*. Both are good candidates for the semiaquatic tank.

Some adult banded water snakes are clad dorsally in scales of uniform olive black, and are off-white ventrally with olive black encroaching onto the sides of the ventral scutes. Other examples may be contrastingly banded in reds, cinnamons, and grays, and have extensive areas of red on the edges of the ventral scales.

That a snake does not have to be exotic to be beautiful is shown by the brilliance of this red-spotted garter snake, Thamnophis sirtalis concinnus, *from the Pacific coast of the United States.*

The red-bellied water snake undergoes extensive color changes with age. Juvenile specimens are prominently banded with brown against tan ground color dorsally. Their bellies are pale orange. With advancing age the dorsal bands fade and the back and sides become a uniform rich brown. The venter deepens in color with virtually every shed, until it, and the upper lips, become a rich reddish orange. There is no denying that a fully adult red-bellied water snake is a spectacular snake.

Diet: Water snakes are easily maintained on a diet of bait store minnows and other *live* fish. **Because of the enzymes they may contain, it is suggested that frozen fish not be used as food fish.** However, because most water snakes will readily accept thawed, frozen fish, if this is a major food item, we suggest that a little liquid multivitamin be injected into the fish's body cavity about once every two weeks.

Ribbon snakes and water snakes prefer fish and frogs as prey items. Garter snakes, on the other hand, seem to prefer worms, slugs, fish, frogs, and toads. To this diet the western forms, and some eastern specimens, add nestling birds and rodents, other snakes, and lizards. Not all individual snakes eat all of these items; some may be more restricted in food preferences. Brown snakes prefer worms and red-bellied snakes eat a preponderance of slugs.

Breeding: Garter snakes, and related natricine species such as brown and water snakes have proven more difficult than many other snake species to breed. Even with an extended period of complete hibernation, many females conceive only every second year and the clutches are often rather small, varying from four to nine in number. Specimens originating from the Deep South may require nothing more than a slight winter cooling to cycle reproductively. The American species are ovoviviparous.

Chapter Eight
Outdoor Cages and Garden Pools

Cage Construction

Determining the most satisfactory caging for various reptiles and amphibians may take some thought. The kind of cage used will necessarily vary according to the amount and kind of space you have available. Will you be keeping your lizards indoors in the limited space of your living room? Indoors, but in a slightly less conspicuous, but more spacious area? On your outdoor patio? Where?

Outdoor Caging Suggestions

We find keeping lizards outdoors infinitely better and more satisfying than keeping them in small indoor terraria. Although at some latitudes, keeping them outside would be only a summer option, and then only with nighttime heat from above-cage heat bulbs, when and where possible we strongly suggest outdoor maintenance. We try always to provide a cage large enough for a breeding colony, and, to provide us opportunity to interact with the lizards, we construct the cages in a manner that allows us easy entry. We call them step-in or walk-in cages.

Caging Basics

The smallest of our outside cages measures 48 inches long × 30 inches wide × 72 inches high (122 × 76 × 183 cm). The larger cages are of similar width and height but are 96 inches (213 cm) long. All are on large casters (wheels) to facilitate easy moving. The uprights of the frames and the door assembly, which measures 2 × 4 feet (61 × 122 cm) are made from 2 × 2s. The top and bottom are solid pieces of marine plywood. The top has had the center removed, leaving a rim about 6 inches (15 cm) wide all the way around. The sides, front, back, door, and top are covered with ⅛-inch (3mm) mesh welded hardware cloth stapled tightly in place. The 30-inch (76 cm) width and the 72-inch (183 cm) height, which includes the casters, allow these cages to be easily wheeled through average interior and exterior doorways. Thus, although it may take some effort, the cages can be wheeled inside during inclement weather, or outside on nice days to allow the lizards natural sunlight and rain. The cage furniture consists of a full-cage-height ficus tree, usually *F. benjamina*, and a number of dead limb perches of suitable diameter.

Cage sizes: While the large—step-in—cages described above are our preference, especially for the water dragons, basilisks, and larger anoles, we have used smaller cages equally well for both large and small species. We have successfully kept small anoles and babies of the larger lizard species in caging as small as 10-gallon (38 L) terraria. Adults of the various basilisks and water dragons should in 55-gallon (208 L) show tanks. We always incorporate potted plants of some type as well as horizontal perching limbs into the decor. Smaller wood and wire cages that offer greater ventilation than converted aquaria can also be constructed. In the high humidity of Florida, we prefer the former.

Vertical caging: A cage containing a pair or trio of Jamaican giant or knight anoles should measure about 4 feet long × 2.5 feet wide × 6 feet high (122 × 62 × 183 cm). A cage containing two pairs or trios should be about 6 feet × 2.5 feet × 6 feet (183 × 62 × 183 cm).

Horizontal caging: We provide vertically oriented terraria/cages for arboreal species, but for lizards that are more terrestrial, we strive to offer a proportionately greater amount of horizontal space. By using ⅛-inch (3 mm) mesh in the cage construction, you will prevent the escape of all but the smallest food insects.

Predators and Fire Ants

It should be mentioned that predators can destroy outside collections virtually overnight. Raccoons and opossums may destroy screen barriers to get at either your herps or your herp's food; rats and mice may do the same. Even if actual predation on the amphibians and reptiles does not occur, cage destruction can result in your pets escaping. Wrapping the bottom 2 feet (61 cm) of the cage in stronger hardware cloth—⅛-inch (3 mm) mesh seems perfect—will dissuade many predators. Hawks, owls, crow family birds (corvids), roadrunners, shrikes, even grackles, may prey on specimens in open-topped cages. Covers preclude this possibility. Burrowing mammals such as shrews, voles, and moles may enter a cage from under and prey upon hibernating, or otherwise quiescent, herps, on clutches of eggs, or newly emerging babies. An 8- to 12-inch-deep (20 to 30 cm) wire, wooden, or aluminum barrier will usually protect your animals from these subterranean species. Wild snakes of many kinds will eat frogs, lizards, or hatchling turtles. *Watch your collection closely.*

Ants of many kinds, but especially the imported fire ants, will quickly and efficiently ravage a collection. So, when situating your outdoor cage, avoid ant-prone areas of your yard, and immediately combat any indication of ant infiltration.

Fenced Areas

Both semiterrestrial turtles and tortoises do well if they're in a fenced enclosure with a sunken water dish. A Pyrex baking dish is sturdy enough to be hosed out or lifted and cleaned and yet shallow enough to allow the turtles to enter and leave at will. The lid of a trash container, sunken to its rim, may be a more suitable water container for multiple or larger specimens. You need to keep the water container fairly shallow because some of the semiterrestrial turtles, such as the box turtle, cannot swim at all, and any turtle or tortoise that becomes overturned in the water dish cannot right itself if the water dish is too deep. A plastic container lid, placed on the ground, will keep food items out of the dirt. A hiding area such as a pile of leaf litter, planted shrubs, or a hiding box will provide your turtle or tortoise with a greater feeling of security.

Turtles and tortoises will quickly learn where their night house is. Even in southern Florida we heated the night house on some of the colder evenings. We accomplished this by using red or blue heat

Heat lamp warms tortoise's night house.

lamps, neither of which seemed to disturb the tortoises' circadian rhythms and breeding cycles in the slightest.

We learned early on that no matter how tightly it is stretched, there is no such thing as tortoise-escape-proof chain link fencing. Large tortoises can walk right under what seems to be a taut, ground-hugging chain link fence. Reinforce the bottom of the fencing by securing ground level rebars—reinforcing bars—lengthwise between the fence posts. An alternative is to run treated 1 × 6s along the bottom of the fence, staking them at 4-foot (122 cm) intervals.

In some areas of the country, cinder block walls are commonly placed around yards and gardens. These are ideal for the chelonians and need no additional preparation at all.

The Outdoor Cage

Although neither of us is a gifted carpenter, we do enjoy building our own cages.

Our outside cages reside in sunlit splendor on a wooden deck. We build all our cages as large as possible and, since we intend them to be used year round, we also proportion them so that they can be rolled inside. If the cage you are planning to build will be used only during the warmth of summer, the lizards being taken indoors during cool/cold weather, movability and dimensions will be less critical.

With that said, we suggest that you first determine how much space you have. Besides determining how big the finished cage will be, the available space should help you decide what kind—or at least what size range—of lizards you'll be keeping. The following instructions and materials list enable you to build a cage with rounded corners approximately 32 inches wide, 48 inches long, and 72 inches high (81 cm wide × 122 cm long × 183 cm high), plus caster height. By not rounding the corners of the bottom and top, you can cut down considerably on your work as well as reduce the number of 2 × 2s needed by four.

Materials Needed

- Two pieces of ¾-inch-thick (9 mm) marine plywood 32 inches × 48 inches (81 cm × 122 cm)
- Straight 2 × 2s—we use treated lumber and have never had problems by doing so. You'll need at least 13 eight-footers.
- Thin wooden or galvanized facing strips to face the inside of the door opening
- ⅛-inch (3 mm) mesh welded wire (hardware cloth). We buy ours by the roll in 36-inch (91 cm) heights. You will need about 30 feet (9 m) per cage.
- Galvanized nails
- A few feet of thin, pliable, single-strand wire
- Staples
- Two sturdy hinges and two hooks and eyes
- Saw, hammer, staple gun, tape measure or yardstick, screwdriver

Since our building methods are not precise, we precut only the ten upright braces to 5 feet 10 inches (176 cm) in length, and the plywood top and bottom. Horizontal braces and door are measured and cut to exact length or size as we build.

We first tackle the top and the bottom of the cage. Because of the perpetual high humidity and frequent rains in Florida, we use marine plywood of ¾-inch (19 mm) thickness for both top and bottom. The dimensions we have settled on for most cages are 32 inches × 48 inches (80 × 122 cm). We round the corners—but this is optional—using an arc on an 8-inch (20 cm) radius. Exactly the same arc must be used to round the corners of both bottom and top—we use a dinner plate. Once the corners are rounded, the bottom is done; however, we cut a sizable panel out of the center of the top; we usually leave a 6-inch (15 cm) rim on all sides and remove the rest. The hole left by the removed panel is, of course, screened.

We build the cage while it is lying on its back. We first nail the inner two uprights in place. Once those are secure, we roll the cage onto a side and nail the next two, and so on. Note that the front has four uprights, the door hanging between the innermost two. We build and screen the door before hanging it. We have found that a width of 2 feet (61 cm) and a height of 4 feet (122 cm) is adequate for the door. The frame is of 2 × 2s.

Because the ⅛-inch (3 mm) hardware cloth we use is in 3-foot (91 cm) heights, and we run it horizontally, horizontal cross braces are necessary between the main uprights. These are positioned about 2 feet 11 inches (90 cm) below the top, or above the bottom of the cage. The wire is over-

Outdoor cages can be large (opposite page) or small, hanging cages; choose the size that best fits your animals' needs (and the space you have available).

lapped slightly and stapled along both its top and bottom edges. The overlapping wire is laced together with pliable single-strand wire along all of the corner arcs.

Ring Cages

Ring cages are made from 3-foot-high (91 cm) aluminum sheeting sunk 1 foot (30 cm) into the ground. They are circular and can be of any desired diameter, but we found that an 8- to 10-foot (24 to 30 m) diameter is ideal. Ring cages are relatively inexpensive.

The easiest way to outline and sink the sheeting is to use a post-hole digger attached to a 4.5-foot (1.37 m) length of twine. The other end of the twine is noosed loosely around a post tapped into the ground at "cage center." By keeping the posthole digger at the outer limit of the twine, it is a relatively simple matter to dig the foot-deep trench needed for the aluminum. The aluminum sheeting is then set into the trench, leveled—this can be painstaking—and the two ends riveted together. The trench is then filled on both sides, with particular care being given to the inside perimeter.

Once the filling of the trench is complete, the cage is essentially done. Hiding places/hibernacula consisting of small-diameter terra-cotta drainage pipes can then be buried several inches below the surface of the ground, and one or more pyramids of stones, logs, or other furniture strategically placed within. Be certain that the inhabitants of the ring cannot leap from the top of the furniture to the top of the ring and escape. Also, remember that after having basked in natural, unfiltered sunlight, a reptile is often more alert and agile than one kept indoors, even if UV has been provided. Where either or both winged and four-footed predators such as hawks, crows, cats, raccoons, or opossums are common, a top must be made for these otherwise open-air cages. We used a higher central stake and draped bird netting over the entire cage.

Garden Pools

What species you are able to successfully keep in an outdoor garden pool or pond will largely depend on where you live. In the far North, water temperatures may remain sufficiently low even in the summer that only temperature-tolerant temperate species can be maintained, and they will have to be hibernated for the several months

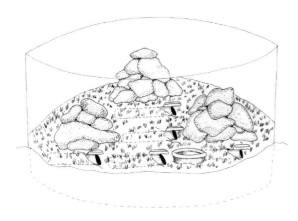

A ring of aluminum makes an escape-proof outdoor cage when sunk into the ground.

of winter. Farther south, where both ground and water temperatures are more moderate, a greater diversity of species can be kept outside for a longer period of time, and, in southern Florida and the Lower Rio Grande Valley, many species, including tropical forms, may be maintained outside year round.

Garden pools can provide ideal, easily maintained quarters for aquatic and basking turtles, and, where legal, small crocodilians. If the environs provide a land area and are enclosed within a sturdy screen house, a pool can also be an excellent enclosure for exotic amphibians, and water-loving lizards.

Like any permanent water source, an unfenced ground-level pool with suitably landscaped environs will often draw a complement of native frogs, toads, and occasionally small snakes. This is especially true in arid areas where open bodies of water are at a premium. Although filtration is optional for all garden pools or ponds, providing filtration will help overcome any water quality mistakes that might be made and will almost certainly improve water clarity. Heating and nighttime lighting is also optional. Always dechlorinate, dechloramine, or age pool water.

Garden pools need not be extravagant. Aquatic turtles and small crocodilians can do quite well in something as simple as a kiddie wading pool. Such a simple setup can be placed on a porch, deck, or in the yard. Buy a pool without a

This pair of black-knobbed sawbacks, Graptemys nigrinoda, *has thrived for years in a cattle tank 7 feet in diameter, planted with tropical water lilies and supplied with basking snags. The blooms of the lilies add a dimension of beauty to the setup.*

ramp leading to its rim, and consider adding a top to prevent either the escape of your animals or their consumption by predatory birds.

Placement of the Pool

Place the pool in a partially shaded area, for although both turtles and crocodilians need and enjoy sun, the small amount of water in the pool will heat up quickly. When situating the pool, also take into consideration the seasonally variable hours of direct sunlight caused by the changing angle of the sun. Create sunning areas for the turtles by positioning logs and/or smooth rocks in the center of the pool, and add the water with a garden hose. You can probably see already how much less work an outdoor enclosure will be than an indoor terrarium. Keep the water level high enough so the inhabitants can totally submerge, but not so deep that they can lever themselves over the edge of the pond. Gauge feed amounts carefully, for uneaten food will quickly cause bacterial buildup in the pool. Clean the pool every couple of days or as needed. You can hose off the algae or wipe the pool down as part of the cleaning process but don't add any sort of chemicals to kill or inhibit the algae.

If you can devote any type of yard space to the pool, you can submerge it to its rim in the soil, and add a low fence, with a several-inch overhang, about 3 feet (91 cm) from the edge of the pool. Plant shrubbery and other types of cover, especially if the pool receives more than a couple of hours of direct sun each day. This will enable your reptiles to wander about at will on the dry land, and, should a female be carrying eggs, she can easily dig a hole to bury her eggs.

Besides turtles and crocodilians, these simple pools will suffice for aquatic toads and frogs, and some salamanders, as well. Since most amphibians lay their eggs in the water, they can breed successfully with no land area available.

If you have more yard space, are artistically inclined, and have some degree of construction ability, your pool can be as elaborate as you wish. A free-form pool that we constructed while in central Florida was about 20 feet (6 m) long and a dozen feet (3.6 m) wide, was spanned by a functional bridge, and overlooked by a large elevated deck. We sat for long periods observing the many turtles it contained. Its depth varied from about 18 inches (46 cm) at the deepest point to only some 12 inches (30 cm) at the shallow end, and the edges were on a gentle incline to permit the turtles to haul out anywhere. The pool was made of cement reinforced with hog wire, and was troweled to a smooth finish to assure that the turtles did not abrade their plastrons while entering or leaving the water.

We had far less elaborate pools while we were in southwest Florida. They were merely 8-feet-diameter (2 m), galvanized cattle watering tanks. In these we maintained a water depth of about 18 inches (46 cm) and centered some large pieces of driftwood and sunken logs for haulout perches. In one pool that housed the basically nonherbivorous map turtles, we were able to grow hardy water lilies as well as some potted emergent vegetation, thus enjoying both the activities of the turtles and the beauty of the plants. In these pools, electrolysis will eventually remove the galvanizing, allowing rusting. When this happens the tank can be lined with a PVC liner of appropriate size, or the interior of the tank can be fiber-glassed.

Inground Pools

In-ground garden pools with plastic liners are now used extensively by reptile and amphibian enthusiasts. Explicit directions for making these pools are available in the same garden shops where the liners are sold. In some areas of the United States, a water-impervious, easily worked clay is available with which you can line the depression that is to be your pool. Pools of these types can be variably tiered and decorated in the deeper parts with potted lilies and spatterdock, or with submerged plants, and on the tiers with potted emergents such as Saint-John's-wort, cattails, and blue flags.

Inhabitants

What species of volunteer herps take up residency in your garden pool will depend on where you live. In the North, it is not unusual for various toads, green frogs, or northern leopard frogs to populate the immediate surroundings of the pool. Garter and brown snakes may also be drawn to its environs.

Pacific tree frogs, Pseudacris regilla, *like other amphibians, can sense water over considerable distances and a new pond is an irresistible lure.*

Further south, green and squirrel tree frogs, and southern leopard frogs are drawn to garden pools like a magnet. Ring-necked snakes and local newts and salamanders may also wander in. In the far West, Pacific tree frogs and red-legged frogs may colonize a garden pool.

In southern Florida, giant toads, Cuban tree frogs, greenhouse frogs, and southern leopard frogs are almost commonplace in even the simplest of pools. In the Lower Rio Grande Valley, the expected species are Mexican tree frogs, Rio Grande chirping frogs, and, if you're lucky, black-striped snakes.

The In-ground Pool

Materials Needed
- Wheelbarrow or Bobcat tractor
- Shovel
- A 12-foot (3.7 m) straight 2 × 4 or 2 × 6 level
- Sand and cement or a heavy-gauge pool liner
- Reinforcing bars (rebars) if necessary, or heavy-gauge hogwire
- Pool filter (optional)
- Draining mechanisms and materials if needed
- Rocks or boards for enclosure walls
- Suitable plants, both aquatic and terrestrial
- Limbs, logs, rocks, and other enclosure furniture

And, if you elected to use the wheelbarrow and shovel rather than the Bobcat, a great deal of energy, enthusiasm, and perseverance.

Setup Procedure

1 Excavate the pool site to the desired depth and contour. If you are preparing the site for a pool liner, be sure to follow the manufacturer's suggestions for the pool depth.

2 Level and contour the rim (lip) of the pool. The level can be determined by laying a straight 2 × 4 or 2 × 6 from side to side and checking with a level.

Excavate pool site and level rim of pool (top left and right). Fill pool and introduce plants.

3 Remove all sharp roots, limbs, rocks, or other foreign objects from the excavation.

4 Line the excavation with a thin coating of clean sand.

5 If the pool is to be of reinforced concrete, lay rebar or hogwire on the sand, perfectly contouring the ground. (If a pool liner is to be used, skip this step.)

6 Pour cement or lay the liner in place. If cement is used, trowel smooth to prevent shell abrasions.

7 If cement was used, wait for 36 to 48 hours for the cement to set and harden. We then prefer to scrub the entire surface with a strong vinegar solution and stiff brush. Fill with water, allow to sit for a day, rinse thoroughly, refill, then rinse again in 24 hours, and

refill again. Check and modify the pH as necessary.

8 Start filtration.

9 Place potted plants where desired and introduce specimens. If the pH is too high or low, treat the water, recheck, allow it to stabilize, then add plants and herps.

The Partially In-ground Pool

Materials Needed
- As above, plus fill dirt, gravel, and sand
- Landscaping timbers of railroad ties and hardware to join them at corners.

This style is usually used with a cattle tank or other metal, or plastic, above-ground pool.

Setup Procedure

1 Remove dirt to the depth desired.

2 Put the pool in place and level it.

3 Build a retaining wall with railroad ties or landscaping timbers.

4 Add fill dirt around the pool.

5 Add a pool liner if the pool is rusty.

6 Check the water quality, modify as necessary, and start the filters.

7 Add plants, then animals.

The Wood-frame Pool

Materials Needed

- Long straight 2 × 6
- Level
- Hammer, circular saw, power drill
- Shovel
- Railroad ties or landscape timbers
- Chosen corner fastener spikes or rebars (reinforcing rods used in concrete)
- Power drill and large diameter bit—to drill holes in overlapping timber ends to accommodate the rebar.
- Thin plywood cut to the inside size of the four retaining walls.
- Pool liner

Besides a garden location, this pool can also be used on a patio, sunporch, or in another large room.

Setup Procedure

1 Cut, stack, and affix the edging timbers carefully and tightly. The ends can be held together with large nails, or drilled to allow one or two sections of rebar to be run from top to bottom.

2 Place a piece of thin plywood vertically against each inner edge of the retaining timbers.

3 Carefully position the pool liner, taking care that no wood splinters, nailheads, or other such objects puncture it.

4 Fill to the desired level.

5 Test and adjust the pH as necessary. Dechlorinate/dechloramine the water.

6 Activate the filter.

7 Add river rock to the bottom, if desired; position aquatic plants and pool furniture, taking care that the inhabitants cannot reach the edge from their basking logs and escape.

Metal Above-ground Pool

Materials Needed

- Long straight 2 × 6
- Level
- Shovel
- Stock tank or other pool
- Pool liner, if necessary

Trowel cement smooth.

Of the four types of garden pools, this is the easiest to set up and maintain. Most stock tanks have a stoppered drain on the side near the bottom. If the pool is oriented with the drain very slightly lower than the opposite side, nearly complete drainage can be had for water changes. This reduces the need for strong filtration, and assures that suitable water quality can be easily provided.

Setup Procedure

1 Prepare the site so that the pool tilts very slightly downward with the drainage bung the lowest.

2 If your pool is galvanized and is scratched or rusted, place a pool liner inside.

3 Fill to the desired level with water.

4 Check and adjust the pH, if necessary. Dechlorinate/dechloramine the water.

5 Activate the pool filter, if any.

6 Place potted aquatic plants, haulout limbs, and other pool furniture where desired. Be sure that the haulout limbs are not so close to the pool sides that the animals can escape.

Creatures for Ponds

Painted Turtles, Sliders, Cooters, Pond Turtles, and Reeve's Turtles

All these turtles are inveterate baskers. If they are northern, they become active each spring soon after most of the ice has melted from their ponds, and remain active until the ice has virtually mantled their ponds again the following winter. Spotted turtles may estivate in the hottest weather. Southern forms are active all year.

The husbandry of the hatchlings of some of these turtles is discussed in the semiaquatic section of this book, starting on page 133.

In garden ponds, turtles such as this southern painted turtle, Chrysemys picta dorsalis, *seek protruding snags and rocks for basking.*

Painted Turtles

The four races of the painted turtle are small and colorful. The southern painted, *Chrysemys picta dorsalis*, identified by a prominent orange vertebral stripe, is the smallest—to 5.5 inches (14 cm)—of the four races. The western painted turtle, *C. p. bellii*, which occasionally exceeds 9 inches (23 cm) in carapace length, but is usually smaller, is the largest race. It has a netlike reticulum of light, sometimes red, lines on the carapace and a red plastron that bears a light-centered dark central blotch with arms that follow the scute seams, sometimes to the edge of the plastron. The two remaining races, the eastern, *C. p. picta*, and the midland, *C. p. marginata*, are between the southern and western painted turtles in size.

It can be hard to differentiate between the eastern and midland painted turtles. This is especially true in areas where intergradation is common. The range of the eastern painted turtle closely follows the eastern seaboard from Nova Scotia to central North Carolina, where it then follows the Piedmont and mountain province inland to central Georgia. The midland painted is found essentially east of the eastern's range, from Canada southward to Tennessee, and dipping down to Alabama and northeast Georgia. The eastern painted turtle has plain plastron and the carapacial scutes are bordered with olive and arranged pretty much in straight rows. The midland painted turtle has a solid lengthwise dark blotch on the plastron—no outward extending arms—and the vertebrals are not in line crossways with the costal scutes.

Sliders

Sliders are perhaps the world's most popular pet turtle, if not the best known. The distinctive red or yellow patch behind each eye is an indication that you're dealing with *Trachemys*, the sliders. *Trachemys scripta scripta* and *T.s. elegans* are, respectively, the yellow-belly and the red-eared slider. They prefer almost still waters and heavy vegetative growth. The yellow-belly is a denizen of the southeastern states, while the red-eared ranges not only through the southeastern states westward to New Mexico, but has a relict population in Ohio. Released captive specimens and their progeny have turned up in essentially every state, many European countries, and Japan. These turtles grow to about 1 foot (30 cm) in length, and many become suffused with melanin as they mature. Identifying a largely black turtle can be challenging.

Selective breeding and temperature manipulation during incubation have yielded a color morph called "pastel," but these young sliders often have malformed scutes and fail to thrive.

Cooters

Cooters are turtles from the southeastern states that prefer moving water, no matter how slowly it moves. They are members of the genus *Psuedemys*. The common name cooter is derived from kuta, an African name for turtle brought to America during the slave trade. The genus includes two kinds of red-bellied turtles.

The cooters and red-bellieds may be confused with painted turtles and sliders in the field, especially when the shells are obscured by algae and you cannot get close enough to distinguish the characteristic facial markings. Although they may look asleep when piled three deep on a sunlit snag, one move from a potential predator—you—sends them all headlong into the water. For an individual turtle, identification is greatly aided if you know its geographical origin.

Both the cooters and red-bellied turtles have a flattened lower jaw when viewed head on, compared to the sliders' rounded jaw. The Florida red-bellieds have a distinct cusp to the front of the jaw.

Cooters have a light vertical line (*P. floridiana* and *P. texana*) or C-shaped marking (*P. concinna*) on the second costal scute on the carapace. Red-bellieds lack any lighter marking on that scute. Cooters have plain-colored plastrons with numerous dark markings; the red-bellieds have a red, coral, or orange plastron.

The most commonly encountered species are the hieroglyphic cooter, *Psuedemys concinna hieroglypica*, and the peninsula cooter, *P. floridana peninsularia*. Hatchlings of each are little green turtles with variable yellow markings on the face, neck, limbs, and carapace. With adulthood, the hieroglyphic cooter, from the river systems of the Gulf drainage, develops distinctive dots, dashes, circles, and bars—hieroglypics—on its carapace. The subdult to adult peninsular cooter is from waterways of peninsular Florida, and wears twin hairpinlike markings on top of its head, the closed end of the hairpins near the eyes.

The prettiest of the cooters is the Florida red-bellied turtle, *P. nelsoni*. Adults are typically cooter-size at 12 to 14 inches (30 to 36 cm), but their darkened carapace bears a ruddy red or orange vertical bar on each scute. There are only a few yellow markings on the head.

The Florida cooter, *P. floridana floridana*, is distinguished by small circular markings along the junction of the plastron and carapace. The plastron is unmarked.

The spotted turtle, Clemmys guttata, *is a denizen of woodland and meadow ponds. To protect the declining numbers in the wild, only hatchlings from established captive colonies should be purchased.*

All the cooters are water foragers, swallowing while submerged. Adults are omnivorous, feeding on water plants, floating romaine leaves, and earthworms, tadpoles, frogs, fish eggs, and carrion. Hatchlings tend to be more carnivorous, but both adults and babies will soon eat the listed foods as well as trout chow, commercial floating turtle foods and bananas. When adult, the sliders (genus *Trachemys*), the cooters, and red-bellied turtles (genus *Pseudemys*) may exceed 10 inches (25 cm) in shell length.

Spotted and Wood Turtles

These turtles, both members of the pond turtle group, are favorites of hobbyists. Other turtles in this group are the Pacific pond and bog turtles. Most are now protected throughout their range and the bog turtle is listed as a federally threatened species. Check the legalities pertaining to collecting, keeping, interstate transportation, and sale carefully before purchasing any of these species.

The Spotted Turtle

The spotted turtle, *Clemmys guttata*, is a 4-inch-long (10 cm) denizen of wooded ponds and bogs of eastern North America. It is most common in slightly acidic seeps that are heavily vegetated with sphagnum. In the early spring of the year, while the weather is still chilly, the males may wander across country roadways in search of females. A few weeks later, egg-laden (gravid) females may wander the same areas looking for suitable nesting sites. It is at these times that spotted turtles are most often encountered.

Hatchlings, which are just over 1 inch (2.5 cm) in length when emerging from the egg, usually bear just a single yellow spot on each of the large dark black carapacial scutes. Additional spots usually appear with advancing age and some old specimens are actually profusely speckled. Orange spots may occur on the neck and head, and the forelimbs and leg axes may vary in color from black to extensively orange.

Spotted turtles may estivate during the hottest part of the year and hibernate during the cold of winter.

The spotted turtle is primarily an aquatic species and captives should be provided with a rather extensive, but not necessarily deep, water area. The turtles should be able to access the land area easily and at all points.

The Wood Turtle

The wood turtle, *Clemmys insculpta*, a species of the northeastern United States and immediately adjacent Canada, is now considered rare to imperiled.

Although often treated as a terrestrial turtle species by many hobbyists, the wood turtle is very much a semi-aquatic. Although it often wanders and forages in woodlands and brushy meadows far from water, it swims readily, often breeds while in the water, and spends its lengthy period of dormancy in aquatic situations.

At 7.5 inches (19 cm) in length, the "woodie" is the largest species of the genus. The carapacial color is of some shade of earthen brown as are the top and sides of the head. The chin, neck, limbs, and tail vary—largely by geographic origin—from pale yellowish green in the westerly populations to brilliant red-orange in the easterly populations.

Asian Pond (Reeve's) Turtle

Chinemys reevesi is found over much of Japan, China, and Korea.

The carapace is strongly tricarinate. Concentric growth rings are retained throughout the turtle's life. Although specimens with shell lengths of more than 9 inches (23 cm) have been found, most are much smaller.

The carapace of this basking species may vary from brown to nearly black. Males are often darker than females. The head is dark with a yellow stripe on each side of the crown and variable reticulations on the cheeks and chin. The limbs are dark. The plastron is brown blotched yellow.

Females of 5 inches (13 cm) can breed successfully and often nest several times annually. From three to nine eggs are laid each time. Males are somewhat smaller than adult females and have a heavy, long tail. A weak plastral concavity is sometimes present. The elongate hatchlings are under 1 inch (2.5 cm) in length. They are very hardy.

Although quite cold-tolerant, we suggest that in captivity, Reeve's turtles should be treated like a southern slider. They can be wintered outdoors in the southern states but should be brought in in the North.

Except for the wood turtle, which wanders and feeds extensively on land, all these turtles are highly aquatic basking turtles. They forage and swallow while in the water, using both sight and smell to find food. The adults of all are quite omnivorous, consuming quantities of vegetation as well as animal matter. Captives eat trout and catfish, dog, cat, and turtle chows, worms, and vegetables such as romaine, escarole, kale, collard, turnip greens, and watercress, as well as melons and other soft, pulpy fruit. Iceberg lettuce and bananas are of no benefit to these or any other turtle. Feed your pet turtles the dark leafy vegetables mentioned above.

These are ideal garden pool turtles. If kept in clean, quasi-natural conditions, their lifespan may exceed 15 years. The known record for a captive is 20 years. Those from the more temperate areas of the United States are quite cold-tolerant; tropical races and those from the Florida peninsula and Lower Rio Grande Valley are less so. Southern animals should be brought into an indoor aquarium during periods of cold weather. If the pond does not freeze all the way to the bottom, the more northerly forms can be kept out year round in most areas.

Since basking is both psychologically and physiologically important to turtles in these genera, it is important that the garden pool be located in a sunlit area. Soft sunny banks and snags projecting over and from the water should be provided.

Breeding: Breeding occurs in the water. Courtship varies by species and subspecies. The males of some forms have elongated claws and hover in the water in front of the female, caressing her face and anterior shell with trembling claws. The males of short-clawed forms pursue the female, nipping at the trailing edge of her shell. In both cases, when the female becomes quiescent, copulation occurs.

Nesting in well drained areas, females may multiclutch. Smaller species may lay from two to eight eggs, while the larger ones may lay more then 20. Some species of cooter dig a dummy nest on each side of the main nesting chamber. Depending on temperature and nest humidity, incubation can vary from about two months to nearly three. Incubation temperatures should be maintained between 82° and 87°F (28° to 30.5°C) (see comments on incubation temperatures, page 00).

Eastern American and Asian Box Turtles

Box turtles are probably the most readily recognized turtles in America. They derive their common name from the ability of the adults to draw the plastron upward against the bottom of the carapace to protect the withdrawn head, limbs, and tail. The cartilaginous hinge in the plastron is undeveloped at hatching, but becomes fully developed by the time the turtle is about one quarter grown. During times of plenty, however, when worms and grasshoppers are abundant and the berry season is in full swing, box turtles may become so corpulent that they are unable to close their plastron entirely.

Although certain sexual characteristics may vary subspecifically, most adult males have a thicker and somewhat longer shell than that of the female, and the males of all but the three-toed box turtle have a plastral concavity in the rear lobe of the plastron. This concavity may or may not be present on male three-toed box turtles. Additionally, adult males of the eastern and Gulf Coast box turtles often have red irises, while those of the females are yellow or brown. Males of all subspecies tend to have curved, hook-like claws on their hind feet. The claws of the females are straighter.

The various races of the eastern box turtle are protected by law in most of the states in which they occur. Be certain of the legalities of collecting or keeping a box turtle.

The Florida Box Turtle

This turtle has an elongate carapace that is black or nearly black and that is patterned on each scute with radiating yellow markings. The rear of the carapace flares outward. There are two yellow lines, sometimes fragmented, on each side of the head. Damp, open woodlands, damp meadows, marshes, and swamp edges are favored habitats of *T. c. bauri*. They are poor swimmers. This usually three-toed race is largely restricted to Florida.

The Gulf Coast Box Turtle

This four-toed subspecies, in contrast to the other races, has a dully colored carapace that is often devoid of strongly contrasting colors. *T .c. major* often enters water. It is the largest of the eastern box turtle subspecies, and although highly domed, has the carapace rather flattened centrally, and the marginals widely flared along the posterior edges. Old males often have a chalk-white mustache or mustache and sideburn facial markings. This

The eastern box turtle, Terrapene c. carolina, *has been reported to live for more than a century.*

The ornate and Eastern box turtles have highly domed shells and can often be seen crossing roadways in the early morning hours.

turtle is restricted in distribution to the eastern Gulf Coast.

The Three-toed Box Turtle

The most divergent subspecies, it ranges widely from Missouri and Alabama to eastern Texas and Kansas. Although some specimens of *T. c. triunguis* may be rather brightly colored, many show a tendency toward a unicolored olive brown, olive tan or horn-colored carapace. Adult males may have a fair amount of red or maroon on the head.

The Eastern Box Turtle

This turtle, *T. c. carolina,* is found from northern Florida to Massachusetts and from Michigan to northwestern Mississippi. Although it is often found near pond and lake edges as well as along woodland and damp meadow streams, the eastern box turtle is a weak swimmer and seldom enters deep water voluntarily. Many specimens are prettily colored in contrasting yellows, oranges, and warm browns; others may be quite drab. This race usually has four claws on the rear feet.

Breeding: The courtship of the eastern box turtle is similar to that of many other turtles and tortoises. The male circles and butts the females he encounters, nipping at the front of their shell, limbs, and head. If the female is receptive, she allows copulation.

A month to six weeks later, the female digs a nest in a root-free area in relatively soft, well-drained soil that receives sunlight for at least part of the day. From two to eight—often four or five—eggs are laid. Multiple clutches, laid at three- to four-week intervals, are normal.

All of the eastern box turtles require a high to moderate relative humidity, with the prairie populations of the three-toed species requiring least.

Western Box Turtles

The Ornate Box Turtle

This turtle is now the form most often seen in the American pet trade. Superficially, the ornate box turtle, *T. o. ornata,* looks much like a Florida box turtle, but generally has a lighter carapacial color, coarser yellow radiations, is mid-dorsally flattened, and lacks precise yellow facial stripings. The dark plastron of ornate box turtles is heavily patterned with bold light lines; the plastron of Florida box turtles is light, occasionally with a few dark markings. If present, these markings are best defined along the scute sutures and on the anterior lobe of the plastron.

Desert Box Turtle

This more westerly race has more, thinner, and less contrasting carapacial markings that tend to fade even more with advancing age.

Unfortunately, *T. o. luteola* is even more difficult to acclimate and establish in captivity than its eastern relatives.

These are turtles of open plains, prairies, and related scrub and low brush thickets. Although the desert race inhabits the driest habitats, it often chooses irrigated areas and the environs of waterholes and river edges for its microhabitat. *T. o. ornata* occurs in patches of suitable habitat from Indiana and South Dakota to the Lower Rio Grande Valley. *T. o. luteola* ranges over much of far western Texas, westward to New Mexico, and southward across the Rio Grande into adjacent Mexico.

Breeding: Unlike the reproductive strategies of the eastern box turtles, which involve much courtship, the breeding sequence of the western box turtle is far more straightforward. Some males sniff the rear margin of the female's shell, others may sniff and butt the female, but many, especially captives, dispense with all courtship formalities.

The innermost toe of the male ornate box turtle is enlarged and angled differently than the others, which helps him in positioning during breeding. The nesting sequence and clutch size is similar to that of the eastern box turtle.

Except in the Lower Rio Grande Valley, where the ornate box turtle is active for all but a few days of the year, both races of the western box turtle hibernate.

Yellow-margined Box Turtle

The most popular Asian box turtle with hobbyists is *Cuora flavomarginata*, the yellow-margined box turtle. Most specimens available in the pet trade are wild-collected and imported from China.

The shell of this basically terrestrial species is moderately to highly domed and the concentric growth rings remain prominent, unless physically worn from the shell by abrasion. The carapacial color of the yellow-rimmed box turtle is somewhat variable, in brown, olive brown, or black. There is usually a prominent vertebral stripe and the

The yellow-margined box turtle, Cuora flavomarginata, *is one of the prettiest and most responsive of the Asian terrestrial species.*

marginals are yellow on their under-sides, the yellow rim from which both common and specific names are derived. The head is nicely col-ored. The olive gray to olive brown of the crown is separated from the yellow-green of the cheeks by a yellow—sometimes greenish yel-low—stripe thinly delineated by a darker edging. The lower cheeks and chin shade to a pale peach to brighter yellow. The legs are dark, the axilla yellowish. This is another of the very difficult to sex turtle species. The tail of both sexes is short, but that of the male is com-paratively wider at the base. The posterior lobe of the male's plas-tron is straight in side view and rounded when viewed from above. The corresponding plastral lobe of the female is slightly more angular and the posterior tip may curve slightly upward when viewed from the side. Most of our adults are between 4.5 and 5.5 inches (11 to 14 cm) in carapace length.

This is an omnivorous turtle species. Ripe and overripe fruits, worms, cat foods, mice, and nearly any other edible object are eagerly consumed.

Breeding: Female yellow-mar-gined box turtles nest yearly. Sev-eral nestings of either one or a pair of eggs occur yearly. The nests are very shallow and the layings are separated by from 10 to 18 days. In Florida we have always allowed nature to take its course and find hatchlings in the yard from late summer to very late fall. The cycling and nesting are all accomplished naturally.

Feeding: To induce a recalcitrant newly acquired eastern box turtle to feed, try a nightcrawler. The box tur-tle will usually almost jump on the worm in its haste to feed! Western box turtles are less enthusiastic about worms, but are usually instantaneously interested in crick-ets, locusts, and especially dung beetles. Once the turtle is feeding, it can be weaned over to canned cat foods and various fruit, berries, and mushrooms.

Seasonal changes: At any lati-tude box turtles will thrive outdoors during summer weather; however, preparation for winter will vary by species, latitude, and whether or not you are cycling them for breed-ing. Yellow-margined, Gulf Coast, Florida, and southernmost individu-als of other species and subspecies require little or no hibernation for any purpose; therefore, at northern lati-tudes, these types are best housed indoors for the winter. If you live in the Lower Rio Grande Valley or peninsular Florida, however, modifications can be made that will enable you to keep the turtles outside all year. Although more northerly examples seldom need hibernating for general maintenance, they may require a period of winter dormancy to cycle for breeding.

Not for Novices

Spectacled Caiman

This comparatively small but aggressive crocodilian attains an adult size of 5 to 7 feet (1.5 to 2.1 m), and occasionally reaches more than 8 feet (2.4 m). It is the "baby alligator" now sold in United States pet stores. The color is yellowish to olive when young, to olive drab in adults, with black crossbands. This species can change color extensively, and is darker by day, when cold, or when frightened, than at night or when content. The common name is derived from the curved bony ridge resembling the bridge of a pair of eyeglasses that crosses the snout immediately anterior to the eyes. The scientific name is *Caiman crocodilus* ssp. The upper eyelids are corrugated and bear a slightly raised knob posteriorly. There may be several dark spots along each side of the lower jaw.

The habitat of the spectacled caiman includes open areas and exposed banks of rivers, oxbows,

Feistiness is a trademark of the neotropical spectacled caiman, Caiman crocodilus. *Adults can attain a length of more than 7 feet!*

lakes, and other permanent water sources throughout much of the neotropics. It is now also established in small breeding colonies in the canal systems of southern Florida.

Although manageable when young, the spectacled caiman is immensely powerful and entirely unsuitable for most private collections once it exceeds 30 to 36 inches (76 to 91 cm) in total length. Placing a young adult of this size or greater in a zoo or nature center is extremely difficult. Before you consider acquiring a caiman, ask the advice of a knowledgeable, experienced herpetologist.

Breeding: This species builds a nest of vegetable debris. More than 30 eggs may be laid per clutch. Females protect the nest, but their exact role in assisting in the hatching of the young and the escape of the young from the nest is poorly understood. Hatchlings are 6.5 to 8 inches (16.5 to 20 cm) in total length.

A greenhouse woodland theme containing day geckos from the island of Madagascar will provide you with hours of enjoyable observations. Pictured are the spotted day gecko, **Phelsuma guttata** *(top), the neon day gecko,* **P. klemmeri** *(middle), and the giant day gecko,* **P. madagascariensis grandis** *(bottom).*

Chapter Nine
Greenhouses

Styles

Greenhouses of many styles, constructed from several types of materials, are readily available today. These vary from simple, self-standing, fully constructed types available from dealers, to myriad do-it-yourself kits, to elaborate and decorative commercial kinds that are generally best left to contractors to set up. Greenhouses are becoming ever more popular and are increasingly used by both hobbyists and commercial reptile and amphibian breeders. Greenhouses are especially in favor with the breeders of amphibia and humidity-loving lizards such as basilisks and water dragons.

What could be better for a dedicated hobbyist than having an enclosure not only dedicated to your amphibians and reptiles, but in which, after it is thoughtfully set up, you can actually place yourself as well? It is necessary to know that in many areas, greenhouses are considered permanent structures and a building permit is required to legally install one.

Securing Your Greenhouse

Although building a greenhouse can be an enjoyable project, securing it as a herp haven can be tedious. Even amphibians and reptiles of the most sedate behavior are especially talented escape artists. In time, the tiniest of apertures in the foundation, the most minuscule of cracks around the ventilation fans, electrical outlets, or doorway, or the tiniest of punctures in a window screen will be found and exploited. When installing or outfitting a greenhouse, you cannot give too much attention to detail.

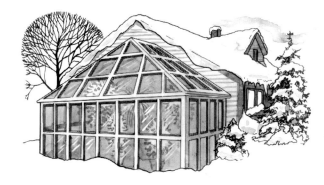

Absolute security is essential and, additionally, heating and cooling units must be entirely screened from the inside to prevent injury to the inhabitants. Securing even those fixtures well above ground level is especially important when climbing species such as tree frogs or anoles are to be kept. Double-entry doors should be considered as an enhanced containment system. Instantaneous escape reactions of skittish species such as basilisks and sail-tailed dragons can be triggered by even the slow opening of a door. Once outside, an aroused lizard can be difficult or impossible to recapture.

In all cases, double glazing should be endorsed both as an energy-saving option and as a way to help control temperature extremes. We further suggest that the base of the unit either be flush against a concrete slab, affixed to a concrete or brick wall, or be sunk a foot (30 cm) or more below the surface of the ground. This will preclude easy access by outside predators and escape by the creatures with which you are working. It is necessary to remember that in the confines of a greenhouse, creatures like white-footed and deer mice that are normally considered innocuous can actually become active predators or may chew and destroy cherished plantings. Normally predatory species such as weasels and shrews can wreak overnight destruction. The solution is in absolute prevention of intru-

sion, not in the eradication of predators once they have gained access to your greenhouse.

Choosing a Theme

Greenhouses often exemplify the adage that the grass is always greener elsewhere. Seldom does a greenhouse portray local conditions; rather, it is usually exactly the opposite. A desert theme will be seen in the humid Southeast, a tropical rainforest theme is portrayed in the snowbelt, or a seasonally wet southeastern swampland may be desired by a herper in the desertlands. Whatever the theme, it is important to provide the appropriate plantings, watering, heating and lighting systems, and cage furniture. The possibility and feasibility of providing a small pond and waterfall, often much-wanted accessories, should be well thought out from the start. While ponds and waterfalls can be wonderful additions to a woodland or rainforest greenhouse, they may not always be appropriate for aridland themes. For example, while a small, shallow pond may not raise the humidity of a desert greenhouse unduly if you happen to live in a normally dry region, should you live instead in a fogbelt or in a normally humid region, it is not likely that you will want the additional humidity created by even the smallest of ponds. In fact, to successfully keep some of the more specialized desert

Greenhouse with Regional Themes

South Africa

Plants	Herps
Haworthia	Flattened rock lizards *(Platysaurus)*
Aloe	Girdle-tailed lizards *(Cordylus)*
Lithops	African treefrog *(Chiromantis)*
	African house snakes *(Lamprophis)*—will eat frogs and lizards

Neotropics

Plants	Herps
Philodendrons	Basilisks *(Basiliscus)*
Anthuriums	Red-eyed treefrog complex *(Agalychnis)*
Prayer plants	Rainbow boas *(Epicrates)*—will eat frogs and lizards, especially when young
Begonias	Tricolored hognosed snakes *(Lystrophis)*—will eat frogs and lizards

Southwestern United States

Plants	Herps
Cacti	Desert iguana *(Dipsosaurus)*
Agaves	Chuckwallas *(Sauromalus)*
Palo verde	Canyon treefrog *(Hyla arenicolor)*
Mesquite trees	Gopher snake complex *(Pituophis)*—will eat frogs and lizards
Creosote bush	Whipsnakes *(Masticophis)*—will eat frogs and lizards

herps in humid regions, it may be necessary to install a dehumidifier. Conversely, if you intend to keep basilisks or emerald tree boas in normally dry areas, both a pond and a humidifier may be welcome—almost mandatory—additions.

Choosing the theme can be accomplished in one of two ways: either by deciding on the herp species with which you wish to work and then researching and recreating its habitat, or by first building the habitat you most wish to see recreated, then adding the appropriate herp species.

If you wish to be a habitat purist, you can use the regional approach—South African plants with South African herps, neotropical plants with neotropical herps, and so on. To accomplish this, you'll need to do considerable research, but it can be a fun and satisfying approach.

When landscaped with imagination, the interior of even a small greenhouse can be your own bit of desert, rainforest, or other chosen habitat and, as such, can provide a healthy and secure habitat for your amphibians and reptiles.

Whether you choose to replicate a craggy desert escarpment, fissured and planted with cacti and succulents, a tropical waterfall bedecked with mosses, ferns, selaginellas and episcias, a small pond replete with blooming tropical water lilies, lush growths of philodendrons, epipremnums, and syngoniums, or a weathered tree skeleton festooned with small orchids, bromeliads, and other greenery, it is only your imagination and your budget that will limit the possibilities.

Creatures for Greenhouses

Great Green Iguana and Black Spiny-Tailed Iguana— for a Savanna Greenhouse

Baby great green iguanas, *Iguana iguana*, are currently one of the most readily available lizards in the pet trades of the world. Most are now produced on iguana farms in Latin America, but many are also collected from the wild. A few are domestically raised by hobbyists.

Juveniles of the black spiny-tailed iguana, *Ctenosaura similis*, are also available. Most are wild-collected.

Both common names are misnomers at some point in the lives of these lizards. Actually, both species are a bright leaf green at hatching, and although the green iguana rapidly pales and becomes suffused with grays, it definitely remains the greener of the two. Some sexually mature males become suffused with a vivid orange, at least anteriorly, during the breeding season. Others become a brighter green. The black spiny-tailed iguana, however, darkens rapidly with age, and while often not truly black, may become nearly so. Except in the breeding season when they become suffused with orange, dominant males are the darkest in color. Adult males of the green iguana may exceed 6 feet (1.8 m) in total length. The tail is long and whiplike, and does not bear whorls of spiny-tipped scales. Females are noticeably smaller. Males of the black spiny-tailed iguana may exceed 4 feet (1.2 m) in length, but have proportionately stout tails that bear whorls of spiny scales. Females are smaller. Both species have crests of elongate scales on the nape and along their back, with the crests of the males being best developed. Both species are capable of some color change, and are darkest when cold.

Never, not even for humanitarian reasons, choose an iguana with dull, sunken eyes and listless mien, or severely protruding hip bones. It

Is a great green iguana, Iguana iguana, *truly the pet lizard for you? We urge that you read about these difficult neotropical lizards* before purchase.

will probably not survive. Always choose an iguana from a clean cage that has in evidence ample fresh drinking water, a warmed and well-illuminated basking area, and full-spectrum lighting (discussed in section on lighting).

Despite its ready availability, the great green iguana is not an easily kept lizard; quite the opposite, in fact. Green iguanas can be quite a problem to keep and to keep well. To successfully keep one over a period of time, you must be a dedicated and knowledgeable owner.

Diet. The importance of a proper diet for these folivores (leaf eaters) cannot be overemphasized. Although many iguanas will consume insects

and even an occasional baby mouse, long-term studies have proven that the healthiest and longest-living iguanas are those that are fed a nutritional and varied *vegetable diet.* This diet can be augmented with a little fruit. *The inclusion of insects, dog food, and monkey chow (all once thought to be healthful foods), in the diet of your iguana for anything other than a very occasional treat, is contraindicated.* In fact, they don't even need these items as a treat! Always think iguana health foods, not iguana fast foods. By so doing you will save your lizard from a bout with gout, kidney dysfunction, or metabolic bone disease. The diet of the black spiny-tailed iguana is similar to that of its green cousin, but might include a slightly greater proportion of insects. Also, spiny-tailed iguanas are cannabalistic, even consuming their own offspring.

Vitamin D_3 and calcium are mandatory dietary additives for both species. This is especially true during periods of rapid growth and if your specimen does not have access to unfiltered, natural sunlight. Ultraviolet rays (UV-B) are necessary to promote the synthesizing of vitamin D_3 and metabolism of calcium by all iguanas. Less D_3 and calcium are necessary when access to unfiltered, natural sunlight is allowed. Your iguana's diet should contain approximately twice as much calcium as phosphorus, and three to four times more calcium than phosphorus is better yet.

Breeding: When their hormones start churning at sexual maturity—and especially during the actual spring to early summer breeding season—adult male iguanas of both species may become so intractable that they become impossible to handle. There is no simple answer to this dilemma, but, during this period of dominate or be dominated, many keepers decide that this is not a lizard they wish to have for a pet!

Reproductive readiness is triggered by a lengthening photoperiod, higher relative humidity, warmer ambient temperatures, and, perhaps, other more subtle cues.

Female iguanas dig deep nests in which to deposit their clutches, and can be allowed to nest in the dirt floor of the greenhouse—you might be able to induce your female to do so by loosening and moistening two square feet of the floor—or provide her with a covered nesting barrel or box containing, besides the necessary access hole in the top, a foot (30 cm) or more of nesting material. The nesting material, either sand, or a sand-peat mixture, must be slightly moistened to allow the female to nest without the substrate collapsing around her.

Clutches normally number between 10 and 30 eggs, but more than 50 are occasionally laid. At a temperature of about 85°F (29°C), the incubation period is about two months.

Support domestic herpetocultural efforts. If you decide you want an iguana, buy iguanas that have been captive bred and hatched domestically. Domestically raised iguanas are less stressed than imports and, although perhaps somewhat more expensive than imports, will host fewer parasites or may, perhaps, be temporarily parasite free.

Additionally, the purchase of captive bred/captive hatched iguanas may be considered a conservation tool, assuring there is no additional draw on wild iguana populations.

Prehensile-tailed Giant Skink—for a Tropical Rainforest Greenhouse

At a slender-tailed length of somewhat more than 2 feet (61 cm), the prehensile-tailed skink, *Corucia zebrata*, is one of the larger, if not the largest, skinks. Its tail is strongly prehensile. Females of this biennially breeding species give birth to a single proportionately *huge* baby or, rarely, a set of slightly smaller twins. The prehensile-tailed skinks offered in the pet trade are, in all but rare instances, wild-collected, imported adults. Although they can become accustomed to handling, many will bite ferociously if carelessly handled.

Prehensile-tailed skinks are imposing but not colorful. They are clad mostly in scales of olive and gray. The head of some specimens has an attractive (to some) yellow flush. Despite the reference to banding made by the specific name, if bands are present they are often discontinuous and irregular. An irregular dark blotching is more common.

A Solomon Islands endemic, this skink is primarily crepuscular in its activity patterns. In the wild, it hides in tree hollows and other such areas of seclusion. Captives should be provided with hollow limbs or parrot nesting boxes in which to hide. Some prehensile-tailed skinks may be active by day in densely shaded areas or during cloudy weather.

Maintenance: This is a vegetarian species that feeds largely on the leaves and fruits of vining *Epipremnum* in the wild, and, when housed in a tropical rainforest greenhouse, will readily eat the leaves of philodendrons and pothos. Therefore, these skinks are best kept caged within the greenhouse rather than

The prehensile-tailed giant skink, Corucia zebrata, *of the Solomon Islands, is a livebearing, crepuscular vegetarian with immensely powerful jaws.*

being allowed to roam freely through the vegetation.

An elevated water dish, such as a shallow, easily sterilized heavy plastic birdbath, is more readily used than a ground-level bowl. These skinks also drink copiously from rain pooling on their logs during sprinklings. Daytime temperatures should not exceed the mid- to high 90's F (35° to 37°C) and nighttime lows of 72° to 76°F (22° to 24°C) seem fine.

If you supply greenhouse grown pothos to your *Corucia*, be sure that you have kept the pothos long enough, watering them with plain water, to purge them of all potentially harmful chemicals such as fertilizers and systemic insecticides.

Diet: Prehensile-tailed skinks thrive on a diet of diced fruit and vegetables and an occasional snail. The benefits, or potential harm, of animal protein in the diet of this species has not been fully explored. We think that if animal protein is given at all, it should be only in minuscule amounts, as animal protein, even in small amounts, has recently been implicated in the development of reptilian gout and kidney disorders in other herbivorous lizard species.

Breeding: These are difficult skinks to sex. Males have broader temporal areas and a shorter nose than the females, but this is a variable and comparative feature.

Maternal and colonial protection of the neonates is marked. As parturition approaches, the gravid females become positively pugnacious toward human intrusion, and short tempers are manifested by

most specimens in the colony after parturition. Fast-growing young and gravid females need much more frequent vitamin D_3 and calcium supplements than would be otherwise necessary.

Corucia kept colonially develop a hierarchy. The introduction of a new adult specimen to a peacefully coexisting group will cause disorder and occasional fighting until the new hierarchy has been established. Be sure to provide sufficient separate areas of seclusion for all specimens.

Blue-Tongued Skink—for a Savanna or Aridland Greenhouse

Both captive bred and imported blue-tongued skinks are readily available to hobbyists today. These are livebearing, slow moving, short legged, terrestrial skinks with a heavy body and a short, nonprehensile tail. When moving slowly they propel themselves with their legs. When rushed they often fold the legs against the body and move with side-to-side undulations. They are clad in many color combinations, from the grays, olives, and salmons of Australia's eastern and northern blue-tongues, *Tiliqua s. scincoides* and *T. s. intermedia*, respectively, to the olive and blacks of the New Guinea blue-tongued skink, *T. gigas*.

Sexing some of these species can be difficult. Adult males of most have broader temporal areas than similarly sized females. Sexually

The northern subspecies, Tiliqua scincoides intermedia, *is the most colorful of Australia's common blue-tongued skinks.*

active males of many populations of eastern blue-tongued skinks (*T. scincoides*) and blotched blue-tongued skinks (*T. nigrolutea*) have brilliant orange irises; those of adult females are olive to pale orange.

Behavior: When kept colonially in cages with numerous visual barriers, one type, the eastern blue-tongued skink, is a rather peaceful, easily bred form. There is very little serious squabbling, even among males at breeding time, and the litters are large—between 10 and 22 young being produced by each female. However, heavily gravid females, and those that have recently given birth, and the neonates, can be very quarrelsome. Adult males may injure or eat newborns. In contrast to the eastern race, when kept communally, northern blue-tongues begin fighting as soon as they see another blue-tongue, and often elevate the fights to active physical clashes where tail tips and legs are injured or amputated. The litters of the northern blue-tongues are smaller, usually numbering between 5 and 12. The young are even more quarrelsome than the adults and are eager to injure each other. They should be kept in individual containers.

Like the northern blue-tongued skink, the New Guinea blue-tongue can be very quarrelsome. It attains some 15 to 18 inches (38 to 46 cm) in total length. This species breeds reasonably well, but seemingly with less consistency than the various Australian species. The clutches number from 6 to 12 babies. If they are to be maintained together, you will need to incorporate many visual barriers into the caging design. Even then the lizards must be monitored very carefully. Severe injuries can be inflicted by one specimen upon another in just a matter of seconds.

Of these three skinks, the eastern blue-tongue is the most cold-tolerant. It will become dormant during very cold weather and can tolerate temperatures that would be fatal to both the more tropical northern and New Guinea blue-tongues. Daytime temperatures for all can be in the high 80°s F (30° to 32°C) to mid-90°s F (35° to 36°C) and nighttime temperatures may be allowed to drop to the high 60°s F (19° to 21°C) or low 70°s F (21° to 22°C).

On a diet of fresh fruits, vegetables, and high-quality canned cat food, the various blue-tongued skinks may attain ages of more than 20 years. Gravid females, and the neonates, which grow very quickly, must be provided with calcium-D_3 additives once or twice a week to prevent the onset of metabolic bone disease (MBD).

Black and White Tegu and Red Tegu—for the Savanna or Open Woodland Greenhouse

Although the black and gold species, *Tupinambis teguixin*, is the most readily available of the tegus, it is usually difficult to handle and not particularly desirable as a pet. Both the black and white, *T. merianae*,

For hobbyists with large facilities, a captive bred black and white tegu, Tupinambis merianae, *may be a good choice. These hardy lizards can attain a length of 4 feet.*

These are composed of (usually) three barely protruding ventrolateral scales. Although small, the spurs are easily visible if the lizard is in hand.

Both the black and white—colored as its name suggests—and the red—black with extensive markings of pale to bright red—are quite cold-tolerant.

Diet: Tegus are opportunistic feeders both in nature and in captivity. Rodents, insects, nestling birds, some prepared foods, and some vegetation are accepted. They seem to prefer succulent fruit to leafy vegetables. Tegus require fresh water and if their dish is large enough may submerge, then curl up contentedly and soak for hours. They may also defecate in their water dish; therefore, water quality must be closely monitored.

Temperatures: Overall summer daytime cage temperatures should be in the 77° to 85°F (25° to 30°C) range with an illuminated basking area of 95° to 103°F (35° to 40°C) on one end. Night temperatures can be allowed to drop somewhat.

It would seem that a period of cooling, and quite probably, hibernation, is very important when cycling the red and the black and white tegus reproductively. A natural photoperiod is probably only slightly less important. Humidity and rainfall changes that effectively simulate the rainy and dry seasons may also be important.

During the months of winter, more or less protected facilities are provided for the lizards. Both species

and the red tegus, *T. rufescens*, are much more satisfactory and are now captive bred in some numbers. Old males develop heavy jowls and a massive body bulk. In gross external appearance the tegus most closely resemble a shiny-scaled monitor lizard. The tail is unkeeled with scales arranged in prominent whorls.

Tegus are preferentially terrestrial, but are well able to climb. They are powerful diggers that construct both home burrows and sub-surface nesting chambers. Unless the foundation of your greenhouse is very deep, it will be necessary to bury a layer of strong, nonrusting, wire a foot (30 cm) or so beneath the surface of the ground to prevent the escape of these lizards.

Male tegus may be identified by the presence of a small postanal spur on each side of the tail base.

have been allowed to hibernate naturally in burrows as far north as the latitude of Birmingham, Alabama. The tegus may burrow to a depth of 2 feet (61 cm) or more.

Breeding: The lizards breed shortly after emerging from hibernation. Female tegus are quite unlike most other lizards, because they actually construct a nest of leaves, straw, and other ground debris to accommodate their eggs. In captivity, the observed females nudge and drag nesting material either into the nesting shelters provided for them or into the nest they had dug. Once nestmaking is completed, the females lay and cover the eggs and make an "attendance" chamber above the eggs in which the female tightly coils. From 15 to 52 eggs have been recorded.

At 80° to 85°F (27° to 29°C) incubation lasts for 65 to 92 days. The hatchlings of the black and white tegu are suffused dorsally and laterally with a bright green. This distinctive color fades rapidly and may be gone entirely after the second shedding. Hatchlings of the red tegu are suffused with a variable amount of brownish red. This is retained throughout life and may intensify with advancing age. The hatchlings measure nearly 10 inches (25 cm) in total length.

Savanna Monitor—for the Savanna or Aridland Greenhouse

The African savanna monitor, *V. exanthematicus,* is a moderately large monitor that is immensely popular in the pet trade. It is a grayish species with darker and lighter markings and much enlarged, roughened nuchal (nape) scales. The dorsal markings of juveniles often take the form of crossbands made up of light-centered dark ocelli and russet vermiculate lines. The tail is prominently banded. Frightened specimens inflate their body and gular area alarmingly and lash with their tail. Tame specimens are not apt to do this and will often actually crawl onto their owner's lap. Savanna monitors quickly learn to associate the presence of a human with food. Be careful when initially reaching for them. A bite, intended or not, by a large specimen, can be a painful ordeal! Besides biting and tail lashing, savanna monitors employ several other defensive ploys. These are raking whatever or whomever is grasping them with their sharp and powerful claws, voiding odoriferous cloacal contents, and playing dead. Because of their feeding habits, the jaws and claws of monitors are often reservoirs of bacteria. Lacerations caused by either should be promptly and vigorously cleansed with an antibacterial soap and treated with a topical antibiotic.

The savanna monitor is a proportionately stocky, dry land species. It commonly attains a length of about 5 feet (1.5 m) and some specimens may near 6 feet (1.8 m). With advanced age, during times of plenty, savanna monitors can become grossly obese. It is probably no more healthy for a monitor to be profoundly overweight than it is for a human to be so.

Diet: Despite the conventional wisdom that mice and other rodents are the preferred diet of this big lizard, this may be an erroneous assumption. It would seem that insects make up most of the diet of wild specimens, and that this preference should be echoed in captivity. Savanna monitors will definitely eat rodents if offered, but the high fat content of the mammals may not be conducive to the lizard's living a long, healthy life.

Breeding: Although monitors of many kinds are considered difficult to breed, both private hobbyists and zoological gardens have succeeded with the savanna monitor a few times.

Tiger ratsnakes, Spilotes pullatus, *may vary in color from nearly solid black to nearly solid yellow. The strongly banded phase of this 9-foot-long snake is one of the prettiest.*

In captivity, savanna monitors often breed during the hottest days of summer, often in conjunction with a passing storm system that rapidly lowers the barometric pressure.

Clutches of up to 50 eggs have been recorded, but most clutches number half that or fewer. A chamber dug into the side of a termitarium may occasionally be used, but, apparently, over much of its range the savanna monitor merely digs a hole in suitably moist, easily worked earth. At an incubation temperature of 83° to 85°F (28° to 29°C), hatchlings emerge in four to five months. Lower, or more variable, temperatures result in a longer incubation period.

Tiger Rat Snake—for a Savanna Greenhouse

This is a slender neotropical snake that is an accomplished tree climber. Although pretty, tiger rat snakes, *Spilotes pullatus* ssp., are often bad-tempered snakes that will, if sufficiently provoked or carelessly handled, deliver a rapid series of slashing bites. Because of this, we consider them snakes most suitable for advanced herpetoculturists. When on the defensive, the tiger snake often inflates its throat vertically before striking. Most tiger rat snakes available in the American pet trade are collected from the wild, and many are both rather severely dehydrated and heavily parasitized when imported. These snakes can near 10 feet (3 m) in length.

In its several subspecies, *S. pullatus* ranges southward from tropical Mexico through much of South America. These are black snakes that are variably banded or speckled with yellow. In some cases the coloration is reversed and we have a primarily yellow snake with black bands or speckles. Occasionally, solid black specimens and, even more rarely, solid yellow or orange specimens are seen.

Tiger rat snakes are well suited for dry savanna and tropical woodland greenhouses. Once acclimated, they can be quite hardy as captives. They are agile and active climbers that, apparently, normally range over an extensive home territory. They should be provided with sizable, vertically oriented cages equipped with numerous horizontal limbs. High temperatures—80° to 90°F (27° to 32°C)—high relative humidity, and ample fresh drinking water should be provided. Nighttime temperatures can be allowed to drop by a few degrees. Opportunistic feeders, these snakes eat rodents, birds, amphibians, and other reptiles.

They grasp their prey in their strong jaws and immobilize it by throwing a loop of their body over it. That this is not always an effective way of subduing rodents is displayed by the anterior scars borne by many specimens.

Breeding: *Spilotes* has proven a problematic breeder. Occasional successes have been recorded by both private hobbyists and zoological gardens. Clutches recorded have been rather small in egg number, most ranging from 6 to 17 eggs. The hatchlings are long—16 to 20 inches (41 to 51 cm)—and slender, and feed readily on small mice. Hatchlings are minireplicas of the adults.

Red-footed Tortoise and Yellow-footed Tortoise—for a Savanna or Open Woodland Greenhouse

These two species do well in humid situations. The red-foot is both a savanna and forest species while the yellow-foot seems more restricted to forests.

The natural range of the red-footed tortoise is from Panama to Argentina, mostly east of the Andes. Within that range there is much variation in adult size and color. You may see reference to Paraguayan red- (or cherry-) headed

The red-footed tortoise, Geochelone carbonaria, *is a pretty and responsive neotropical species of moderate size.*

red-foots, or Paraguayan dwarfs, the same as the red-headed ones, or Bolivian giants or Colombians—these latter have prominently concave shell sides—or any of several other designations. Some are more expensive than others, but none are inexpensive.

Although many are smaller, red-foots often attain 1 foot (30 cm) in length and some near 18 inches (46 cm). The elongate shell is highly domed, of a dark ground color, and, when viewed from above, has parallel to concave sides. The anterior marginals, even of hatchlings, are non-serrate. There is a light, yellow to orange spot in the center of each of the costal and vertebral scutes, and a less well-defined light spot often occurs on each marginal. The scales of the head and forelimbs may vary from yellow through orange to red. Typically, the scales of the forelimbs are brighter than those of the head.

Yellow-footed tortoises attain a much greater size than the rather closely allied red-foot. In bygone days some of the yellow-footed tortoises in the pet trade were close to 30 inches (76 cm) in shell length. Apparently they came from the forested, tricountry area of Amazonian Colombia, Peru, and Brazil. Today, only seldom are wild-collected specimens of any size available. Almost all specimens offered for sale are captive-bred and -hatched hatchlings. Babies are round when viewed from above but more elongate when mature.

The carapace color is yellowish, often with gray or brown overtones. The scales of the head and forelimbs are yellow.

Diet: Captive red-footed and yellow-footed tortoises will eagerly eat dark leafy vegetables such as romaine and escarole, pulpy fruit such as squashes, fruits such as apples, pears, kiwis, and a very small portion of prepared tortoise diet or dog kibble. There are several tortoise diets now on the market that claim to be a complete diet, but we would still recommend that they be augmented with vegetables and fruit. We also suggest that a D_3/calcium supplement be periodically added to the food. Vitamin/mineral supplements are given to rapidly growing young tortoises more frequently than to adults.

Both the red- and yellow-footed tortoises are very hardy and pretty species that we strongly recommend as starter tortoises. Of course, there are many very advanced hobbyists who covet these species, too. We do urge that you acquire captive-hatched babies whenever possible. Even the hatchlings are hardy and readily accept a variety of food.

Breeding: As the tortoises approach sexual maturity, you will note that males remain less highly domed and have a broader carapace than the females. Males also have concave plastra and a heavier, longer tail than females. Courtship involves a species-specific series of head bobs and nods as well as a series of chuckling vocalizations.

After immobilizing the female by nipping her shell and limbs, the male mounts and breeds her.

At most latitudes, breeding sequences by both of these tortoise species seem stimulated by lengthening photoperiods and the onset of the spring and summer rainy season. Low barometric pressure, if accompanied by suitably warm temperatures, may stimulate breeding year round.

Nesting can be a lengthy process. Some females dig nests just deep enough to contain the eggs; others may dig so deeply that the eggs are covered with several inches of earth. Small to moderate clutches of 3 to 10 eggs are usually produced by adult females. In the "humid" incubator at 82° to 86°F (28° to 30°C), incubation varies from 100 to nearly 180 days. Hatchlings are usually very similar to the adults, but may be more brightly colored. Most retain a prominent umbilical egg sac when emerging from the egg. This is absorbed within a day or two and the plastron closes over the umbilical area.

Leopard Tortoise for the Aridland Greenhouse

The eastern leopard tortoise, *Geochelone pardalis babcocki,* is the tortoise most often seen in the pet trade. It is the smaller, more highly domed, and more widely distributed of the two races. It occurs over much of southern Africa, except the southwest. Although some specimens may attain slightly more than a 2-foot (61 cm) shell length, most are much smaller. Females of only 1 foot (30 cm) in length are perfectly able to produce viable eggs. Sexual differences are rather slight. Adult males do have a weak plastral concavity, not present in females, and their tails are somewhat longer and heavier than those of the females.

The natural habitat of the leopard tortoise includes open woodlands, scrub, grasslands, and savannas. It prefers arid, well-drained areas. Some specimens readily adapt to humid conditions such as in the southeastern United States or isolated fogbelts elsewhere, but many will require lengthy acclimatization. We have found that this species seems rather susceptible to respiratory problems when it is maintained in humid areas, especially when temperatures cool; however, once acclimatized, and if otherwise properly cared for, these tortoises will live for several decades in captivity.

In coloration leopard tortoises may vary from sparsely to heavily patterned. The namesake leopard spots are present only on juvenile specimens. These fragment with advancing age, and other more irregular markings may form. The edges of each scute are usually the lightest in color. The ground color is tan, yellow, or, when adult, some shade of dusty brown. The smudges are black.

Breeding: Multiple clutches are usually produced by each sexually active female. They are laid at three- to four-week intervals and may number from 4 to 14 (small females) to more than 30 (larger females) in each clutch. They incubate easily in a low-humidity incubator, hatching in about three months at 86°F (30°C).

Spur-thighed Tortoise for the Aridland Greenhouse

Geochelone sulcata is one of the largest—20 to 30 inches (51 to 76 cm)—and most prolific of the world's mainland tortoises. Virtually unknown in the American pet trade only 20 years ago, the big spur-thighed tortoise is now probably the species most frequently bred by hobbyists. It is not a brightly colored tortoise. Adults are an unmarked tan to brown coloration dorsally often darker on scute edges. This species is hardy, adaptable, and amiable. The sexes are difficult to differentiate, but females are smaller than males, have a smaller tail, and do not have the weak plastral concavity typical of most males.

Hatchlings are of comparatively brighter hue than adults. When properly cared for, hatchlings grow very rapidly. They reach large sizes and sexual maturity in just a few years.

The range of this tortoise is roughly delineated in the north by the southern edge of the Sahara Desert. From there it ranges southward to southern Mauritania and

Senegal; thus, in nature it is an aridland species. Additionally, it is an accomplished digger that may construct burrows up to 4 feet (1.2 m) deep and more than 20 feet (6.1 m) long. Many specimens, though, will merely push their way under shrubs and make a shallow pallet to which they will regularly retire.

Breeding: Like the leopard tortoise, female *G. sulcata* dig well-formed, deep nesting holes. The clutch size varies from 5 to about 18 eggs but 7 to 10 seems most common. Females often dig well down into the soil with their forefeet before reversing position and digging the actual nesting chamber with their rear feet. At temperatures of 83° to 86°F (28° to 30°C), incubation lasts approximately three months. In nature, incubation durations of up to seven months have been reported.

Both the leopard and spur-thighed tortoises are preferentially vegetarians. Wild specimens eat many types of grasses, succulents, and fungi. Captives eat many kinds of available greens, pulpy vegetables, and fruits. A very small amount of dog chow can also be offered. Excesses of animal protein in the diet have now been linked to reptilian gout and abnormal carapacial growth (pyramiding). The carapaces of both species normally retain prominent growth rings.

Chapter Ten
Screenhouses

In the sunbelt of the United States, in southern Europe, and in other subtropical and tropical areas of the world, outdoor screenhouses are an option in caging reptiles and amphibians. As with other outside facilities, screenhouses will work well as summer quarters for many reptiles and amphibians, even in most temperate regions.

Rick and Lynn Russell, breeders of many lizard and tree frog species in southwest Florida, construct screenhouses with a floor space of 10 × 10 feet (3 × 3 m) and a height of 8 feet (2.4 m). The Russells choose to use a relatively nonabrasive fiberglass screen on the sides and a 75 percent shade cloth on the top of these enclosures. In these they maintain cold-tolerant subtropical species of amphibians and reptiles year round, and cold-sensitive species for more than nine months of the year. The screenhouses are elaborately planted with orchids, bromeliads, ferns, and aroids, and decorated with large hanging baskets of plants. They are crisscrossed with limbs that form basking and displaying perches for the animals and have large rocks, limbs, and small pools of water on the cage floor. Crickets are capable of chewing through the fiberglass screen sides, but usually don't. The Russells watch the screen carefully for the occasional small cricket hole and patch it *immediately*.

During the winter months, when they may need to be brought quickly to warmer quarters, the cold-sensitive species are moved to smaller cages—2 feet long × 2 feet

Screenhouses, like these of Rick and Lynn Russell of Florida, can be the nucleus of captive breeding programs that will supply reptiles and amphibians for hobbyists of the future.

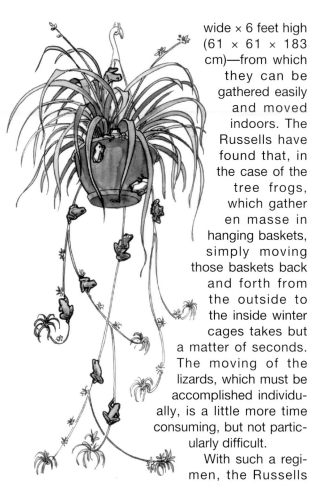

wide × 6 feet high (61 × 61 × 183 cm)—from which they can be gathered easily and moved indoors. The Russells have found that, in the case of the tree frogs, which gather en masse in hanging baskets, simply moving those baskets back and forth from the outside to the inside winter cages takes but a matter of seconds. The moving of the lizards, which must be accomplished individually, is a little more time consuming, but not particularly difficult.

With such a regimen, the Russells breed, among other species, painted-bellied monkey frogs, maroon-eyed tree frogs, red-headed basilisks, and frilled lizards.

Creatures for Screenhouses

Frilled Lizard

The frilled lizard, *Chlamydosaurus kingii*, is the world's only lizard species to have the trademark distensible neck frill. The frill is erected when the lizard is startled or displaying. Two thirds of this lizard's 32 inches (81 cm) is tail. It is a species of the dry northern Australian and southern New Guinean woodlands. In its natural habitat it is often seen clinging to the trunk of a tree, perched jauntily on top of an anthill or termite mound, or on other such vantage points. These lizards climb readily and run speedily. They are bipedal once up to speed. Reproductive activity seems stimulated as much by the advent of the seasonal summer rains as by lengthened photoperiods and higher average temperatures.

It was not until the 1990s that this coveted species became readily available to hobbyists. It is now captive bred in fair numbers, often in outdoor facilities, both in Europe and America.

Frilled lizards have proven hardy and unexpectedly quiet captives. Once acclimated, most will allow themselves to be gently handled, showing no inclination to dart away or bite. It is often difficult to induce them to erect the frill for which they are so famous.

Frilled lizards are dark in color, especially when they are cold. When they are warm, a suffusion of light pigment often dominates. The frill, which is narrowest beneath the throat and divided nuchally may have red, yellow or tan, and black highlights. Frilled lizards are oviparous and lay from 4 to more than 15 eggs.

Although strongly insectivorous, frilled lizards also consume nestling birds, rodents and other lizards.

Frilled lizards will drink droplets on leaves and limbs and water from shallow dishes and will soak for long periods when given a water receptacle large and deep enough for them to submerge in.

A minimum suggested cage size for a pair or trio of adults would be 4 feet wide × 8 feet long × 6 feet high (1.2 × 2.4 × 1.8 m). Adequate visual barriers may help prevent the lizards being inadvertently startled.

Red-headed Basilisk

Basiliscus galeritus is the most divergent of the four species of basilisks. It occurs only in Ecuador and Colombia. It has a well-developed cranial crest but the vertebral and caudal crests are represented by a series of enlarged flattened scales, each separated from the next by several small scales. The ground color of this pretty lizard is russet brown, brightest anteriorly. Olive green highlights are present on the head and anterior trunk.

Although wild-collected specimens are nervous and easily stressed, captive-born young seem to acclimate readily. These lizards are active, running and climbing readily. They are best suited to large outdoor cages. Natural sunlight and a varied insect diet, high in beta and other carotenes and calcium, seems best for these lizards.

Adult males develop the larger cranial crest and size and the

Two increasingly popular lizard species are the Australian frilled dragon, Chlamydosaurus kingii *(top), and the Ecuadorian red-headed basilisk,* Basiliscus galeritus, *(bottom).*

brighter colors. Large males are about 18 inches (46 cm) in length, of which two thirds is tail length. Females are several inches shorter.

Day Geckos

The day geckos commonly seen in the pet trade are active arborealists that are difficult to handle, but easy to keep and breed. They have rather exacting dietary requirements, but these, too, are easily met. They must be provided with

Day Gecko Delight

⅓ jar of mixed fruit, papaya, peach, or apricot strained baby food

1 teaspoon of honey

⅓ eyedropper of Avitron, liquid bird vitamins

½ teaspoon of Osteoform powdered multivitamins

Add water to proper consistency

A small amount of bee pollen can be added

vitamin/mineral supplements. Vitamin D_3 and calcium are the two most important additives. Besides insects, day geckos eat fruit exudates and pollen, and lap at sap.

In the box is an easily made formula suitable for virtually all species of day geckos.

Besides the vitamin-enhanced fruit mixture, we provide the geckos with calcium-dusted crickets, waxworms, and an occasional giant mealworm.

During inclement weather or in indoor facilities, full-spectrum lighting is also necessary. Day geckos, especially the males, are extremely territorial. Although most hobbyists raise many juveniles in the same enclosure, as all reach sexual maturity, males will develop aggressive behavior. Subordinate males will need to be removed to their own individual terraria. Day geckos do well in pairs but we have found two or three females to a single male seems a better ratio. Such groupings are more visible, seem to thrive better, and there is, undeniably, a potential for more eggs.

Chapter Eleven

Photographing Amphibians and Reptiles in Their Terraria

Photographing amphibians can be an enjoyable and fulfilling pursuit. Today, there is a burgeoning number of reptile and amphibian photographers, some of whom may specialize in a particular discipline such as field photography, zoo photography, or one group, such as snakes. Many hobbyists see photography as the best way to document captive or wild behavior patterns. It is a pursuit that we enjoy immensely, but getting suitable images of amphibians and reptiles, even those of common ones, on film is not always as easy as would be imagined. Stealth and field knowledge must be combined with the discipline of photography. Toting photographic equipment into the field in inclement weather, as might be necessary if you hope to photograph chorusing frogs or toads, can be a tedious undertaking. As you progress, each photo will help you to see how the next could be improved. Getting started is easy.

The equipment required will depend upon a number of variables. Among these are whether you will be indulging in both long distance field photos and staged closeups.

Photographic Hints

For staged photography, create a small natural setting by placing rocks, mosses, leaves, or bark—whichever is most appropriate for the species you're photographing—on a stage. Use a small lazy Susan as a stage. This enables you to rotate the stage with the animal on it for different photographic angles. This works, providing that you move *v e r y   s l o w l y*, both in your own actions and in rotating the stage. If you don't have a lazy Susan, just arrange the setting items on a tabletop or on a tree stump—outdoors or in, depending on where you are at the time—put the specimen in place, focus and shoot. Having a photo

Basic Equipment Needs

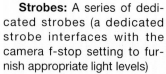

We suggest a sturdy 35 mm camera body with interchangeable lenses. You don't necessarily need a brand-new camera body and lenses; we've used quality second-hand equipment for many of our photographic ventures. However, you *do* need a photo supply dealer who can accurately advise you about the condition of the equipment you're buying, and who can tell you about some features of that particular lens or body. Usually, second-hand camera equipment does not come with manuals of any sort.

Lenses: The lenses we use include:

- 28 mm wide angle for habitat photos

Choose the right lenses for your needs.

- 50 mm standard for habitat photos
- 100 mm macro for closeups (suitable for almost every purpose)
- 75 to 205 mm zoom lens for variable field work
- 400 mm fixed focal length telephoto lens for field work
- 120 to 600 zoom lens for distant but variable field work

Capturing reptiles on film requires patience.

Strobes: A series of dedicated strobes (a dedicated strobe interfaces with the camera f-stop setting to furnish appropriate light levels)

Lens adapter: ×1.25 power magnifier or ×2 doubler.

Film: ISO 50-slide film is slower and less grainy than higher-speed films. This slower film will give you the best results, but also requires a bright day or electronic flashes to compensate for the slow speed. The higher the ISO, the less light you will need to photograph, but the grainier your pictures will be. If you are taking pictures for publication, use ISO 50-slide film. If you are taking photos merely for your own enjoyment, use either slide or print film.

Tripod: A sturdy tripod—an absolute necessity for the telephoto lenses—will hold your camera steady while you squeeze off that once-in-a-lifetime shot. Camera equipment with lenses is heavy, especially if you're out in the field and have slogged through hip-deep water, then scaled a couple of hillsides. The equipment is heavy even if you're indoors.

Camera body: After having a camera body malfunction on occasion, we now always have at least one spare body available.

assistant to help pose or catch the subject if it becomes frightened and attempts to escape is very helpful.

We created a backing for our stage with the top half of a round trash can. We first cut it to size, then firmly bolted it in place. Black velvet clipped into place around the inside surface of the background provides a good backdrop. The result is an easily moved, eminently serviceable, stage.

Field photography can be considerably more trying than staged photography. To successfully accomplish the former, it is almost mandatory that you have an assistant.

Approaching a nocturnal amphibian or reptile with a camera while keeping the beast in a flashlight beam can be truly exasperating. A small flashlight held in place on the bracket or flash unit with a strip of Velcro is a great way to free your hands. Generally, if you move very slowly, the subject of your interest will remain in place long enough to permit you to get a few shots. You, or your partner, will need to move quickly to capture the specimen if it moves, replace it where you wish to photograph it, then move slowly to refocus and shoot.

If you're trying field photography, approach the animal slowly and obliquely. Avoid eye contact. If the amphibian or reptile notices you, as it almost certainly will, freeze for a moment, then begin moving again. Eventually, if you are lucky, you will be close enough to make the field shot for which you were hoping.

When finished, retrace your steps carefully, disturbing as little habitat as possible, and leaving nothing behind—nothing that is but your footprints and the specimen you just successfully photographed.

Glossary

agamid: a lizard of the family Agamidae.

albino: lacking black pigment.

allopatric: not occurring together but often adjacent.

ambient temperature: the temperature of the surrounding environment.

amplexus: the breeding embrace of most anurans and some salamanders.

anerythristic: lacking red pigment.

anterior: toward the front.

anus: the external opening of the cloaca; the vent.

aposematic: brilliantly contrasting colors that may warn predators of toxicity or other dangers.

arboreal: tree-dwelling.

autotomize: the ability to break easily or voluntarily cast off and usually to regenerate a part of the body. This is used with tail breakage in lizards.

boid: boas and pythons.

brille: the transparent "spectacle" covering the eyes of snakes and some lizards.

brumation: similar to hibernation.

bufonid: a toad or toad relative.

caudal: pertaining to the tail.

cloaca: the common chamber into which digestive, urinary, and reproductive systems empty and that itself opens exteriorly through the vent or anus.

colubrid: the largest grouping of snakes, including such forms as garter snakes, rat snakes, bull snakes, and kingsnakes.

con...: as used here, a prefix to several words (generic, specific) indicating "the same." Congeneric refers to species in the same genus; conspecific indicates the same species.

constricting: to wrap tightly in coils and squeeze.

convergent evolution: similarity of two unrelated species as the result of environmental or other conditions.

crepuscular: active at dawn and/or dusk.

cryptic: as used here, having an outline and/or color that blends with a chosen and specific background.

dendrobatid: an arrow-poison or torrent frog.

deposition: as used here, the laying of the eggs.

deposition site: the spot chosen by the female in which to lay her eggs.

dichromatic: two color phases of the same species, often sex-linked.

dimorphic: a difference in form, build, or coloration involving the same species; often sex-linked.

direct development: amphibian larvae that metamorphose within the egg capsule.

diurnal: active in the daytime.

dorsal: pertaining to the back; upper surface.

dorsolateral: pertaining to the upper sides.

dorsum: the upper surface.

ecological niche: the precise habitat utilized by a species.

ectothermic: poikilothermic; cold-blooded.

endemic: confined to a specific region.

estivation: a period of warm weather inactivity, often triggered by excessive heat or drought.

eublepharine: an eyelidded gecko (leopard gecko relatives).

femoral pores: specialized enlarged, pheromone-releasing modified glandular structures beneath the femur.

femur: the part of the leg between the hip and the knee.

form: an identifiable species or subspecies.

fossorial: adapted for burrowing or digging.

fracture planes: softer areas in the tail vertebrae that allow the tail to break easily if seized.

gekkonid: a typical gecko.

genus: a taxonomic classification of a group of species having similar characteristics. The genus falls between the next higher designation of *family* and the next lower designation of *species*. Genera is the singular of genus. The generic name is always capitalized when written.

glottis: the opening of the windpipe.

gravid: the reptilian equivalent of mammalian pregnancy.

gular: pertaining to the throat.

heliothermic: pertaining to a species that basks in the sun to thermoregulate.

hemipenes: the dual copulatory organs of male lizards and snakes.

hemipenis: the singular form of hemipenes.

hibernaculum: a hibernation chamber.

hybrid: offspring resulting from the breeding of two species.

hydrate: to restore body moisture by drinking or absorption.

hylid: a treefrog.

iguanid: iguanas and related lizards.

insular: as used here, island-dwelling.

intergrade: offspring resulting from the breeding of two subspecies.

juvenile: a young or immature specimen.

keel: a ridge along the center of a scale.

labial: pertaining to the lips.

lamella: modified transverse scales beneath the toes of some lizards.

lateral: pertaining to the side.

lateral line organs: sensory organs imbedded in the lateral lines of some amphibians.

leptodactylid: a frog of the family leptodactylidae.

melanism: a profusion of black pigment.

metamorph: amphibian recently transformed from the larval stage.

metamorphosis: the transformation from one stage of life to the next.

microhylid: a frog of the narrow-mouthed toad family.

middorsal: pertaining to the middle of the back.

midventral: pertaining to the center of the belly or abdomen.

monotypic: containing but one type.

natricine: water, garter, ribbon, brown, and related snakes.

nocturnal: active at night.

nuptial pad: the roughened pads developed on thumbs and/or forelimbs during the breeding season by male frogs.

opisthoglyphid: rear-fanged.

oviparous: reproducing by means of eggs that hatch after laying.

ovoviviparous: producing eggs that develop within the maternal body.

parotoid gland: the toxin-producing shoulder glands of some anurans.

photoperiod: the hours of daylight relative to the hours of darkness.

phyllomedusine: a neotropical subgroup of treefrogs with opposable thumbs; the leaf or monkey frogs.

poikilothermic: a species with no internal body temperature regulation; the old term was *cold-blooded*.

polliwog: a tadpole.

postocular: to the rear of the eye.

posterior: toward the rear.

race: a subspecies.

ranid: a true frog.

rostral: the often modified scale on the tip of the snout; pertaining to the tip of the snout.

rugose: wrinkled or tuberculate.

saxicolous: rock-dwelling.

sclerophyll: scrubby plants with modified leaves resistant to water loss.

scansorial: capable of or adapted for climbing.

scute: scale, often referring to the ventral scales of a snake or the shields of a turtle's shell.

species: a group of similar creatures that produce viable young when breeding; the taxonomic designation that falls beneath *genus* and above *subspecies*.

subcaudal: under the tail.

subdigital: under the toes.

subspecies: the subdivision of a species; a race that may differ slightly in color, size, scalation, or other criteria.

SVL: snout-vent length.

sympatric: occurring together.

taxonomy: the science of classification of plants and animals.

termitarium: a termite nest.

terrestrial: land-dwelling.

thermoregulate: to regulate (body) temperature by choosing a warmer or cooler environment.

tricarinate: three keels or ridges.

tuberculate: pertaining to tubercles.

tubercles: warty protuberances.

tympanum: the external eardrum.

vent: the external opening of the cloaca; the anus.

venter: the underside of a creature; the belly.

ventral: pertaining to the undersurface or belly.

ventrolateral: pertaining to the sides of the venter (=belly).

viviparous: live-bearing species with modified placenta.

xeric: relating to or requiring only a small amount of moisture.

Useful Addresses and Literature

Books

Arnold, E. N. and J. A. Burton. *A Field Guide to the Reptiles and Amphibians of Britain and Europe.* London: Collins, 1978.

Bartlett, Richard D. *In Search of Reptiles and Amphibians.* Leiden: E. J. Brill, 1988.

____. *Digest for the Successful Terrarium.* Morris Plains, NJ: TetraPress, 1989.

____. and Patricia P. Bartlett. *Corn Snakes and Other Rat Snakes, A Complete Pet Owner's Manual.* Hauppauge, NY: Barron's Educational Series, Inc., 1996.

____. *Turtles and Tortoises, A Complete Pet Owner's Manual.* Hauppauge, NY: Barron's, 1996.

____. *Lizard Care from A to Z.* Hauppauge, NY: Barron's, 1997.

Bartlett, Patricia P. and Ernie Wagner. *Pythons, A Complete Pet Owner's Manual.* Hauppauge, NY: Barron's, 1997.

Bishop, Sherman C. *Handbook of Salamanders.* Ithaca, NY: Comstock, 1943.

Conant, Roger and Joseph T. Collins. *A Field Guide to Reptiles and Amphibians; Eastern and Central North America.* Boston: Houghton Mifflin Co., 1998.

Ernst, Carl H. and George R. Zug. *Snakes in Question: The Smithsonian Answer Book.* Washington, DC: Smithsonian Institution Press, 1996.

Greene, Harry W. *Snakes: The Evolution of Mystery in Nature.* Berkeley: Univ. of California Press, 1997.

Indiviglio, Frank. *Newts and Salamanders, A Complete Pet Owner's Manual.* Hauppauge, NY: Barron's, 1997.

Markel, Ronald G. and R. D. Bartlett. *Kingsnakes and Milksnakes, A Complete Pet Owner's Manual.* Hauppauge, NY: Barron's, 1995.

Marshall, Samuel D. *Tarantulas and Other Arachnids, A Complete Pet Owner's Manual.* Hauppauge, NY: Barron's, 1996.

Mehrtens, John M. *Living Snakes of the World in Color.* New York: Sterling Pub., 1987.

Peters, James A. *Dictionary of Herpetology.* New York: Hafner Publishing Co., 1964.

Pope, Clifford H. *The Reptiles of China.* New York: Amer. Mus. Nat. Hist., 1935.

Smith, Hobart M. *Handbook of Lizards.* Ithaca, NY: Comstock, 1946.

Smith, Malcolm A. *The Fauna of British India, Ceylon and Burma, Reptilia and Amphibia, Vol. III—Serpentes.* London: Taylor and Francis Ltd., 1943.

Herp Websites
American Society of Ichthologists and Herpetologists
www.utexas.edu/depts/asih/

Society for the Study of Reptiles and Amphibians
http://falcon.cc.ukans.edu/~gpisani/SSAR.html

Herp pictures
http://gto.ncsa.uinc.edu/pingleto/lobby.html

Michigan Museum of Zoology
http://www.ummz.lsa.imich.edu/herps/

International public library ready reference
http://www.ipl.org/ref/RR/static/ent6580.html

Stebbins, Robert C. *A Field Guide to Western Reptiles and Amphibians.* Boston: Houghton Mifflin Co., 1985.

Wagner, Doug. *Boas, A Complete Pet Owner's Manual.* Hauppauge, NY: Barron's, 1996.

Wareham, David C. *The Reptile and Amphibian Keeper's Dictionary.* London: Blandford, 1993.

Wright, Albert H. and A. A. Wright. *Handbook of Snakes: Vols. I and II.* Ithaca, NY: Comstock, 1957.

____. *Handbook of Frogs and Toads.* Ithaca, NY: Comstock, 1949.

Magazines
Reptile and Amphibian Magazine
RD 3, Box 3709-A
Pottsville, PA 17901

Reptiles Magazine
P. O. Box 6050
Mission Viejo, CA 92690-6050

The Vivarium
P.O. Box 300067
Escondido, CA 92030-0067
(Available by membership in American Federation of Herpetoculturists)

Reptilian
22 Firs Close
Hazlemere, High Wycombe
Bucks HP15 7TF, England

Reptile Hobbyist
P.O. Box 427
Neptune, NJ 07753

The following professional journals are available only to members of the societies or, occasionally, through used book sellers.

Herpetological Review and the *Journal of Herpetology*
The Society for the Study of Reptiles and Amphibians
Department of Zoology
Miami University
Oxford, OH 45056

Copeia
The American Society of Ichthyologists and Herpetologists
Department of Zoology
Southern Illinois University
Carbondale, IL 62901-6501

Herpetologica
c/o Maureen A. Donnelly
College of Arts and Sciences
Florida International University
North Miami, FL 33181

Index